Favorite Brand Name

Classic
Recipe Collection

pil

Publications International, Ltd.

Favorite Brand Name Recipes at www.fbnr.com

 Publications International, Ltd.

Microwave Cooking: Microwave ovens vary in wattage. Use the cooking times as guidelines and check for doneness before adding more time.

Preparation/Cooking Times: Preparation times are based on the approximate amount of time required to assemble the recipe before cooking, baking, chilling or serving. These times include preparation steps such as measuring, chopping and mixing. The fact that some preparations and cooking can be done simultaneously is taken into account. Preparation of optional ingredients and serving suggestions is not included.

Contents

191

279

73

15

Great Beginnings

CREAMY ROASTED RED PEPPER DIP

1 package (8 ounces) PHILADELPHIA® Cream Cheese, softened
3 tablespoons milk
½ cup chopped, drained, roasted red peppers
½ teaspoon dried thyme leaves
⅛ teaspoon ground black pepper

MIX cream cheese and milk with electric mixer on medium speed until smooth. Blend in remaining ingredients. Refrigerate.

SERVE with NABISCO® Crackers or assorted cut-up vegetables.   *Makes 1½ cups*

Prep: 5 minutes plus refrigerating

GRILLED ANTIPASTO PLATTER

16 medium scallops
16 medium shrimp, shelled and deveined
12 mushrooms (about 1 inch diameter)
 3 ounces thinly sliced prosciutto or deli-style ham
16 slender asparagus spears
 1 jar (6½ ounces) marinated artichoke hearts,
    drained
 2 medium zucchini, cut lengthwise into slices
 1 large or 2 small red bell peppers, cored, seeded
    and cut into 1-inch-wide strips
 1 head radicchio, cut lengthwise into quarters
    (optional)
   Lemon Baste (recipe follows)
   Lemon wedges

Soak 12 long bamboo skewers in water for at least 20 minutes to keep them from burning. Thread 4 scallops on each of 4 skewers and 4 shrimp on each of another 4 skewers. Thread 6 mushrooms on each of 2 more skewers. Cut prosciutto into 2×1-inch strips. Wrap 2 asparagus spears together with 2 strips of prosciutto; secure with a toothpick. Repeat with remaining asparagus spears. Wrap each artichoke heart in 1 strip of prosciutto; thread on 2 remaining skewers. Place ingredients except radicchio and lemon wedges on a baking sheet. Reserve ¼ cup Lemon Baste. Brush remaining Lemon Baste liberally over ingredients on baking sheet.

Spread medium KINGSFORD® Briquets in a wide single layer over the bed of the grill. Oil hot grid to help prevent sticking. Grill skewers, asparagus bundles, zucchini and red peppers, on an uncovered grill, 7 to 12 minutes until vegetables are tender, seafood firms up and turns opaque and prosciutto around wrapped vegetables is crisp, turning once or twice. Remove each item from grill to a large serving platter as it is done. Pour remaining baste over all. Serve hot or at room temperature. Garnish with radicchio and lemon wedges.

Makes 4 main-dish servings or 8 appetizer servings

LEMON BASTE

½ cup olive oil
¼ cup lemon juice
½ teaspoon salt
¼ teaspoon black pepper

Whisk together all ingredients in small bowl until well blended. *Makes about ¾ cup*

GRILLED ANTIPASTO PLATTER

ORANGE ICED TEA

2 SUNKIST® oranges
4 cups boiling water
5 tea bags
   Ice cubes
   Honey or brown sugar to taste

With vegetable peeler, peel each orange in continuous spiral, removing only outer colored layer of peel (eat peeled fruit or save for other uses). In large pitcher, pour boiling water over tea bags and orange peel. Cover and steep 5 minutes. Remove tea bags; chill tea mixture with peel in covered container. To serve, remove peel and pour over ice cubes in tall glasses. Sweeten to taste with honey. Garnish with orange quarter-cartwheel slices and fresh mint leaves, if desired. *Makes 4 (8-ounce) servings*

MUSHROOM PARMESAN CROSTINI

MUSHROOM PARMESAN CROSTINI

1 tablespoon olive or vegetable oil
1 clove garlic, finely chopped
1 cup chopped mushrooms
1 loaf Italian or French bread (about 12 inches long), cut into 12 slices and toasted
¾ cup RAGÚ® Pizza Quick® Sauce
¼ cup grated Parmesan cheese
1 tablespoon finely chopped fresh basil leaves *or* 1 teaspoon dried basil leaves

Preheat oven to 375°F. In 8-inch nonstick skillet, heat oil over medium heat and cook garlic 30 seconds. Add mushrooms and cook, stirring occasionally, 2 minutes or until liquid evaporates.

On baking sheet, arrange bread slices. Evenly spread Ragú® Pizza Quick Sauce on bread slices, then top with mushroom mixture, cheese and basil. Bake 15 minutes or until heated through. *Makes 12 crostini*

Recipe Tip: Many varieties of mushrooms are available in supermarkets and specialty grocery stores. Shiitake, portobello and cremini mushrooms all have excellent flavor.

SOUTHWESTERN QUESADILLAS

3 (8-inch) flour tortillas
   I CAN'T BELIEVE IT'S NOT BUTTER!® Spray
¼ teaspoon chili powder, divided
⅛ teaspoon ground cumin, divided
1 cup shredded Monterey Jack or Cheddar cheese
   (about 4 ounces)
1 can (4 ounces) chopped green chilies, drained
1 can (2¼ ounces) sliced pitted ripe olives, drained
2 tablespoons chopped cilantro (optional)

Generously spray one side of one tortilla with I Can't Believe It's Not Butter! Spray. Sprinkle with ½ of the chili powder and cumin. On baking sheet, arrange tortilla spice-side down, then top with ½ of the cheese, chilies, olives and cilantro. Top with second tortilla. Repeat layers, ending with tortilla. Spray top tortilla generously with I Can't Believe It's Not Butter! Spray, then sprinkle with remaining chili powder and cumin. Grill or broil until tortillas are golden and cheese is melted. Cut in wedges and serve, if desired, with salsa.

Makes 4 servings

SOUTHWESTERN QUESADILLAS

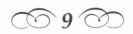

SUNRISE PUNCH

1 tub **CRYSTAL LIGHT TROPICAL PASSIONS®** Strawberry Kiwi Flavor Low Calorie Soft Drink Mix
2 **cups cold water**
2 **cups chilled unsweetened pineapple juice**
1 **bottle (1 liter) chilled seltzer**
   Ice cubes

PLACE drink mix in large plastic or glass pitcher. Add water and juice; stir to dissolve. Refrigerate.

JUST before serving, pour into large punch bowl. Stir in seltzer. Serve over ice.

Makes 2 quarts or 8 (1-cup) servings

Prep: 5 minutes plus refrigerating

CHEESY POTATO SKINS WITH BLACK BEANS & SALSA

6 **medium potatoes (6 ounces each), baked**
¾ **cup GUILTLESS GOURMET® Black Bean Dip (Spicy or Mild)**
¾ **cup (3 ounces) grated Cheddar cheese**
¾ **cup GUILTLESS GOURMET® Salsa (Roasted Red Pepper or Southwestern Grill)**
¾ **cup low fat sour cream**
   Fresh cilantro sprigs (optional)

Preheat oven to 400°F. Cut baked potatoes in half lengthwise and scoop out potato pulp, leaving ¼-inch pulp attached to skin (avoid breaking skin). (Save potato pulp for another use, such as mashed potatoes.) Place potato skins on large baking sheet, skin sides down; bake 5 minutes.

Fill each potato skin with 1 tablespoon bean dip and 1 tablespoon cheese. Return to oven; bake 10 minutes. Remove from oven; let cool 5 minutes. Dollop 1 tablespoon salsa and 1 tablespoon sour cream onto each potato. Garnish with cilantro, if desired. Serve hot.

Makes 12 servings

BUFFALO CHICKEN WINGS

24 chicken wings
1 teaspoon salt
¼ teaspoon ground black pepper
4 cups vegetable oil for frying
¼ cup butter or margarine
¼ cup hot pepper sauce
1 teaspoon white wine vinegar
   Celery sticks
1 bottle (8 ounces) blue cheese dressing

Cut tips off wings at first joint; discard tips. Cut remaining wings into two parts at the joint; sprinkle with salt and pepper. Heat oil in deep fryer or heavy saucepan to 375°F. Add half the wings; fry about 10 minutes or until golden brown and crisp, stirring occasionally. Remove with slotted spoon; drain on paper towels. Repeat with remaining wings.

Melt butter in small saucepan over medium heat; stir in pepper sauce and vinegar. Cook until thoroughly heated. Place wings on large platter. Pour sauce over wings. Serve warm with celery and dressing for dipping.

Makes 24 appetizers

Favorite recipe from **National Chicken Council**

CALIFORNIA QUESADILLAS

1 small ripe avocado
2 packages (3 ounces each) cream cheese, softened
3 tablespoons *Frank's® RedHot®* Cayenne Pepper Sauce
¼ cup minced fresh cilantro leaves
16 (6-inch) flour tortillas (2 packages)
1 cup (4 ounces) shredded Cheddar or Monterey Jack cheese
½ cup finely chopped green onions
   Sour cream (optional)

Halve avocado and remove pit. Scoop out flesh into food processor or bowl of electric mixer. Add cream cheese and *Frank's RedHot* Sauce. Cover and process, or beat, until smooth. Add cilantro; process, or beat, until well blended. Spread rounded tablespoon avocado mixture onto each tortilla. Sprinkle half the tortillas with cheese and onions, dividing evenly. Top with remaining tortillas; press gently.

Place tortillas on oiled grid. Grill over medium coals 5 minutes or until cheese melts and tortillas are lightly browned, turning once. Cut into triangles. Serve with sour cream, if desired. Garnish as desired.

Makes 8 appetizer servings

Note: You may serve avocado mixture as a dip with tortilla chips.

Prep Time: 20 minutes
Cook Time: 5 minutes

POT STICKERS

1 boneless, skinless chicken breast, finely chopped
1 cup cooked rice
½ cup finely chopped fresh mushrooms
1 carrot, finely shredded
2 green onions, finely chopped
1 tablespoon white wine
1 teaspoon cornstarch
1 teaspoon dark sesame oil
¼ teaspoon salt
¼ teaspoon ground white pepper
50 wonton skins
5 tablespoons vegetable oil, divided
2½ cups water, divided
    Soy sauce, Chinese hot mustard or sweet and
    sour sauce

Combine chicken, rice, mushrooms, carrot, onions, wine, cornstarch, sesame oil, salt and pepper in medium bowl. Cut corners from wonton skins with knife or round cookie cutter to make circles. Place 1 teaspoon chicken mixture on center of each circle. Fold circles in half, pressing edges together with fork. Heat 1 tablespoon vegetable oil in large skillet until very hot. Place 10 pot stickers in single layer in skillet; fry 2 minutes or until bottoms are golden brown. Add ½ cup water to skillet. Cover and cook 6 to 7 minutes or until water is absorbed. Repeat with remaining pot stickers, adding 1 tablespoon vegetable oil and ½ cup water per batch. Serve warm with your choice of sauce for dipping. *Makes 50 appetizers*

Favorite recipe from **USA Rice Federation**

CHAMPAGNE PUNCH

1 orange
1 lemon
¼ cup cranberry-flavored liqueur or cognac
¼ cup orange-flavored liqueur or triple sec
1 bottle (750 mL) pink or regular champagne or
    sparkling white wine, well chilled
    Fresh cranberries (optional)
    Citrus strips for garnish

Remove colored peel, not white pith, from orange and lemon in long thin strips with citrus peeler. Refrigerate orange and lemon for another use. Combine peels and cranberry- and orange-flavored liqueurs in glass pitcher. Cover and refrigerate 2 to 6 hours.

Just before serving, tilt pitcher to one side and slowly pour in champagne. Leave peels in pitcher for added flavor. Place a cranberry in bottom of each glass. Pour into champagne glasses. Garnish with citrus strips tied in knots, if desired. *Makes 4 cups, 6 to 8 servings*

Nonalchoholic Cranberry Punch: Pour 3 cups well-chilled club soda into ⅔ cup (6 ounces) cranberry cocktail concentrate, thawed. Makes 3½ cups, 6 servings.

CLASSIC CHICKEN PUFFS

1 box UNCLE BEN'S® Long Grain & Wild Rice
   Original Recipe
2 cups cubed cooked TYSON® Fresh Chicken
½ can (10¾ ounces) condensed cream of mushroom
   soup
⅓ cup chopped green onions
⅓ cup diced pimientos or diced red bell pepper
⅓ cup diced celery
⅓ cup chopped fresh parsley
⅓ cup chopped slivered almonds
¼ cup milk
1 box frozen prepared puff pastry shells, thawed

COOK: CLEAN: Wash hands. Prepare rice according to package directions. When rice is done, add remaining ingredients (except pastry shells). Mix well. Reheat 1 minute. Fill pastry shells with rice mixture.

SERVE: Serve with a mixed green salad and balsamic vinaigrette, if desired.

CHILL: Refrigerate leftovers immediately.

Makes 6 servings

Tip: This recipe is a great way to use up leftover chicken.

Prep Time: none
Cook Time: 20 minutes

CLASSIC CHICKEN PUFF

BAKED BRIE

½ **pound Brie cheese, rind removed**
¼ **cup chopped pecans**
¼ **cup KARO® Dark Corn Syrup**

1. Preheat oven to 350°F.

2. Place cheese in shallow oven-safe serving dish. Top with pecans and corn syrup.

3. Bake 8 to 10 minutes or until cheese is almost melted. Serve warm with plain crackers or melba.

Makes about 8 servings

Prep Time: 5 minutes
Bake Time: 8 minutes

HOLIDAY EGGNOG

   2 **cups skim milk**
   2 **tablespoons cornstarch**
3½ **teaspoons EQUAL® FOR RECIPES** *or* **12 packets EQUAL® sweetener** *or* **½ cup EQUAL® SPOONFUL™**
   2 **eggs, beaten**
   2 **teaspoons vanilla**
   ¼ **teaspoon ground cinnamon**
   2 **cups skim milk, chilled**
   ⅛ **teaspoon ground nutmeg**

Mix 2 cups milk, cornstarch and Equal® in small saucepan; heat to boiling. Boil 1 minute, stirring constantly. Mix about half of milk mixture into eggs; return egg mixture to remaining milk in saucepan. Cook over low heat until slightly thickened, stirring constantly. Remove from heat; stir in vanilla and cinnamon. Cool to room temperature; refrigerate until chilled. Stir 2 cups chilled milk into custard mixture; serve in small glasses. Sprinkle with nutmeg.

Makes 8 (4-ounce) servings

Variation: Stir 1 to 1½ teaspoons rum or brandy extract into eggnog, if desired.

• Classic Tip •

Brie is considered one of the world's greatest cheeses. It is a soft-ripened cheese which means it is neither cooked or pressed. As it ripens it develops a powdery white rind that is edible.

SPICY SHRIMP COCKTAIL

2 tablespoons olive or vegetable oil
¼ cup finely chopped onion
1 tablespoon chopped green bell pepper
1 clove garlic, minced
1 can (8 ounces) CONTADINA® Tomato Sauce
1 tablespoon chopped pitted green olives, drained
¼ teaspoon red pepper flakes
1 pound cooked shrimp, chilled

1. Heat oil in small skillet. Add onion, bell pepper and garlic; sauté until vegetables are tender. Stir in tomato sauce, olives and red pepper flakes.

2. Bring to a boil; simmer, uncovered, for 5 minutes. Cover.

3. Chill thoroughly. Combine sauce with shrimp in small bowl. *Makes 6 servings*

Prep Time: 6 minutes
Cook Time: 10 minutes

DELUXE FAJITA NACHOS

1 tablespoon vegetable oil
4 boneless, skinless chicken breast halves (about 1 pound), thinly sliced
1 package (1.27 ounces) LAWRY'S® Spices & Seasonings for Fajitas
⅓ cup water
8 ounces tortilla chips
1¼ cups (5 ounces) shredded Cheddar cheese
1 cup (4 ounces) shredded Monterey Jack cheese
1 large tomato, chopped
1 can (2¼ ounces) sliced black olives, drained
¼ cup sliced green onions
   Salsa

In medium skillet, heat oil. Add chicken and cook over medium-high heat 5 to 8 minutes. Add Spices & Seasonings for Fajitas and water; mix well. Bring to a boil over medium-high heat; reduce heat to low and simmer 7 minutes. In large shallow ovenproof platter, arrange chips. Top with chicken mixture and cheeses. Place under broiler to melt cheeses. Top with tomato, olives, green onions and desired amount of salsa.

Makes 4 appetizer or 2 main-dish servings

Serving Suggestion: Garnish with guacamole and sour cream.

Hint: For a spicier version, add sliced jalapeños.

Substitution: 1¼ pounds cooked ground beef can be used in place of shredded chicken.

CORNED BEEF & SWISS APPETIZERS

1 package (8 ounces) PHILADELPHIA® Cream
    Cheese, softened
2 teaspoons Grey Poupon® Dijon Mustard
¼ pound corned beef, chopped
½ cup (2 ounces) KRAFT® Shredded Swiss Cheese
2 tablespoons chopped green onion
36 slices cocktail rye bread, toasted

MIX cream cheese and mustard with electric mixer on medium speed until smooth.

BLEND in meat, Swiss Cheese and onion. Spread on toast slices. Place on cookie sheet.

BROIL 2 to 3 minutes or until lightly browned.

Makes 3 dozen

To Make Ahead: Prepare as directed except for broiling. Place on cookie sheet. Freeze 1 hour or until firm. Place in freezer-safe zipper-style plastic bags. Freeze up to 1 month. When ready to serve, thaw 10 minutes. Broil as directed.

Prep Time: 20 minutes
Broil Time: 3 minutes

CRISPY ORIENTAL WONTONS

½ pound ground pork
1 cup VELVEETA® Mild Cheddar Shredded
    Pasteurized Process Cheese Food
2 tablespoons green onion slices
1 teaspoon minced peeled gingerroot
1 teaspoon sesame oil (optional)
32 wonton wrappers
    Sesame seeds
    Dipping Sauce

• Preheat oven to 425°F.

• Brown meat; drain. Mix together meat, process cheese food, onion, gingerroot and sesame oil.

• For each wonton, place scant tablespoonful meat mixture in center of one wonton wrapper. Bring corners together over meat mixture; twist and pinch together, enclosing meat mixture in dough. Flatten bottom slightly. Place on cookie sheet. Brush lightly with water; sprinkle with sesame seeds.

• Bake 10 to 12 minutes or until golden brown. Serve warm with Dipping Sauce. *Makes 32 appetizers*

Prep Time: 25 minutes
Cook Time: 12 minutes

FRUIT SMOOTHIES

1 cup orange juice
1 cup fat-free plain yogurt
1 frozen banana*
1 cup frozen strawberries or raspberries
1¾ teaspoons EQUAL® FOR RECIPES *or* 6 packets
    EQUAL® sweetener *or* ¼ cup EQUAL®
    SPOONFUL™

Peel and cut banana into large chunks. Place in plastic freezer bag, seal and freeze at least 5 to 6 hours or overnight.

• Place all ingredients in blender or food processor. Blend until smooth. *Makes 2 servings*

HOT HUSH PUPPIES

    WESSON® Vegetable Oil
1¾ cups cornmeal
 ½ cup all-purpose flour
 1 teaspoon sugar
 ¾ teaspoon baking soda
 ½ teaspoon salt
 ½ teaspoon garlic salt
 ½ cup diced onion
 ½ to 1 (4-ounce) can diced jalapeño peppers
 1 cup buttermilk
 1 egg, beaten

Fill a large deep-fry pot or electric skillet to half its depth with Wesson® Oil. Heat oil to 400°F. Meanwhile, in a large bowl, sift together cornmeal, flour, sugar, baking soda, salt and garlic salt; blend well. Add onion and jalapeño peppers; stir until well blended. In small bowl, combine buttermilk and egg; add to dry ingredients. Stir until batter is moist and *all* ingredients are combined. Working in small batches, carefully drop batter by heaping tablespoons into hot oil. Fry until golden brown, turning once during frying. Remove and drain on paper towels. Serve with your favorite salsa or dipping sauce. *Makes 36 hush puppies*

FRUIT SMOOTHIES

SPINACH DIP

1 package (10 ounces) frozen chopped spinach, thawed and squeezed dry
1 container (16 ounces) sour cream
1 cup HELLMANN'S® or BEST FOODS® Mayonnaise
1 package KNORR® Recipe Classics™ Vegetable Soup, Dip and Recipe Mix
1 can (8 ounces) water chestnuts, drained and chopped (optional)
3 green onions, chopped

• In medium bowl, combine all ingredients; chill at least 2 hours.

• Stir before serving. Serve with your favorite dippers.

Makes about 4 cups dip

Yogurt Spinach Dip: Substitute 1 container (16 ounces) plain lowfat yogurt for sour cream.

Spinach and Cheese Dip: Add 2 cups (8 ounces) shredded Swiss cheese with spinach.

Prep Time: 10 minutes
Chill Time: 2 hours

PESTO CHICKEN BRUSCHETTA

2 tablespoons olive oil, divided
1 teaspoon coarsely chopped garlic, divided
8 diagonal slices (¼ inch thick) sourdough bread
½ cup (2 ounces) grated BELGIOIOSO® Asiago Cheese, divided
2 tablespoons prepared pesto
¼ teaspoon pepper
4 boneless skinless chicken breast halves
12 slices (¼ inch thick) BELGIOIOSO® Fresh Mozzarella Cheese (8 ounces)
2 tomatoes, each cut into 4 slices

In 10-inch skillet, heat 1 tablespoon olive oil and ½ teaspoon garlic. Add 4 slices bread. Cook over medium-high heat, turning once, 5 to 7 minutes or until toasted. Remove from pan. Add remaining 1 tablespoon oil and ½ teaspoon garlic; repeat with remaining bread slices. Sprinkle ¼ cup BelGioioso Asiago Cheese on bread. In same skillet, combine pesto and pepper. Add chicken, coating with pesto. Cook over medium-high heat, turning once, 8 to 10 minutes or until chicken is brown. Place 3 slices BelGioioso Fresh Mozzarella Cheese on each bread slice; top with tomato slice. Slice chicken pieces in half horizontally. Place on tomato; sprinkle with remaining BelGioioso Asiago Cheese.

Makes 4 servings

SAVORY STUFFED MUSHROOMS

20 medium mushrooms
2 tablespoons finely chopped onion
2 tablespoons finely chopped red bell pepper
3 tablespoons FLEISCHMANN'S® Original
   Margarine
½ cup dry seasoned bread crumbs
½ teaspoon dried basil leaves

1. Remove stems from mushrooms; finely chop ¼ cup stems.

2. Cook and stir chopped stems, onion and pepper in margarine in skillet over medium heat until tender. Remove from heat; stir in crumbs and basil.

3. Spoon crumb mixture loosely into mushroom caps; place on baking sheet. Bake at 400°F for 15 minutes or until hot.

Makes 20 appetizers

Preparation Time: 20 minutes
Cook Time: 15 minutes
Total Time: 35 minutes

CHESAPEAKE BAY BLOODY MARY

1 cup ice
4 ounces MR & MRS T® Bloody Mary Mix
1½ ounces vodka
½ ounce ROSE'S® Lime Juice
¼ teaspoon crab boil seasoning (or favorite seafood
   spice blend)
   Lime wedge (for garnish)
   Celery stick (for garnish)

Fill a tall glass with ice; add next 4 ingredients. Stir well and garnish with lime wedge or celery stick.

Makes 1 serving

• Classic Tip •

Crab boil seasoning is also referred to as shrimp boil and fish boil. It is a mixture of herbs and spices that usually include mustard seeds, peppercorns, bay leaves, whole allspice and cloves, dried ginger pieces and red chilies.

SAVORY STUFFED MUSHROOMS

7-LAYER MEXICAN DIP

1 package (8 ounces) PHILADELPHIA® Cream
  Cheese, softened
1 tablespoon TACO BELL® HOME ORIGINALS®*
  Taco Seasoning Mix
1 cup *each* guacamole, TACO BELL® HOME
  ORIGINALS® Thick 'N Chunky Salsa and
  shredded lettuce
1 cup KRAFT® Shredded Mild Cheddar Cheese
½ cup chopped green onions
2 tablespoons sliced pitted ripe olives

**TACO BELL and HOME ORIGINALS are registered trademarks
owned and licensed by Taco Bell Corp.*

MIX cream cheese and seasoning mix. Spread onto
bottom of 9-inch pie plate or quiche dish.

LAYER guacamole, salsa, lettuce, cheese, onions and
olives over cream cheese mixture; cover. Refrigerate.

SERVE with NABISCO® Crackers or tortilla chips.

Makes 6 to 8 servings

Great Substitutes: If your family doesn't like
guacamole, try substituting 1 cup TACO BELL® HOME
ORIGINALS™ Refried Beans.

Prep: 10 minutes plus refrigerating

SANGRIA

1 cup KARO® Light Corn Syrup
2 lemons, sliced
1 orange, sliced
½ cup brandy
1 bottle (750 ml) dry red wine
2 tablespoons lemon juice
1 bottle (12 ounces) club soda or seltzer, chilled

1. In large pitcher combine corn syrup, lemon and
orange slices and brandy. Let stand 20 to 30 minutes,
stirring occasionally.

2. Stir in wine and lemon juice. Refrigerate.

3. Just before serving, add soda and ice cubes.

Makes about 6 (8-ounce) servings

Prep Time: 10 minutes, plus standing and chilling

• Classic Tip •

*Empanadas are a Spanish
and Mexican specialty. They are usually
a single-serving size turnover with a
pastry crust and savory meat-and-
vegetable filling. They also can be filled
with fruit and served as a dessert.*

BITE SIZE TACOS

1 pound ground beef
1 package (1.25 ounces) taco seasoning mix
2 cups *French's® Taste Toppers™* French Fried
    Onions
¼ cup chopped fresh cilantro
32 bite-size round tortilla chips
¾ cup sour cream
1 cup shredded Cheddar cheese

1. Cook beef in nonstick skillet over medium-high heat 5 minutes or until browned; drain. Stir in taco seasoning mix, *¾ cup water, 1 cup* **Taste Toppers** and cilantro. Simmer 5 minutes or until flavors are blended, stirring often.

2. Preheat oven to 350°F. Arrange tortilla chips on foil-lined baking sheet. Top with beef mixture, sour cream, remaining **Taste Toppers** and cheese.

3. Bake 5 minutes or until cheese is melted and *Taste Toppers* are golden.   *Makes 8 appetizer servings*

Prep Time: 5 minutes
Cook Time: 15 minutes

BITE SIZE TACOS

SPICY TUNA EMPANADAS

1 (3-ounce) pouch of STARKIST® Solid White or
    Chunk Light Tuna, drained and flaked
1 can (4 ounces) diced green chilies, drained
1 can (2¼ ounces) sliced ripe olives, drained
½ cup shredded sharp Cheddar cheese
1 chopped hard-cooked egg
    Salt and pepper to taste
¼ teaspoon hot pepper sauce
¼ cup medium thick and chunky salsa
2 packages (15 ounces each) refrigerated pie crusts
    Additional salsa

In medium bowl, place tuna, chilies, olives, cheese, egg, salt, pepper and hot pepper sauce; toss lightly with fork. Add ¼ cup salsa and toss again; set aside. Following directions on package, unfold crusts (roll out slightly with rolling pin if you prefer thinner crust); cut 4 circles, 4 inches each, out of each crust. Place 8 circles on foil-covered baking sheets; wet edge of each circle with water. Top each circle with ¼ cup lightly packed tuna mixture. Top with remaining circles, stretching pastry slightly to fit; press edges together and crimp with fork. Cut slits in top crust to vent. Bake in 425°F oven 15 to 18 minutes or until golden brown. Cool slightly. Serve with additional salsa.

Makes 8 servings

MINI PIZZAS

CRUST
⅓ cup olive oil
1 tablespoon TABASCO® brand Pepper Sauce
2 large cloves garlic, crushed
1 teaspoon dried rosemary, crumbled
1 (16-ounce) package hot roll mix with yeast packet
1¼ cups hot water

GOAT CHEESE TOPPING
1 large tomato, diced
¼ cup crumbled goat cheese
2 tablespoons chopped fresh parsley

ROASTED PEPPER AND OLIVE TOPPING
½ cup shredded mozzarella cheese
½ cup pitted green olives
⅓ cup roasted red pepper strips

ARTICHOKE TOPPING
½ cup chopped artichoke hearts
½ cup cherry tomatoes, sliced into wedges
⅓ cup sliced green onions

For crust, combine olive oil, TABASCO® Sauce, garlic and rosemary in small bowl. Combine hot roll mix, yeast packet, hot water and 2 tablespoons oil mixture in large bowl; stir until dough pulls away from side of bowl. Turn dough onto lightly floured surface; shape into ball. Knead until smooth, adding additional flour as necessary.

Preheat oven to 425°F. For toppings, combine ingredients in separate bowls. Cut dough into quarters; cut each quarter into 10 equal pieces. Roll each piece into ball. Press each ball into 2-inch round on large cookie sheet; brush each round with remaining oil mixture. Arrange about 2 teaspoons topping on each dough round. Bake 12 minutes or until dough is lightly browned and puffed. *Makes 40 appetizers*

CITRUS COOLER

2 cups fresh squeezed orange juice
2 cups unsweetened pineapple juice
1 teaspoon fresh lemon juice
¾ teaspoon vanilla extract
¾ teaspoon coconut extract
2 cups cold sparkling water

Combine juices and extracts in large pitcher; refrigerate until cold. Stir in sparkling water; serve over ice.

Makes 8 servings

CHEESE STRAWS

½ cup (1 stick) butter, softened
⅛ teaspoon salt
  Dash ground red pepper
1 pound sharp Cheddar cheese, shredded, at room
  temperature
2 cups self-rising flour

Heat oven to 350°F. In mixer bowl, beat butter, salt and pepper until creamy. Add cheese; mix well. Gradually add flour, mixing until dough begins to form a ball. Form dough into ball with hands. Fit cookie press with small star plate; fill with dough according to manufacturer's directions. Press dough onto cookie sheets in 3-inch-long strips. Bake 12 minutes, just until lightly browned. Cool completely on wire rack. Store tightly covered. *Makes about 10 dozen*

SUNDRIED TOMATO CHEESE BALL

8 ounces PHILADELPHIA® Cream Cheese,*
  softened
1 cup KRAFT® Shredded Cheddar Cheese
  (4 ounces)
⅓ cup GREY POUPON® COUNTRY DIJON®
  Mustard
1 teaspoon dried basil leaves
1 clove garlic, crushed
½ teaspoon onion powder
¼ cup sundried tomatoes,** finely chopped
⅓ cup PLANTERS® Walnuts, toasted and chopped
  Assorted crackers, breadsticks and bagel chips

Low-fat cream cheese may be substituted for regular cream cheese.

**If sundried tomatoes are very dry, soften in warm water for 15 minutes. Drain before using.*

1. Mix cheeses, mustard, basil, garlic and onion powder in large bowl with electric mixer at medium speed until blended but not smooth. Stir in sundried tomatoes. Shape cheese mixture into a 5-inch ball; wrap and refrigerate 1 hour. Roll cheese ball in chopped nuts. Wrap and refrigerate until serving time.

2. Serve as a spread with assorted crackers, breadsticks and bagel chips. *Makes 1-pound cheese ball*

POTATO PANCAKE APPETIZERS

3 medium Colorado russet potatoes, peeled and grated
1 egg
2 tablespoons all-purpose flour
1 teaspoon salt
¼ teaspoon black pepper
1 cup grated carrot (1 large)
1½ cups grated zucchini (2 small)
½ cup low-fat sour cream or plain yogurt
2 tablespoons finely chopped fresh basil
1 tablespoon chopped chives *or* 1½ teaspoons chili powder

Preheat oven to 425°F. Wrap potatoes in several layers of paper towels; squeeze to remove excess moisture. Beat egg, flour, salt and pepper in large bowl. Add potatoes, carrot and zucchini; mix well. Oil 2 nonstick baking sheets. Place vegetable mixture by heaping spoonfuls onto baking sheets; flatten slightly. Bake 8 to 15 minutes until bottoms are browned. Turn; bake 5 to 10 minutes more. Stir together sour cream and herbs; serve with warm pancakes.

Makes about 24 appetizer pancakes

Favorite recipe from **Colorado Potato Administrative Committee**

TORTILLA CRUNCH CHICKEN FINGERS

1 envelope LIPTON® RECIPE SECRETS® Savory Herb with Garlic Soup Mix
1 cup finely crushed plain tortilla chips or cornflakes (about 3 ounces)
1½ pounds boneless, skinless chicken breasts, cut into strips
1 egg
2 tablespoons water
2 tablespoons margarine or butter, melted

Preheat oven to 400°F.

In medium bowl, combine savory herb with garlic soup mix and tortilla chips. In large plastic bag or bowl, combine chicken and egg beaten with water until evenly coated. Remove chicken and dip in tortilla mixture until evenly coated; discard bag. On 15½×10½×1-inch jelly-roll pan sprayed with nonstick cooking spray, arrange chicken; drizzle with margarine. Bake, uncovered, 12 minutes or until chicken is done.

Makes about 24 chicken fingers

Tip: Serve chicken with your favorite fresh or prepared salsa.

SPRING ROLLS

½ pound ground pork
1 teaspoon KIKKOMAN® Soy Sauce
1 teaspoon dry sherry
½ teaspoon garlic salt
2 tablespoons vegetable oil
3 cups fresh bean sprouts
½ cup sliced onion
1 tablespoon KIKKOMAN® Soy Sauce
1 tablespoon cornstarch
¾ cup water, divided
8 egg roll wrappers
½ cup quick biscuit mix
1 egg, beaten
   Vegetable oil for frying
   Hot mustard, tomato ketchup and KIKKOMAN®
   Soy Sauce

Combine pork, 1 teaspoon soy sauce, sherry and garlic salt; mix well. Let stand 15 minutes. Heat 2 tablespoons oil in hot wok or large skillet over medium-high heat; brown pork mixture in hot oil. Add bean sprouts, onion and 1 tablespoon soy sauce. Stir-fry until vegetables are tender-crisp; drain and cool. Dissolve cornstarch in ¼ cup water. Place about ⅓ cupful pork mixture on lower half of egg roll wrapper. Moisten left and right edges with cornstarch mixture. Fold bottom edge up just to cover filling. Fold left and right edges ½ inch over; roll jelly-roll fashion. Moisten top edge with cornstarch mixture and seal. Complete all rolls. Combine biscuit mix, egg and remaining ½ cup water in small bowl; dip each roll in batter. Heat oil for frying in wok or large saucepan over medium-high heat to 370°F. Deep-fry rolls, a few at a time, in hot oil 5 to 7 minutes, or until golden brown, turning often. Drain on paper towels. Slice each roll in half. Serve with mustard, ketchup and soy sauce as desired.

Makes 8 appetizer servings

SPRING ROLLS

RICE & ARTICHOKE PHYLLO TRIANGLES

1 box UNCLE BEN'S® Butter & Herb Fast Cook
    Recipe Long Grain & Wild Rice
1 jar (6½ ounces) marinated quartered artichokes,
    drained and finely chopped
2 tablespoons grated Parmesan cheese
1 tablespoon minced onion or 1 green onion with
    top, finely chopped
⅓ cup plain yogurt or sour cream
10 sheets frozen phyllo dough, thawed

1. Prepare rice according to package directions. Cool completely.

2. Preheat oven to 375°F. In medium bowl, combine rice, artichokes, Parmesan cheese and onion; mix well. Stir in yogurt until well blended.

3. Place one sheet of phyllo dough on a damp kitchen towel. (Keep remaining dough covered.) Lightly spray dough with nonstick cooking spray. Fold dough in half by bringing short sides of dough together; spray lightly with additional cooking spray.

4. Cut dough into four equal strips, each about 3¼ inches wide. For each appetizer, spoon about 1 tablespoon rice mixture onto dough about 1 inch from end of each strip. Fold 1 corner over filling to make triangle. Continue folding as you would fold a flag to form a triangle that encloses filling. Repeat with remaining dough and filling.

5. Place triangles on greased baking sheets. Spray triangles with nonstick cooking spray. Bake 12 to 15 minutes or until golden brown.

Makes 40 appetizers

Cook's Tips: To simplify preparation, the rice mixture can be prepared a day ahead, covered and refrigerated until ready to use. Use a pizza cutter to cut phyllo dough into strips.

HAM AND GOUDA QUESADILLA SNACKS

1½ cups shredded smoked Gouda cheese (6 ounces)
  1 cup chopped ham (4 ounces)
  ½ cup pitted ripe olives, chopped
  ¼ cup minced red onion
  ½ cup GREY POUPON® COUNTRY DIJON®
    Mustard
  8 (6- or 7-inch) flour tortillas
    Sour cream, chopped peppers, sliced pitted ripe
    olives and cilantro, for garnish

Mix cheese, ham, olives and onion in small bowl. Spread 1 tablespoon mustard on each tortilla; spread about ⅓ cup cheese mixture over half of each tortilla. Fold tortilla in half to cover filling.

Heat filled tortillas in large nonstick skillet over medium heat for 4 minutes or until cheese melts, turning once. Cut each quesadilla into 3 wedges. Place on serving platter; garnish with sour cream, peppers, olives and cilantro.

Makes 24 appetizers

RICE & ARTICHOKE PHYLLO TRIANGLES

Meat Entrées

CARIBBEAN PORK KABOBS AND RICE

1 cup UNCLE BEN'S® ORIGINAL CONVERTED® Brand Rice
1½ cups peeled, diced sweet potato
2 tablespoons plus 2 teaspoons Caribbean seasoning, divided
1 can (8 ounces) pineapple chunks in pineapple juice
1 (12-ounce) pork tenderloin, cut into 1½-inch cubes
1 red bell pepper, cut into 1-inch squares
1 green bell pepper, cut into 1-inch squares
¼ cup dry-roasted peanuts

1. In medium pan, heat 2 cups water to a boil. Add rice, sweet potato and 2 teaspoons Caribbean seasoning. Cover, reduce heat and simmer 10 minutes or until rice and sweet potato are tender.

2. Drain pineapple chunks, reserving juice. Add pineapple chunks to rice mixture.

3. Preheat broiler. Place remaining 2 tablespoons Caribbean seasoning into large resealable plastic food storage bag. Add pork; seal bag and turn to coat pork with seasoning. Thread pork and bell peppers onto skewers.

4. Broil kabobs 4 minutes on each side. Turn and brush with reserved pineapple juice. Continue cooking 2 minutes on each side until pork is no longer pink.

5. Top rice with peanuts and serve with kabobs.

Makes 4 servings

Meat Entrées

TENDERLOIN DELUXE WITH MUSHROOM SAUCE

10 tablespoons I CAN'T BELIEVE IT'S NOT
    BUTTER!® Spread, divided
¼ cup chopped green onions
1 tablespoon Dijon-style mustard
1 teaspoon soy sauce
2½- to 3-pound beef tenderloin
8 ounces mushrooms, sliced
2 medium onions, finely chopped
2 cloves garlic, finely chopped
⅓ cup dry sherry
4 drops hot pepper sauce
1 cup beef broth

Preheat oven to 425°F.

In small bowl, blend 4 tablespoons I Can't Believe It's
Not Butter! Spread, green onions, mustard and soy
sauce. In 13×9-inch baking or roasting pan, arrange
beef and evenly spread with mustard mixture.

Bake uncovered 15 minutes. Decrease heat to 400°F and
bake 45 minutes or until desired doneness. Let stand
10 minutes before slicing.

Meanwhile, in 12-inch skillet, melt remaining
6 tablespoons I Can't Believe It's Not Butter! Spread
over medium-high heat and cook mushrooms, stirring
occasionally, 3 minutes or until softened. Stir in onions
and cook, stirring occasionally, 12 minutes or until
golden brown. Add garlic and cook 30 seconds. Stir in
sherry and hot pepper sauce and cook 2 minutes. Stir in
broth and simmer 5 minutes or until sauce is slightly
thickened. Serve sauce over sliced beef.

Makes 6 servings

BEEF KABOBS WITH APRICOT GLAZE

1 can (15¼ ounces) DEL MONTE® Apricot Halves
1 tablespoon cornstarch
1 teaspoon Dijon mustard
½ teaspoon dried basil leaves
1 pound sirloin steak, cut into 1½-inch cubes
1 small green bell pepper, cut into ¾-inch pieces
4 medium mushrooms, cut in half
4 to 8 skewers*

*To prevent burning of wooden skewers, soak skewers in water for
10 minutes before assembling kabobs.*

1. Drain apricot syrup into small saucepan. Blend in
cornstarch until dissolved. Cook over medium heat,
stirring constantly, until thickened. Stir in mustard and
basil. Set aside.

2. Thread meat, apricots, green pepper and mushrooms
alternately onto skewers; brush with apricot syrup
mixture. Grill kabobs over hot coals (or broil) about
5 minutes on each side or to desired doneness,
brushing occasionally with additional syrup mixture.
Garnish, if desired.   *Makes 4 servings*

Prep and Cook Time: 25 minutes

TENDERLOIN DELUXE WITH MUSHROOM SAUCE

BEEF & TOMATO STIR-FRY

½ pound boneless tender beef steak (sirloin, rib eye or top loin)
3 tablespoons cornstarch, divided
4 tablespoons KIKKOMAN® Soy Sauce, divided
1 tablespoon dry sherry
1 clove garlic, minced
2 teaspoons minced fresh gingerroot
½ teaspoon sugar
1 cup water
2 tablespoons vegetable oil, divided
2 stalks celery, cut diagonally into ¼-inch-thick slices
1 medium onion, chunked
1 medium-size green bell pepper, chunked
2 medium tomatoes, chunked

Cut beef across grain into thin strips. Combine 1 tablespoon *each* cornstarch, soy sauce and sherry with garlic, gingerroot and sugar in medium bowl; stir in beef. Let stand 15 minutes. Meanwhile, combine water, remaining 2 tablespoons cornstarch and 3 tablespoons soy sauce in small bowl; set aside. Heat 1 tablespoon oil in hot wok or large skillet over high heat. Add beef and stir-fry 1 minute; remove. Heat remaining 1 tablespoon oil in same pan. Add celery, onion and bell pepper; stir-fry 3 minutes. Add beef, soy sauce mixture and tomatoes; cook and stir until sauce boils and thickens and tomatoes are heated through. *Makes 4 servings*

MEXICAN MEATLOAF

1½ pounds lean ground turkey or beef
1 cup GUILTLESS GOURMET® Southwestern Grill Salsa, divided
1 cup (3.5 ounces) crushed GUILTLESS GOURMET® Baked Tortilla Chips (yellow or white corn)
½ medium onion, chopped
3 egg whites, slightly beaten
½ teaspoon coarsely ground black pepper

Preheat oven to 350°F. Mix turkey, ½ cup salsa, crushed chips, onion, egg whites and pepper in large bowl until lightly blended. Shape into loaf and place in 9×5-inch loaf pan.

Bake 1 hour or until firm. Pour remaining ½ cup salsa over top; bake 10 minutes more. Let stand 10 minutes before slicing and serving. *Makes 4 servings*

BEEF & TOMATO STIR-FRY

ITALIAN SAUSAGE LASAGNA

1½ **pounds BOB EVANS® Italian Roll Sausage**
2 **tablespoons olive oil**
2 **green bell peppers, thinly sliced**
1 **large yellow onion, thinly sliced**
4 **cloves garlic, minced and divided**
1 **(28-ounce) can whole tomatoes, undrained**
1 **(8-ounce) can tomato sauce**
2 **teaspoons fennel seeds**
   Salt and black pepper to taste
1 **tablespoon butter or margarine**
1 **large yellow onion, chopped**
2 **(10-ounce) packages chopped frozen spinach,**
   thawed and squeezed dry
1 **cup grated Parmesan cheese, divided**
3 **cups (24 ounces) low fat ricotta cheese**
1 **pound shredded mozzarella or provolone cheese**
9 **uncooked lasagna noodles**

Crumble sausage in large heavy skillet. Cook over medium heat until well browned, stirring occasionally. Remove sausage to paper towels; set aside. Drain off drippings and wipe skillet clean with paper towels. Heat oil in same skillet over medium-high heat until hot. Add green peppers, sliced onion and half the garlic. Cook, covered, over medium heat about 10 minutes or until vegetables are wilted, stirring occasionally. Stir in tomatoes with juice, tomato sauce and fennel seeds, stirring well to break up tomatoes. Bring to a boil. Reduce heat to low; simmer, uncovered, 20 to 30 minutes to blend flavors. Stir in reserved sausage. Season sauce mixture with salt and black pepper; set aside. Melt butter in small saucepan over medium-high heat; add chopped onion and remaining garlic. Cook and stir about 10 minutes or until onion is tender. Stir in spinach and ¼ cup Parmesan; set aside. Combine ricotta, mozzarella and ½ cup Parmesan in medium bowl. Season with salt and black pepper. Cook noodles according to package directions; drain.

Preheat oven to 350°F. Pour ⅓ of reserved sauce mixture into greased 13×9-inch baking dish; spread evenly. Arrange 3 noodles over sauce mixture; spread half the spinach mixture over noodles. Spread half the cheese mixture evenly over spinach. Repeat layers once. Top with remaining 3 noodles and sauce mixture. Sprinkle with remaining ¼ cup Parmesan. Bake about 1 hour or until sauce is bubbly and cheese is browned on top. Let stand 10 to 15 minutes before slicing. Serve hot. Refrigerate leftovers. *Makes 8 servings*

• Classic Tip •

Bring a little taste of Italy to your table tonight. Serve with crusty bread and a tossed salad for a complete meal everyone will love.

GLAZED PORK CHOPS & APPLES

4 boneless pork chops, ½ inch thick
½ cup apple juice
¼ cup *French's*® Hearty Deli Mustard
¼ cup packed brown sugar
1 green or red apple, cut into small chunks

1. Heat *1 tablespoon oil* in nonstick skillet over medium-high heat. Cook pork chops for 5 minutes or until browned on both sides.

2. Add remaining ingredients. Bring to a full boil. Reduce heat to medium. Simmer, uncovered, for 8 to 10 minutes or until pork is no longer pink in center and sauce thickens slightly, stirring occasionally.

3. Serve with noodles, if desired.   *Makes 4 servings*

Prep Time: 5 minutes
Cook Time: 13 minutes

GLAZED PORK CHOP & APPLES

SHEPHERD'S PIE

1 pound ground beef
1 cup chopped onion
1 teaspoon LAWRY'S® Seasoned Salt
1 package (10 ounces) frozen peas and carrots, cooked and drained
1 package (0.88 ounces) LAWRY'S® Brown Gravy Mix
1 cup water
1 egg, beaten
3 cups mashed potatoes
  Paprika

In large skillet, cook ground beef and onion over medium-high heat until beef is browned; drain fat.

Add Seasoned Salt and peas and carrots; mix well. Prepare Brown Gravy Mix with 1 cup water according to package directions. Add some gravy to beaten egg; gradually add egg-gravy mixture to gravy, stirring constantly. Combine gravy with meat. In shallow, 2-quart casserole, place meat; arrange potatoes in mounds over meat. Sprinkle top with paprika. Bake, uncovered, in 400°F oven 15 minutes or until heated.

Makes 6 servings

Serving Suggestion: Serve with tossed green salad.

HERBED ROAST

1 beef top round roast (about 3 pounds)
⅓ cup Dijon-style mustard
1½ teaspoons dried thyme, crushed
1 teaspoon dried rosemary, crushed
1 teaspoon LAWRY'S® Seasoned Pepper
1 teaspoon LAWRY'S® Garlic Powder with Parsley
½ teaspoon LAWRY'S® Seasoned Salt

Brush all sides of roast with mustard. In small bowl, combine remaining ingredients; mix well. Sprinkle on top and sides of roast, pressing into meat. Place roast, fat side up, on rack in roasting pan. Roast in 325°F oven, 50 minutes to 1 hour or until internal temperature reaches 160°F. Remove roast from oven. Let stand, covered, 15 minutes.

Makes 6 to 8 servings

Serving Suggestion: Slice thinly and serve with roasted potato wedges and steamed vegetables.

SWEET 'N' SOUR COUNTRY RIBS

3 pounds country-style pork ribs, fat trimmed

3 large sweet potatoes, peeled and cut into 2-inch chunks
2 cups apple juice
¼ cup cider vinegar
¼ cup *French's®* Worcestershire Sauce
¼ cup packed brown sugar
2 tablespoons *French's®* Hearty Deli Brown Mustard
2 tart green apples, cored and cut into 1-inch chunks
1 tablespoon cornstarch

1. Heat *1 tablespoon oil* in 6-quart saucepot or Dutch oven over high heat. Cook ribs 10 minutes or until well-browned on all sides; drain fat.

2. Add potatoes to ribs. Whisk together apple juice, vinegar, Worcestershire, sugar and mustard. Pour over rib mixture; stir well. Heat to boiling. Reduce heat to low. Cook, covered, 40 minutes or until pork is tender and no longer pink in center, stirring occasionally.

3. Stir in apples; cook 5 minutes or until tender. Transfer ribs, potatoes and apples to platter; keep warm. Combine cornstarch with *2 tablespoons water*. Stir into pot. Heat to boiling, whisking constantly. Cook 1 to 2 minutes or until liquid thickens, stirring often. Serve with corn and crusty bread, if desired.

Makes 6 servings (with 2 cups gravy)

20 Minute Marinade: Marinate 1 pound steak, chicken or chops for 20 minutes in ¼ cup *French's®* Worcestershire Sauce.

Prep Time: 10 minutes
Cook Time: about 1 hour

HERBED ROAST

HONEY WHISKEY CLOVE HAM

¾ **cup honey**
1½ **tablespoons bourbon whiskey***
½ **teaspoon ground cloves**
1 **bone-in ham, fully cooked and spiral sliced (about 5 pounds)**

*2 teaspoons vanilla can be substituted for bourbon.

Combine honey, bourbon and cloves in small bowl until well blended. Place ham, cut-side down, in roasting pan; brush with honey mixture. Cover pan with foil and bake at 275°F about 1 hour or until heated through. Remove foil from ham and increase oven temperature to 425°F. Brush with honey mixture. Bake about 10 minutes more or until ham is golden brown. Remove from oven and place on serving platter. Pour juices over ham. *Makes 10 to 12 servings*

Favorite recipe from **National Honey Board**

SPARERIBS WITH TEX–MEX BARBECUE SAUCE

6 **pounds pork spareribs, cut into 2-rib portions**
½ **cup HELLMANN'S® or BEST FOODS® Real or Light Mayonnaise**
½ **cup ketchup**
¼ **cup Worcestershire sauce**
3 **tablespoons chili powder**
1 **clove garlic, minced or pressed**
⅛ **teaspoon hot pepper sauce**

1. In large shallow roasting pan, arrange ribs on rack in single layer. Roast in 325°F oven 1½ hours or until tender.

2. Meanwhile, prepare Tex-Mex Barbecue Sauce. Using wire whisk, stir mayonnaise, ketchup, Worcestershire sauce, chili powder, garlic and hot pepper sauce in small bowl until smooth.

3. Brush sauce on ribs, turning frequently, during last 20 minutes of roasting time. *Makes 6 servings*

Homestyle Barbecue Sauce: Follow recipe for Tex-Mex Barbecue Sauce, omitting chili powder and garlic and adding ¼ cup prepared mustard and ¼ cup KARO® Dark Corn Syrup or ¼ cup firmly packed brown sugar in step 2.

Sweet and Sour Barbecue Sauce: Follow recipe for Tex-Mex Barbecue Sauce, omitting Worcestershire sauce, chili powder, garlic and hot pepper sauce and adding ¾ cup apricot preserves, ¼ cup soy sauce and 1 teaspoon ground ginger in step 2.

HONEY WHISKEY CLOVE HAM

FRUITED PORK LOIN

1 cup dried apricot halves
½ cup dry sherry
1 (3- to 5-pound) center cut pork rib or loin roast, backbone cracked
1 cup KARO® Light or Dark Corn Syrup
1 tablespoon grated orange peel
½ cup orange juice
¼ cup soy sauce

1. In small saucepan, combine apricots and sherry. Cover and cook over medium heat, stirring occasionally, until liquid is absorbed.

2. Trim excess fat from surface of roast. Cut deep slits in meat directly over rib bones; insert 3 or 4 apricots in each slit. Place roast, bone-side down, on rack in roasting pan.

3. Roast in 325°F oven 1 to 2 hours* or until meat thermometer registers 160°F.

4. Meanwhile, prepare glaze. In small saucepan, stir corn syrup, orange peel, orange juice and soy sauce. Bring to boil; reduce heat and simmer 5 minutes. Set aside half of glaze to serve with pork loin.

5. Brush pork loin frequently with remaining glaze during last 30 minutes of roasting. Serve with reserved glaze.
Makes 6 to 10 servings

Roast pork loin at 325°F for 20 to 25 minutes per pound.

Prep Time: 20 minutes
Bake Time: 1 to 2 hours

DIJON PESTO STEAK

½ cup finely chopped fresh basil or parsley

½ cup PLANTERS® Walnuts, finely chopped
⅓ cup GREY POUPON® Dijon Mustard
1 clove garlic, crushed
1 (2-pound) boneless sirloin or top round steak

Combine basil or parsley, walnuts, mustard and garlic in small bowl.

Broil steak 5 inches from heat source, about 10 minutes, turning once. Spread top of steak with basil or parsley mixture; broil 2 to 3 minutes more or until lightly browned and beef is cooked to desired doneness. Slice and serve.
Makes 6 to 8 servings

• Classic Tip •

Never use cooking sherry in place of dry sherry. It lacks distinction and flavor and sometimes has added salt.

QUICK BEEF BOURGUIGNONNE

3 tablespoons all-purpose flour
½ teaspoon dried thyme
½ teaspoon ground black pepper
¾ pound boneless sirloin or top round steak, cut into 1-inch pieces
2 tablespoons vegetable oil, divided
3 cups (8 ounces) halved or quartered crimini or white mushrooms
⅓ cup thinly sliced shallots or chopped onion
1 (14½-ounce) can beef broth
¼ cup dry red wine or water
1 (4.8-ounce) package PASTA RONI® Garlic Alfredo
¾ cup thinly sliced carrots

QUICK BEEF BOURGUIGNONNE

1. Combine flour, thyme and pepper in resealable plastic food storage bag. Add steak; shake to coat evenly with flour mixture.

2. In large skillet over medium-high heat, heat 1 tablespoon oil. Add steak; cook 3 minutes or until lightly browned on all sides. Remove from skillet; set aside.

3. In same skillet over medium heat, heat remaining 1 tablespoon oil. Add mushrooms and shallots; cook 3 minutes, stirring occasionally.

4. Add ¼ cup water, beef broth and wine; bring to a boil. Add pasta, steak, carrots and Special Seasonings. Reduce heat to medium. Simmer 5 minutes or until pasta is tender. Let stand 5 minutes before serving.

Makes 4 servings

Prep Time: 15 minutes
Cook Time: 20 minutes

CROWN ROAST OF PORK WITH PEACH STUFFING

1 (7- to 8-pound) crown roast of pork (12 to 16 ribs)
1½ cups water
1 cup FLEISCHMANN'S® Original Margarine, divided
1 (15-ounce) package seasoned bread cubes
1 cup chopped celery
2 medium onions, chopped
1 (16-ounce) can sliced peaches, drained and chopped, reserve liquid
½ cup seedless raisins

1. Place crown roast, bone tips up, on rack in shallow roasting pan. Make a ball of foil and press into cavity to hold open. Wrap bone tips in foil. Roast at 325°F, uncovered, for 2 hours; baste with pan drippings occasionally.

2. Heat water and ¾ cup margarine in large heavy pot to a boil; remove from heat. Add bread cubes, tossing lightly with a fork; set aside.

3. Cook and stir celery and onions in remaining margarine in large skillet over medium-high heat until tender, about 5 minutes.

4. Add celery mixture, peaches with liquid and raisins to bread cube mixture, tossing to mix well.

5. Remove foil from center of roast. Spoon stuffing lightly into cavity. Roast 30 to 45 minutes more or until meat thermometer registers 155°F (internal temperature will rise to 160°F upon standing). Cover stuffing with foil, if necessary, to prevent overbrowning. Bake any remaining stuffing in greased, covered casserole during last 30 minutes of roasting. *Makes 12 to 16 servings*

Preparation Time: 45 minutes
Cook Time: 2 hours and 30 minutes
Total Time: 3 hours and 15 minutes

BEEF WITH DRY SPICE RUB

3 tablespoons firmly packed brown sugar
1 tablespoon black peppercorns
1 tablespoon yellow mustard seeds
1 tablespoon whole coriander seeds
4 cloves garlic
1½ to 2 pounds beef top round steak or London Broil, about ½ inch thick
Vegetable or olive oil
Salt

Place sugar, peppercorns, mustard seeds, coriander seeds and garlic in blender or food processor; process until seeds and garlic are crushed. Rub beef with oil; pat on spice mixture. Season generously with salt.

Lightly oil hot grid to prevent sticking. Grill beef on covered grill over medium-low KINGSFORD® Briquets 16 to 20 minutes for medium or until desired doneness, turning once. Let stand 5 minutes before cutting across the grain into thin diagonal slices. *Makes 6 servings*

CROWN ROAST OF PORK WITH PEACH STUFFING

STEAKHOUSE LONDON BROIL

1 package KNORR® Recipe Classics™ Roasted Garlic Herb or French Onion Soup, Dip and Recipe Mix
⅓ cup vegetable or olive oil
2 tablespoons red wine vinegar
1 (1½- to 2-pound) beef round steak (for London Broil) or flank steak

• In large plastic food bag or 13×9-inch glass baking dish, blend recipe mix, oil and vinegar.

• Add steak, turning to coat. Close bag, or cover, and marinate in refrigerator 30 minutes to 3 hours.

• Remove meat from marinade, discarding marinade. Grill or broil, turning occasionally, until desired doneness.

• Slice meat thinly across the grain.

Makes 6 to 8 servings

Garlic Chicken: Substitute 6 to 8 boneless chicken breasts or 3 to 4 pounds bone-in chicken pieces for steak. Marinate as directed. Grill boneless chicken breasts 6 minutes or bone-in chicken pieces 20 minutes or until chicken is no longer pink.

Prep Time: 5 minutes
Marinate Time: 30 minutes to 3 hours
Grill Time: 20 minutes

BLUE CHEESE BURGERS WITH RED ONION

2 pounds ground chuck
2 cloves garlic, minced
1 teaspoon salt
½ teaspoon black pepper
4 ounces blue cheese
⅓ cup coarsely chopped walnuts, toasted
1 torpedo (long) red onion *or* 2 small red onions, sliced into ⅜-inch-thick rounds
2 baguettes (each 12 inches long)
Olive or vegetable oil

Combine beef, garlic, salt and pepper in medium bowl. Shape meat mixture into 12 oval patties. Mash cheese and blend with walnuts in small bowl. Divide cheese mixture equally; place onto centers of 6 meat patties. Top with remaining meat patties; tightly pinch edges together to seal in filling.

Oil hot grid to help prevent sticking. Grill patties and onion, if desired, on covered grill, over medium KINGSFORD® Briquets, 7 to 12 minutes for medium doneness, turning once. Cut baguettes into 4-inch lengths; split each piece and brush cut side with olive oil. Move cooked burgers to edge of grill to keep warm. Grill bread, oil side down, until lightly toasted. Serve burgers on toasted baguettes. *Makes 6 servings*

MARINATED BEEF ROAST WITH ZESTY HORSERADISH GLAZE

Marinated Beef Roast
- 2 cups red wine
- 1 cup diced sweet onion
- ½ cup WESSON® Vegetable Oil
- ½ cup beef broth
- 3 tablespoons steak sauce
- 2 teaspoons GEBHARDT® Chili Powder
- 1 teaspoon dried sweet basil
- 1 teaspoon crushed fresh garlic
- 4½ to 5 pounds sirloin tip roast

Glaze
- ⅓ cup chili sauce
- ¼ cup red wine
- 3 tablespoons prepared horseradish
- 1 teaspoon salt

Gravy (optional)
- ¼ cup all-purpose flour
- Red wine or beef broth
- Salt and pepper to taste

Marinated Beef Roast

In a large resealable plastic food storage bag, combine *all marinade* ingredients; seal and shake well. Add roast; squeeze out air and seal. Place on platter; refrigerate 4 hours or overnight. Bring roast to room temperature. Preheat oven to 350°F. Place roast on roasting rack in the center of a foil-lined drip pan. Pour marinade in drip pan. Roast meat about 2 hours (internal temperature of 140°F with meat thermometer) or until desired doneness.

Glaze

Meanwhile, combine *all glaze* ingredients; blend well. During the last hour of roasting, spoon glaze over roast 3 times using ⅓ glaze each time. Remove roast from oven; cover and let stand 20 minutes before carving.

Gravy

While roast is standing, make a pan gravy with drippings. Pour drippings into a liquid measuring cup; allow drippings to settle. Skim off fat into a saucepan. Heat fat along with 2 to 3 tablespoons flour; mix well. Cook flour mixture until dark brown. Add red wine or beef broth to reserved drippings to equal 3 cups. Whisk liquid into flour mixture, stirring constantly, until gravy is smooth and thickened. Salt and pepper to taste. Slice roast; serve gravy on the side.

Makes 12 to 14 servings

• Classic Tip •

Horseradish is an ancient herb native to eastern Europe. It has green spiky leaves that can be used in salads. However, it is mainly grown for its large, white, spicy roots.

HAM & ASPARAGUS BRUNCH BAKE

2 boxes UNCLE BEN'S® Long Grain & Wild Rice
Original Recipe
1 pound asparagus, cut into 1-inch pieces (about
2½ cups)
2 cups chopped ham
1 cup chopped yellow or red bell pepper
¼ cup finely chopped red onion
1 cup (4 ounces) shredded Swiss cheese

1. In large saucepan, prepare rice mixes according to
package directions, adding asparagus during last
5 minutes of cooking.

2. Meanwhile, preheat oven to 350°F. Grease 11×7½-
inch baking dish.

3. Remove rice mixture from heat. Add ham, bell
pepper and onion; mix well. Place mixture in prepared
baking dish; sprinkle with cheese.

4. Bake 25 to 30 minutes or until mixture is heated
through.   *Makes 8 servings*

Variation: Substitute UNCLE BEN'S® Brand Butter &
Herb Long Grain & Wild Rice for the Original Recipe
Long Grain & Wild Rice.

Tip: This dish can be prepared ahead of time through
step 3. Cover with foil and refrigerate several hours or
overnight. Bake, covered, in preheated 350°F oven for
15 minutes. Remove foil and continue to bake until
heated through, about 10 minutes.

HAM & ASPARAGUS BRUNCH BAKE

LIPTON® ONION BURGERS

1 envelope LIPTON® RECIPE SECRETS® Onion
  Soup Mix*
2 pounds ground beef
½ cup water

*Also terrific with LIPTON® RECIPE SECRETS® Beefy Onion,
Onion Mushroom, Beefy Mushroom, Savory Herb with Garlic or
Ranch Soup Mix.*

1. In large bowl, combine all ingredients; shape into
8 patties.

2. Grill or broil until done.   *Makes about 8 servings*

Prep Time: 10 minutes
Cook Time: 12 minutes

PEPPERED STEAKS WITH BLACKBERRY SAUCE

Steaks
  ⅓ cup lemon juice
  ⅓ cup oil
  ¼ cup chopped onion
  2 cloves garlic, crushed
  4 (4- to 6-ounce) beef tenderloin or eye of round
    steaks, trimmed of fat
  1 tablespoon coarsely ground pepper

Blackberry Sauce
  ½ cup SMUCKER'S® Seedless Blackberry Jam
  ¼ cup red wine vinegar
  ¼ teaspoon onion powder
  ¼ cup fresh or frozen blackberries, thawed

Combine lemon juice, oil, onion and garlic in large
resealable plastic bag; mix well. Place steaks in bag, seal
and refrigerate 6 to 24 hours, turning bag occasionally.

When ready to cook, rub pepper around edges of each
steak.

Heat grill. In small saucepan, combine jam, vinegar and
onion powder. Cook over medium heat until jam is
melted, stirring constantly. Remove from heat.

Oil grill rack. Place steaks on gas grill over medium
heat or on charcoal grill 4 to 6 inches from medium-hot
coals. Cook 8 to 12 minutes or until desired doneness,
turning once halfway through cooking. To serve, spread
steaks with blackberry sauce; top with fresh berries.

Makes 4 servings

Note: Steaks can be cooked in the broiler. Place on oiled
broiler pan. Broil 4 to 6 inches from heat for 7 to
10 minutes or until desired doneness, turning once
halfway through cooking.

MARINATED FLANK STEAK WITH PINEAPPLE

1 can (15¼ ounces) DEL MONTE® Sliced
    Pineapple In Its Own Juice
¼ cup teriyaki sauce
2 tablespoons honey
1 pound flank steak

1. Drain pineapple, reserving 2 tablespoons juice. Set aside pineapple for later use.

2. Combine reserved juice, teriyaki sauce and honey in shallow 2-quart dish; mix well. Add meat; turn to coat. Cover and refrigerate at least 30 minutes or overnight.

3. Remove meat from marinade, reserving marinade. Grill meat over hot coals (or broil), brushing occasionally with reserved marinade. Cook about 4 minutes on each side for rare; about 5 minutes on each side for medium; or about 6 minutes on each side for well done. During last 4 minutes of cooking, brush pineapple slices with marinade; grill until heated through.

4. Slice meat across grain; serve with pineapple. Garnish, if desired.   *Makes 4 servings*

Note: Marinade that has come into contact with raw meat must be discarded or boiled for several minutes before serving with cooked food.

Prep and Marinate Time: 35 minutes
Cook Time: 10 minutes

HARVEST POT ROAST WITH SWEET POTATOES

1 envelope LIPTON® RECIPE SECRETS® Onion
    Soup Mix
1½ cups water
¼ cup soy sauce
2 tablespoons firmly packed dark brown sugar
1 teaspoon ground ginger (optional)
1 (3- to 3½-pound) boneless pot roast (rump, chuck
    or round)
4 large sweet potatoes, peeled, if desired, and cut
    into large chunks
3 tablespoons water
2 tablespoons all-purpose flour

1. Preheat oven to 325°F. In Dutch oven or 5-quart heavy ovenproof saucepot, combine soup mix, water, soy sauce, brown sugar and ginger; add roast.

2. Cover and bake 1 hour 45 minutes.

3. Add potatoes and bake covered an additional 45 minutes or until beef and potatoes are tender.

4. Remove roast and potatoes to serving platter and keep warm; reserve juices.

5. In small cup, with wire whisk, blend water and flour. In Dutch oven, add flour mixture to reserved juices. Bring to a boil over high heat. Boil, stirring occasionally, 2 minutes. Serve with roast and potatoes.

Makes 6 servings

MARINATED FLANK STEAK WITH PINEAPPLE

BEEF AND BROCCOLI

Sauce

　　2 tablespoons oyster sauce

　　¼ cup water

　　1 tablespoon *each*: cornstarch and dry sherry

　　⅛ teaspoon Oriental sesame oil

Beef and Vegetables

　　3 tablespoons LA CHOY® Soy Sauce

　　1 tablespoon cornstarch

　　1 pound flank steak, sliced across grain into thin
　　　　2-inch strips

　　4 tablespoons WESSON® Oil, divided

　　3 cups fresh broccoli flowerettes

　　1 cup julienne-cut carrots

　　1 tablespoon *each:* minced fresh garlic and
　　　　gingerroot

　　1 can (8 ounces) LA CHOY® Sliced Water
　　　　Chestnuts, drained

　　1 can (5 ounces) LA CHOY® Chow Mein Noodles

In small bowl, combine sauce ingredients; set aside. In large bowl, combine soy sauce and cornstarch; mix well. Add beef; toss gently to coat. Cover and marinate 30 minutes. In large nonstick skillet or wok, heat 2 tablespoons oil. Add half of beef mixture; stir-fry until lightly browned. Remove beef from skillet; set aside. Repeat with remaining beef mixture. Heat remaining 2 tablespoons oil in same skillet. Add broccoli, carrots, garlic and ginger; stir-fry 1 to 2 minutes or until vegetables are crisp-tender. Return beef to skillet. Stir sauce; add to skillet with water chestnuts. Cook, stirring constantly, until sauce is thick and bubbly. Reserve a few noodles; serve beef mixture over remaining noodles. Garnish with reserved noodles.

Makes 4 to 6 servings

• Classic Tip •

Oyster sauce is a popular Asian seasoning. It is a dark brown sauce consisting of oysters, brine and soy sauce and cooked until thick and concentrated.

SKILLET STEAK FAJITAS

½ cup A.1.® Steak Sauce
½ cup mild, medium or hot thick and chunky salsa
1 (1-pound) beef flank or bottom round steak, thinly sliced
1 medium onion, thinly sliced
1 medium green bell pepper, cut into strips
1 tablespoon margarine or butter
8 (6½-inch) flour tortillas, warmed

1. Blend steak sauce and salsa. Place steak in glass dish; coat with ¼ cup salsa mixture. Cover; refrigerate 1 hour, stirring occasionally.

2. Cook and stir onion and pepper in margarine in large skillet, over medium-high heat for 3 minutes or until tender. Remove with slotted spoon; set aside.

3. Cook and stir steak in same skillet for 5 minutes or until done. Add remaining salsa mixture, onion and pepper; cook until heated through. Serve with tortillas and your favorite fajita toppings if desired.

Makes 4 servings

SKILLET STEAK FAJITAS

ROASTED GARLIC SWEDISH MEATBALLS

1 pound ground beef
½ cup plain dry bread crumbs
1 egg
1 jar (16 ounces) RAGÚ® Cheese Creations!® Roasted Garlic Parmesan Sauce
1¼ cups beef broth
2 teaspoons Worcestershire sauce
1 teaspoon ground allspice (optional)

In large bowl, combine ground beef, bread crumbs and egg; shape into 20 (1½-inch) meatballs.

In 12-inch nonstick skillet, brown meatballs over medium-high heat.

Meanwhile, in medium bowl, combine Ragú Cheese Creations! Sauce, beef broth, Worcestershire sauce and allspice; stir into skillet. Bring to a boil over high heat. Reduce heat to low and simmer uncovered, stirring occasionally, 10 minutes or until meatballs are done and sauce is slightly thickened. Serve, if desired, over hot cooked noodles or rice.

Makes 4 servings

MUSHROOM–SAUCED STEAK

½ cup sliced onion

2 tablespoons margarine or butter

1½ cups sliced mushrooms

1 cup A.1.® BOLD & SPICY Steak Sauce

½ cup dairy sour cream

2 (8-ounce) beef club or strip steaks, about 1 inch thick

Sauté onion in margarine in medium skillet over medium heat until tender, about 5 minutes. Add mushrooms; sauté 5 minutes more. Stir in steak sauce; heat to a boil. Reduce heat and simmer 5 minutes; stir in sour cream. Cook and stir until heated through (do not boil); keep warm.

Grill steaks over medium heat 5 minutes on each side or until done. Serve steaks topped with mushroom sauce.

Makes 4 servings

HAM & BARBECUED BEAN SKILLET

1 tablespoon vegetable oil

1 cup chopped onion

1 teaspoon bottled minced garlic

1 can (15 ounces) red or pink kidney beans, rinsed and drained

1 can (15 ounces) cannellini or Great Northern beans, rinsed and drained

1 cup chopped green bell pepper

½ cup firmly packed light brown sugar

½ cup catsup

2 tablespoons cider vinegar

2 teaspoons dry mustard

1 fully cooked smoked ham steak (about 12 ounces), cut ½ inch thick

1. Heat oil in large deep skillet over medium-high heat until hot. Add onion and garlic; cook 3 minutes, stirring occasionally.

2. Add kidney beans, cannellini beans, bell pepper, brown sugar, catsup, vinegar and mustard; mix well.

3. Trim fat from ham; cut into ½-inch pieces. Add ham to bean mixture; simmer over medium heat 5 minutes or until sauce thickens and mixture is heated through, stirring occasionally.

Makes 4 servings

Serving suggestion: Serve with a Caesar salad and crisp breadsticks.

Prep and Cook Time: 20 minutes

MUSHROOM-SAUCED STEAK

Meat Entrées

SWEET AND SOUR PORK

¾ pound boneless pork
1 teaspoon vegetable oil
1 bag (16 ounces) BIRDS EYE® frozen Farm Fresh
    Mixtures Pepper Stir Fry vegetables
1 tablespoon water
1 jar (14 ounces) sweet and sour sauce
1 can (8 ounces) pineapple chunks, drained

• Cut pork into thin strips.

• In large skillet, heat oil over medium-high heat.

• Add pork; stir-fry until pork is browned.

• Add vegetables and water; cover and cook over
medium heat 5 to 7 minutes or until vegetables are
crisp-tender.

• Uncover; stir in sweet and sour sauce and pineapple.
Cook until heated through.   *Makes 4 servings*

Serving Suggestion: Serve over hot cooked rice.

Birds Eye Idea: For a quick sweet and sour sauce for
chicken nuggets or egg rolls, add sugar and vinegar to
taste to jarred strained apricots or peaches.

Prep Time: 5 minutes
Cook Time: 15 to 18 minutes

BEEF SIRLOIN IN RICH ITALIAN SAUCE

2 tablespoons olive or vegetable oil
1 pound top sirloin, cut into thin strips
2 cloves garlic, cut in half
1 can (14.5 ounces) CONTADINA® Recipe Ready
    Diced Tomatoes, undrained
2 tablespoons chopped fresh parsley *or*
    2 teaspoons dried parsley flakes
2 tablespoons dry red wine or beef broth
½ teaspoon dried thyme leaves, crushed
¼ teaspoon dried rosemary leaves, crushed
¼ teaspoon salt
¼ teaspoon ground black pepper
    Additional chopped fresh parsley (optional)

1. Heat oil over high heat in large skillet. Add meat
and garlic; cook for 1 to 2 minutes or until meat is
browned, stirring occasionally. Remove meat from
skillet; discard garlic.

2. Add undrained tomatoes, parsley, wine, thyme,
rosemary, salt and pepper to skillet; stir. Bring to a boil.
Reduce heat to low.

3. Return meat to skillet; cover. Simmer for 5 minutes.
Sprinkle with additional fresh parsley, if desired.

Makes 4 servings

Prep Time: 8 minutes
Cook Time: 9 minutes

SWEET AND SOUR PORK

 64

BARBECUED RIBS

1 cup ketchup
½ cup GRANDMA'S® Molasses
¼ cup cider vinegar
¼ cup Dijon mustard
2 tablespoons Worcestershire sauce
1 teaspoon garlic powder
1 teaspoon hickory flavor liquid smoke (optional)
¼ teaspoon ground red pepper
¼ teaspoon hot pepper sauce
4 to 6 pounds baby back ribs

1. Prepare grill for direct cooking. While coals are heating, combine all ingredients except ribs in large bowl; mix well. Place ribs on grid over medium hot coals. Cook ribs 40 to 45 minutes or until they begin to brown; turning occasionally.

2. Once ribs begin to brown, begin basting them with sauce. Continue to cook and baste ribs with sauce an additional 1 to 1½ hours or until tender and cooked through.*   *Makes 4 to 6 servings*

Do not baste during last 5 minutes of grilling.

PORK SPIEDINI

2 pounds boneless pork loin, cut into 1-inch cubes
¾ cup cider vinegar
¾ cup olive oil
4 tablespoons lemon juice
1 tablespoon Worcestershire sauce
1 tablespoon dried oregano
1 teaspoon dried thyme
2 cloves garlic, minced
2 teaspoons black pepper, ground
1 teaspoon salt
½ teaspoon cayenne
6 thick slices Italian bread

Combine all ingredients, except bread, in resealable plastic food storage bag; refrigerate 4 to 24 hours. Remove pork cubes from marinade; thread pork onto skewers (if using bamboo skewers, soak in water for 1 hour to prevent burning). Grill over hot coals, basting with reserved marinade, for 4 to 5 minutes. Turn kabobs and grill 4 minutes. Serve by pulling meat off of skewer onto Italian bread.   *Makes 6 servings*

Preparation Time: 15 minutes
Cooking Time: 10 minutes

*Favorite recipe from **National Pork Board***

ONIONY BBQ MEATLOAF

2 pounds ground beef
**1⅓ cups *French's*® *Taste Toppers*™ French Fried
Onions, divided**
1 cup barbecue sauce, divided
½ cup dry seasoned bread crumbs
2 eggs
¼ cup *French's*® Worcestershire Sauce

1. Preheat oven to 350°F. Combine beef, ⅔ *cup Taste
Toppers*, *½ cup* barbecue sauce, bread crumbs, eggs and
Worcestershire in large bowl; stir with fork until well
blended.

2. Place meat mixture into greased 2-quart shallow
baking dish; shape into 9×5-inch loaf. Bake 1 hour or
until no longer pink; drain. Pour remaining *½ cup* sauce
over meatloaf and top with remaining ⅔ *cup Taste
Toppers*. Bake 5 minutes or until *Taste Toppers* are
golden.

3. Cut into slices. Serve with deli coleslaw and rolls, if
desired.   *Makes 6 to 8 servings*

Tip: For a change of pace use ketchup, tomato sauce or
marinara sauce for the barbecue sauce.

Prep Time: 10 minutes
Cook Time: about 1 hour

ONIONY BBQ MEATLOAF

ROAST BEEF WITH RED WINE GRAVY

2 tablespoons oil
Salt and black pepper
1 sirloin tip roast (3 to 4 pounds)
2 tablespoons all-purpose flour
1 jar (7 ounces) cocktail onions, drained
1 can (14½ ounces) beef broth
2 tablespoons HOLLAND HOUSE® Red Cooking Wine

Heat oven to 350°F. Heat oil in Dutch oven. Season roast to taste with salt and pepper; brown on all sides.

Remove from Dutch oven. Drain excess fat, reserving ¼ cup drippings in Dutch oven. Sprinkle flour over reserved drippings. Cook over medium heat until lightly browned, stirring constantly. Add roast and onions to Dutch oven. Cook for 1¾ to 2¼ hours or until desired doneness. Remove roast onto cutting board. Let stand 5 to 10 minutes before slicing. Gradually stir in beef broth and cooking wine. Bring to a boil; reduce heat. Cook until gravy thickens. Slice roast and arrange with onions on serving platter. Serve with gravy.

Makes 6 servings

OLD-FASHIONED BEEF POT PIE

1 pound ground beef
1 can (11 ounces) condensed beef with vegetables and barley soup
½ cup water
1 package (10 ounces) frozen peas and carrots, thawed and drained
½ teaspoon seasoned salt
⅛ teaspoon garlic powder
⅛ teaspoon ground black pepper
1 cup (4 ounces) shredded Cheddar cheese, divided
1⅓ cups *French's® Taste Toppers™* French Fried Onions, divided
1 package (7.5 ounces) refrigerated biscuits

Preheat oven to 350°F. In large skillet, brown ground beef in large chunks; drain. Stir in soup, water, vegetables and seasonings; bring to a boil. Reduce heat and simmer, uncovered, 5 minutes. Remove from heat; stir in ½ cup cheese and ⅔ cup *Taste Toppers*.

Pour mixture into 12×8-inch baking dish. Cut each biscuit in half; place, cut side down, around edge of casserole. Bake, uncovered, 15 to 20 minutes or until biscuits are done. Top with remaining cheese and ⅔ cup *Taste Toppers*; bake, uncovered, 5 minutes or until *Taste Toppers* are golden brown.

Makes 4 to 6 servings

ROAST BEEF WITH RED WINE GRAVY

JAMAICAN BABY BACK RIBS

2 tablespoons sugar

2 tablespoons fresh lemon juice

1 tablespoon salt

1 tablespoon vegetable oil

2 teaspoons black pepper

2 teaspoons dried thyme leaves, crushed

¾ teaspoon *each* ground cinnamon, nutmeg and allspice

½ teaspoon ground red pepper

6 pounds well-trimmed pork baby back ribs, cut into 3- to 4-rib portions

Barbecue Sauce (recipe follows)

1. For seasoning rub, combine all ingredients except ribs and Barbecue Sauce in small bowl; stir well. Spread over all surfaces of ribs; press with fingertips so mixture adheres to ribs. Cover; refrigerate overnight.

2. Prepare grill for indirect cooking. While coals are heating, prepare barbecue sauce.

3. Baste ribs generously with Barbecue Sauce; grill 30 minutes more or until ribs are tender and browned, turning occasionally.

4. Bring remaining Barbecue Sauce to a boil over medium-high heat; boil 1 minute. Serve ribs with remaining sauce.

Makes 6 servings

BARBECUE SAUCE

2 tablespoons butter

½ cup finely chopped onion

1½ cups ketchup

1 cup red currant jelly

¼ cup apple cider vinegar

1 tablespoon soy sauce

¼ teaspoon each ground red and black peppers

Melt butter in medium saucepan over medium-high heat. Add onion; cook and stir until softened. Stir in remaining ingredients. Reduce heat to medium-low; simmer 20 minutes, stirring often.

Makes about 3 cups

Ovenbaked Jamaican Ribs: Preheat oven to 350°F. Prepare ribs as directed in step 1. Place ribs in foil-lined roasting pan. Cover with foil; bake 1 hour. Uncover; baste with Barbecue Sauce. Bake, uncovered, 30 minutes more. Continue as directed in step 4.

Poultry Aplenty

GRILLED LEMON CHICKEN DIJON

⅓ cup **HOLLAND HOUSE**® **White with Lemon Cooking Wine**
⅓ **cup olive oil**
2 **tablespoons Dijon mustard**
1 **teaspoon dried thyme leaves**
2 **whole chicken breasts, skinned, boned and halved**

In shallow baking dish combine cooking wine, oil, mustard and thyme. Add chicken and turn to coat. Cover; marinate in refrigerator for 1 to 2 hours.

Prepare grill for direct cooking. Drain chicken, reserving marinade. Grill chicken over medium coals 15 to 20 minutes or until cooked through, turning once and basting with marinade.*   *Makes 4 servings*

Do not baste during last 5 minutes of grilling.

ROASTED CORNISH HENS WITH DOUBLE MUSHROOM STUFFING

2 Cornish hens (about 1½ pounds each)
½ teaspoon salt
¼ teaspoon ground black pepper
3 tablespoons I CAN'T BELIEVE IT'S NOT BUTTER!® Spread
1 tablespoon finely chopped shallot or onion
2 teaspoons chopped fresh tarragon leaves *or* ½ teaspoon dried tarragon leaves, crushed (optional)
½ lemon, cut in 2 wedges
Double Mushroom Stuffing (recipe follows)
1 tablespoon all-purpose flour

Preheat oven to 425°F. Season hens and hen cavities with salt and pepper.

In small bowl, blend I Can't Believe It's Not Butter! Spread, shallot and tarragon. Evenly spread under skin, then place 1 lemon wedge in each hen.

In 18×12-inch roasting pan, on rack, arrange hens breast side up; tie legs together with string. Roast uncovered 15 minutes.

Meanwhile, prepare Double Mushroom Stuffing.

Decrease heat to 350°F and place Double Mushroom Stuffing casserole in oven with hens. Continue roasting hens 30 minutes or until meat thermometer inserted in thickest part of the thigh reaches 180°F and stuffing is golden. Remove hens to serving platter and keep warm. Remove rack from pan.

Skim fat from pan drippings. Blend flour with reserved broth from stuffing; stir into pan drippings. Place roasting pan over heat and bring to a boil over high heat, stirring frequently. Reduce heat to low and simmer, stirring occasionally, 1 minute or until gravy is thickened. Serve gravy and stuffing with hens.

Makes 2 servings

DOUBLE MUSHROOM STUFFING

3 tablespoons I CAN'T BELIEVE IT'S NOT BUTTER!® Spread
½ cup chopped onion
2 cups sliced white and/or shiitake mushrooms
2½ cups fresh ½-inch Italian or French bread cubes
1 can (14½ ounces) chicken broth
2 tablespoons chopped fresh parsley

In 12-inch nonstick skillet, melt I Can't Believe It's Not Butter! Spread over medium-high heat and cook onion, stirring occasionally, 2 minutes or until softened. Add mushrooms and cook, stirring occasionally, 4 minutes or until golden. Stir in bread, ¾ cup broth (reserve remaining broth) and parsley. Season, if desired, with salt and ground black pepper. Spoon into greased 1-quart casserole.

During last 30 minutes of roasting, place stuffing casserole in oven with hens. Cook until stuffing is heated through and golden. *Makes 2 servings*

ROASTED CORNISH HEN WITH DOUBLE MUSHROOM STUFFING

MINI CHICKEN POT PIES

MINI CHICKEN POT PIES

1 container (about 16 ounces) refrigerated reduced-fat buttermilk biscuits
1½ cups milk
1 package (1.8 ounces) white sauce mix
2 cups cut-up cooked chicken
1 cup frozen assorted vegetables, partially thawed
2 cups shredded Cheddar cheese
2 cups *French's® Taste Toppers*™ French Fried Onions

1. Preheat oven to 400°F. Separate biscuits; press into 8 (8-ounce) custard cups, pressing up sides to form crust.

2. Whisk milk and sauce mix in medium saucepan. Bring to boiling over medium-high heat. Reduce heat to medium-low; simmer 1 minute, whisking constantly, until thickened. Stir in chicken and vegetables.

3. Spoon about ⅓ cup chicken mixture into each crust. Place cups on baking sheet. Bake 15 minutes or until golden brown. Top each with cheese and *Taste Toppers*. Bake 3 minutes or until golden. To serve, remove from cups and transfer to serving plates.

Makes 8 servings

Prep Time: 15 minutes
Cook Time: about 20 minutes

TURKEY ROULADE

1 pound (10 slices) uncooked, boneless turkey breast
1 container (15 ounces) ricotta cheese
1½ cups (6 ounces) shredded mozzarella cheese, divided
1 package (10 ounces) frozen chopped spinach, thawed, squeezed dry
1 teaspoon garlic salt
1 tablespoon olive or vegetable oil
1 cup chopped onion
2 cloves garlic, minced
1 can (14.5 ounces) CONTADINA® Recipe Ready Diced Tomatoes, undrained
1 can (6 ounces) CONTADINA® Tomato Paste
1 cup chicken broth
1 teaspoon Italian herb seasoning
1 teaspoon salt
1 teaspoon ground black pepper

TURKEY ROULADE

1. Pound turkey slices between 2 pieces of plastic wrap to ⅛-inch thickness.

2. Combine ricotta cheese, 1 cup mozzarella cheese, spinach and garlic salt in medium bowl. Spread ⅓ cup cheese mixture onto each turkey slice; roll up. Secure with toothpick. Place rolls in 13×9-inch baking dish.

3. Heat oil in large skillet. Add onion and garlic; sauté for 2 minutes. Add tomatoes and juice, tomato paste, broth, Italian seasoning, salt and pepper. Bring to a boil.

4. Reduce heat to low; simmer for 10 minutes. Spoon sauce over rolls; cover.

5. Bake in preheated 425°F oven for 20 to 25 minutes or until turkey is no longer pink in center. Sprinkle with remaining mozzarella cheese. Bake for additional 5 minutes or until cheese is melted.

Makes 10 servings

Prep Time: 20 minutes
Cook Time: 43 minutes

TURKEY–OLIVE RAGOÛT EN CRUST

½ pound boneless white or dark turkey meat, cut into 1-inch cubes
1 clove garlic, minced
1 teaspoon vegetable oil
¼ cup (about 10) small whole frozen onions
½ cup reduced-sodium chicken bouillon or turkey broth
½ teaspoon dried parsley flakes
⅛ teaspoon dried thyme leaves
1 small bay leaf
1 medium red potato, skin on, cut into ½-inch cubes
10 frozen snow peas
8 whole small pitted ripe olives
1 can (4 ounces) refrigerated crescent rolls
½ teaspoon dried dill weed

1. Preheat oven to 375°F.

2. In medium skillet over medium heat, cook and stir turkey in garlic and oil 3 to 4 minutes or until no longer pink; remove and set aside. Add onions to skillet; cook and stir until lightly browned. Add bouillon, parsley, thyme, bay leaf and potato. Bring mixture to a boil. Reduce heat; cover and simmer 10 minutes or until potato is tender. Remove and discard bay leaf.

3. Combine turkey mixture with potato mixture. Stir in snow peas and olives. Divide mixture between 2 (1¾-cup) individual ovenproof casseroles.

4. Divide crescent rolls into 2 rectangles; press perforations together to seal. If necessary, roll out each rectangle to make dough large enough to cover top of each casserole. Sprinkle dough with dill weed, pressing lightly into dough. Cut small decorative shape from each dough piece; discard cutouts or place on baking sheet and bake in oven with casseroles. Place dough over turkey-vegetable mixture in casseroles. Trim dough to fit; press dough to edge of each casserole to seal. Bake 7 to 8 minutes or until pastry is golden brown.   *Makes 2 individual deep-dish pies*

Lattice Crust Variation: With pastry wheel or knife, cut each rectangle lengthwise into 6 strips. Arrange strips, lattice-fashion, over turkey-vegetable mixture; trim dough to fit. Press ends of dough to edge of each casserole to seal.

Note: For more golden crust, brush top of dough with beaten egg yolk before baking.

Favorite recipe from **National Turkey Federation**

RANCH CRISPY CHICKEN

¼ cup unseasoned dry bread crumbs or cornflake crumbs
1 packet (1 ounce) HIDDEN VALLEY® Original Ranch® Salad Dressing & Recipe Mix
6 bone-in chicken pieces

Combine bread crumbs and salad dressing & recipe mix in a gallon-size Glad® Zipper Storage Bag. Add chicken pieces; seal bag. Shake to coat chicken. Bake chicken on ungreased baking pan at 375°F. for 50 minutes or until no longer pink in center and juices run clear.

Makes 4 to 6 servings

RANCH CRISPY CHICKEN

CRISPY DUCK

1 whole duck (about 5 pounds)
1 tablespoon dried rubbed sage
1 teaspoon salt
¼ teaspoon black pepper
3 cups vegetable oil
1 tablespoon butter or margarine
2 large Granny Smith or Rome Beauty apples, cored and cut into thin wedges
½ cup clover honey
Fresh sage sprigs and crab apples for garnish

1. Remove neck and giblets from duck. Cut wing tips and second wing sections off duck; wrap and freeze for another use. Trim excess fat and excess skin from duck; discard. Rinse duck and cavity under cold running water; pat dry with paper towels. Cut duck into quarters, removing backbone and breast bone.

2. Place duck in 13×9-inch baking pan. Combine sage, salt and black pepper. Rub duck with sage mixture. Cover; refrigerate 1 hour.

3. To steam duck, place wire rack in wok. Add water to 1 inch below rack. (Water should not touch rack.) Cover wok; bring water to a boil over medium-high heat. Arrange duck, skin sides up, on wire rack. Cover; steam 40 minutes or until fork-tender. (Add boiling water to wok to keep water at same level.)

4. Transfer cooked duck to plate. Carefully remove rack from wok; discard water. Rinse wok and dry. Heat oil in wok over medium-high heat until oil registers 375°F on deep-fry thermometer. Add ½ of duck, skin sides down. Fry 5 to 10 minutes or until crisp and golden brown, turning once. Drain duck on paper towels. Repeat with remaining duck, reheating oil.

5. Pour off oil. Melt butter in wok over medium heat. Add apples; cook and stir 5 minutes or until wilted. Stir in honey and bring to a boil. Transfer apples with slotted spoon to warm serving platter. Arrange duck on apples. Drizzle honey mixture over duck. Garnish, if desired. *Makes 4 servings*

SUMMER RASPBERRY CHICKEN

4 boneless, skinless chicken breast halves (about 1 pound), pounded to ¼-inch thickness
¾ cup LAWRY'S® Dijon & Honey Marinade with Lemon Juice, divided
1 cup fresh or frozen raspberries
½ cup walnut pieces

Grill or broil chicken 10 to 15 minutes or until no longer pink in center and juices run clear when cut, turning once and basting often with ½ cup Dijon & Honey Marinade. *Do not baste during last 5 minutes of cooking.* Discard any remaining marinade. Cut chicken into strips. In food processor or blender, process raspberries and additional ¼ cup Dijon & Honey Marinade 10 seconds. Drizzle raspberry sauce over chicken; sprinkle with walnuts. *Makes 4 servings*

Serving Suggestion: Serve chicken on field greens or angel hair pasta. Garnish with fresh raspberries, if desired.

SUMMER RASPBERRY CHICKEN

TURKEY SCALOPPINE

1 pound turkey cutlets or 4 boneless, skinless
    chicken breast halves (about 1 pound),
    pounded to ⅛-inch thick
2 tablespoons all-purpose flour
1½ teaspoons LAWRY'S® Seasoned Salt, divided
1 teaspoon LAWRY'S® Lemon Pepper
3 tablespoons olive oil, divided
1 medium-sized green bell pepper, cut into strips
1 cup sliced butternut squash or zucchini
½ cup sliced fresh mushrooms
1 teaspoon cornstarch
½ teaspoon LAWRY'S® Garlic Powder with Parsley
¼ cup dry white wine
⅓ cup chicken broth
1 tablespoon plus 1½ teaspoons lemon juice

In large resealable plastic food storage bag, combine
flour, ¾ teaspoon Seasoned Salt and Lemon Pepper.
Add turkey, a few pieces at a time, to plastic bag; seal
bag. Shake until well coated. In large skillet, heat
2 tablespoons oil. Add turkey and cook over medium-
high heat about 5 minutes on each side or until no
longer pink in center. Remove from skillet; keep warm.
In same skillet, heat remaining 1 tablespoon oil. Add
bell pepper, squash and mushrooms and cook over
medium-high heat until bell peppers are crisp-tender.
Reduce heat to low. In small bowl, combine cornstarch,
Garlic Powder with Parsley and remaining ¾ teaspoon
Seasoned Salt; mix well. Stir in combined wine, broth
and lemon juice. Add to skillet. Bring just to a boil over
medium-high heat, stirring constantly. Simmer
1 minute. Garnish, if desired. *Makes 4 servings*

Serving Suggestion: On platter, layer vegetables,
turkey or chicken and top with sauce.

TURKEY SCALOPPINE

COUNTRY FRENCH CHICKEN SKILLET

      2 tablespoons margarine or butter
  1½ pounds boneless, skinless chicken breast halves
      1 cup water
      1 package KNORR® Recipe Classics™ Vegetable or
        Spring Vegetable Soup, Dip and Recipe Mix
      ¼ teaspoon dried dill weed (optional)
      ½ cup sour cream

• In large skillet, melt margarine over medium-high heat and brown chicken, turning occasionally, 5 minutes.

• Stir in water, recipe mix and dill weed. Bring to a boil over high heat. Reduce heat to low and simmer covered, stirring occasionally, 10 minutes or until chicken is no longer pink. Remove chicken to serving platter and keep warm.

• Remove skillet from heat; stir in sour cream. Spoon sauce over chicken and serve, if desired, with noodles.

Makes 4 to 6 servings

Prep Time: 5 minutes
Cook Time: 16 minutes

COUNTRY FRENCH CHICKEN SKILLET

HERB ROASTED TURKEY

1 (12-pound) turkey, thawed if frozen
½ cup FLEISCHMANN'S® Original Margarine,
   softened, divided
1 tablespoon Italian seasoning

Preparation Time: 20 minutes
Cook Time: 3 hours and 30 minutes
Cooling Time: 15 minutes
Total Time: 4 hours and 5 minutes

1. Remove neck and giblets from turkey cavities. Rinse turkey; drain well and pat dry. Free legs from tucked position; do not cut band of skin. Using rubber spatula or hand, loosen skin over breast, starting at body cavity opening by legs.

2. Blend 6 tablespoons margarine and Italian seasoning. Spread 2 tablespoons herb mixture inside body cavity; spread remaining herb mixture on meat under skin. Hold skin in place at opening with wooden picks. Return legs to tucked position; turn wings back to hold neck skin in place.

3. Place turkey, breast-side up, on flat rack in shallow open pan. Insert meat thermometer deep into thickest part of thigh next to body, not touching bone. Melt remaining 2 tablespoons margarine; brush over skin.

4. Roast at 325°F for 3½ to 3¾ hours. When skin is golden brown, shield breast loosely with foil to prevent overbrowning. Check for doneness; thigh temperature should be 180°F to 185°F. Transfer turkey to cutting board; let stand 15 to 20 minutes before carving. Remove wooden toothpicks just before carving.

Makes 12 servings

• Classic Tip •

A whole frozen turkey must be thawed in the refrigerator. When thawing a whole turkey, remember it is a lengthy process. Estimate 24 hours of thawing time for every 5 pounds of bird. Never thaw a turkey at room temperature.

HERB ROASTED TURKEY

BROCCOLI, CHICKEN AND RICE CASSEROLE

1 box UNCLE BEN'S CHEF'S RECIPE™ Broccoli Rice Au Gratin Supreme
2 cups boiling water
4 boneless, skinless chicken breasts (about 1 pound)
¼ teaspoon garlic powder
2 cups frozen broccoli
1 cup (4 ounces) reduced-fat shredded Cheddar cheese

1. Heat oven to 425°F. In 13×9-inch baking pan, combine rice and contents of seasoning packet. Add boiling water; mix well. Add chicken; sprinkle with garlic powder. Cover and bake 30 minutes.

2. Add broccoli and cheese, continue to bake, covered, 8 to 10 minutes or until chicken is no longer pink in center.

Makes 4 servings

SAUTÉED TURKEY MEDALLIONS

2 tablespoons chopped shallots
¼ cup margarine or butter, divided
2 cups chicken broth
2 tablespoons reduced sodium soy sauce
2 tablespoons balsamic vinegar
½ cup GREY POUPON® Dijon Mustard
¼ cup heavy cream
6 (4-ounce) turkey cutlets
1 medium red onion, sliced
6 sundried tomatoes,* cut into thin slices (about ⅓ cup)
⅓ cup seedless raisins, soaked in 1 tablespoon cognac for 1 hour

If sundried tomatoes are very dry, soften in warm water for 15 minutes. Drain before using.

1. Sauté shallots in 1 tablespoon margarine or butter in medium skillet over medium heat until tender. Add chicken broth, soy sauce and vinegar; heat to a boil. Reduce heat; simmer until liquid is reduced by half. Stir in mustard and cream; heat through. Remove from heat; keep warm.

2. Brown turkey on both sides in 2 tablespoons margarine or butter in another skillet over medium heat, about 5 to 7 minutes; remove from skillet and keep warm.

3. Sauté red onion in remaining margarine or butter in same skillet until tender. Add tomatoes and drained raisins; cook for 2 minutes more. Top turkey cutlets with onion mixture and warm sauce. Garnish as desired.

Makes 6 servings

BROCCOLI, CHICKEN AND RICE CASSEROLE

HIDDEN VALLEY FRIED CHICKEN

HIDDEN VALLEY FRIED CHICKEN

1 broiler-fryer chicken, cut up (2 to 2½ pounds)
1 cup prepared HIDDEN VALLEY® Original Ranch® Salad Dressing
¾ cup all-purpose flour
1 teaspoon salt
½ teaspoon freshly ground black pepper
Vegetable oil

Place chicken pieces in shallow baking dish; pour salad dressing over chicken. Cover; refrigerate at least 8 hours. Remove chicken. Shake off excess marinade; discard marinade. Preheat oven to 350°F. On plate, mix flour, salt and pepper; roll chicken in seasoned flour. Heat ½ inch oil in large skillet until small cube of bread dropped into oil browns in 60 seconds or until oil is 375°F. Fry chicken until golden, 5 to 7 minutes on each side; transfer to baking pan. Bake until chicken is tender and juices run clear, about 30 minutes. Serve with corn muffins, if desired.

Makes 4 main-dish servings

COUNTRY CHICKEN POT PIE

1 package (1.8 ounces) white sauce mix
2¼ cups milk
2 to 3 cups diced cooked chicken*
3 cups BIRDS EYE® frozen Mixed Vegetables
1½ cups seasoned croutons**

No leftover cooked chicken handy? Before beginning recipe, cut 1 pound boneless skinless chicken into 1-inch cubes. Brown chicken in 1 tablespoon butter or margarine in large skillet, then proceed with recipe.

**For a quick homemade touch, substitute 4 bakery-bought biscuits for croutons. Split and add to skillet, cut side down.*

• Prepare white sauce mix with milk in large skillet according to package directions.

• Add chicken and vegetables. Bring to boil over medium-high heat; cook 5 minutes or until heated through, stirring occasionally.

• Top with croutons; cover and let stand 5 minutes.

Makes about 4 servings

Serving Suggestion: Serve with a green salad.

Prep Time: 5 minutes
Cook Time: 15 minutes

SIMMERED TUSCAN CHICKEN

2 tablespoons olive or vegetable oil
1 pound boneless, skinless chicken breasts, cut into 1-inch cubes
2 cloves garlic, finely chopped
4 medium potatoes, cut into ½-inch cubes (about 4 cups)
1 medium red bell pepper, cut into large pieces
1 jar (26 to 28 ounces) RAGÚ® Old World Style® Pasta Sauce
1 pound fresh or frozen cut green beans
1 teaspoon dried basil leaves, crushed
Salt and ground black pepper to taste

In 12-inch skillet, heat oil over medium-high heat and cook chicken with garlic until chicken is no longer pink. Remove chicken and set aside.

In same skillet, add potatoes and bell pepper. Cook over medium heat, stirring occasionally, 5 minutes. Stir in remaining ingredients. Bring to a boil over high heat. Reduce heat to low and simmer covered, stirring occasionally, 35 minutes or until potatoes are tender. Return chicken to skillet and heat through.

Makes 6 servings

SIMMERED TUSCAN CHICKEN

GRILLED GAME HENS, TEXAS-STYLE

1 can (8 ounces) tomato sauce
¼ cup vegetable oil
1½ teaspoons chili powder
1 teaspoon paprika
¼ teaspoon garlic powder
¼ teaspoon ground red pepper
4 Cornish game hens (1 to 1½ pounds each), cut into halves

In small bowl, combine all ingredients except game hens. Brush hens generously with tomato mixture. Grill hens, on covered grill, over medium-hot KINGSFORD® with Mesquite Charcoal Briquets 45 to 50 minutes or until fork-tender, brushing frequently with tomato mixture.

Makes 4 servings

CRANBERRY ORANGE GAME HENS WITH VEGETABLE STUFFING

Game Hens

    4 small Cornish game hens (16 ounces each)
    1 carrot, finely diced
    1 stalk celery, finely diced
    2 cups bread stuffing mix
    1 teaspoon poultry seasoning
    1 cup chicken stock or broth
    Salt and pepper

Sauce

    1 cup fresh or frozen cranberries, chopped
    1 cup (12-ounce jar) SMUCKER'S® Sweet Orange
       Marmalade
    ¼ cup water
    1 teaspoon lemon juice
    Lemon wedges for garnish (optional)

Remove as much fat as possible from game hens. Combine carrot, celery, stuffing mix, poultry seasoning and chicken stock. Season with salt and pepper. Fill cavity of each hen with stuffing; place on roasting pan. Bake at 400°F for 45 minutes.

Meanwhile, prepare sauce. In medium saucepan, combine all sauce ingredients. Cook over medium-high heat for 5 to 8 minutes until cranberries have released their juice. Set aside.

Remove game hens from oven. Spread sauce over top and sides of hens. Reserve any extra sauce to serve later with hens. Return hens to oven and continue baking 10 to 15 minutes.

To serve, place game hens on 4 serving plates. Spoon some of stuffing onto each plate. Spoon additional sauce over hens. Garnish with lemon wedges, if desired. *Makes 4 servings*

• Classic Tip •

To quickly and easily chop cranberries, place in a food processor or blender and pulse on and off a few times until the desired size is achieved.

CRANBERRY ORANGE GAME HEN
WITH VEGETABLE STUFFING

CREOLE CHICKEN

1½ tablespoons vegetable oil
1 whole chicken, cut up or 2 pounds chicken
   pieces
1½ tablespoons butter or margarine
1 medium onion, thinly sliced
2 teaspoons LAWRY'S® Garlic Powder with
   Parsley
1½ teaspoons LAWRY'S® Seasoned Salt
1 teaspoon LAWRY'S® Seasoned Pepper
1 can (8 ounces) tomato sauce
½ cup red wine
3 medium tomatoes, chopped
1 red bell pepper, sliced into strips
1 green bell pepper, sliced into strips
3 cups hot cooked rice

In large skillet, heat oil. Add chicken and cook over medium-high heat until brown, about 5 minutes. Remove and set aside. In same skillet, heat butter. Add onion and cook over medium-high heat until tender. Add Garlic Powder with Parsley, Seasoned Salt and Seasoned Pepper. Return chicken pieces to skillet. Add remaining ingredients except rice. Cover and simmer over low heat 30 to 40 minutes until chicken is cooked. Serve over rice. *Makes 4 to 6 servings*

Serving Suggestion: Just add a couple of corn bread muffins to the plate and the meal is complete.

HIDDEN HERB GRILLED TURKEY BREAST

1 (3- to 9-pound) BUTTERBALL® Breast of Young
   Turkey, thawed
¼ cup coarsely chopped fresh parsley
2 tablespoons chopped mixed fresh herbs such as
   thyme, oregano and marjoram
2 tablespoons grated Parmesan cheese
1 teaspoon olive oil
½ teaspoon lemon juice
½ teaspoon salt
¼ teaspoon garlic powder
¼ teaspoon black pepper
   Vegetable oil

Prepare grill for indirect-heat grilling. Combine parsley, herbs, Parmesan cheese, oil, lemon juice, salt, garlic powder and pepper in medium bowl. Gently loosen and lift turkey skin from surface of meat. Spread herb blend evenly over breast meat. Replace skin over herb blend. Brush skin with vegetable oil. Place turkey breast skin side up on prepared grill. Cover grill and cook 1½ to 2½ hours for a 3- to 9-pound breast or until internal temperature reaches 170°F and meat is no longer pink in center. *Number of servings varies*

Prep Time: 15 minutes plus grilling time

CREOLE CHICKEN

CHICKEN AND BROCCOLI CRÊPES

10 prepared Basic Crêpes (recipe follows)
½ cup half-and-half
½ cup all-purpose flour
½ teaspoon garlic salt
1¼ cups chicken broth
2 cups (8 ounces) shredded Wisconsin Cheddar
    cheese, divided
½ cup (2 ounces) shredded Wisconsin Monterey
    Jack cheese
1½ cups dairy sour cream, divided
2 tablespoons diced pimiento
1 tablespoon parsley flakes
1 teaspoon paprika
2 tablespoons butter
1 can (4 ounces) sliced mushrooms, drained
2 packages (10 ounces each) frozen broccoli spears,
    cooked and drained
2 cups cubed cooked chicken

Prepare Basic Crêpes; set aside. Combine half-and-half, flour and garlic salt in medium saucepan; beat with wire whisk until smooth. Blend in chicken broth. Stir in 1 cup Cheddar cheese, Monterey Jack cheese, ½ cup sour cream, pimiento, parsley and paprika. Cook sauce over medium-low heat until mixture thickens, stirring constantly. Remove from heat; set aside. Melt butter in small skillet over medium-high heat. Cook and stir mushrooms in butter.

On half of each crêpe, place equally divided portions of cooked broccoli, chicken and mushrooms. Spoon 1 to 2 tablespoons cheese sauce over each. Fold crepes. Place in large, shallow baking dish. Pour remaining cheese sauce over crêpes. Top with remaining 1 cup sour cream and 1 cup Cheddar cheese. Bake, uncovered, in preheated 350°F oven 5 to 10 minutes or until cheese melts. Garnish with chopped fresh parsley, if desired. *Makes 10 crêpes*

CHICKEN AND BROCCOLI CRÊPES

BASIC CRÊPES

3 eggs
½ teaspoon salt
2 cups plus 2 tablespoons all-purpose flour
    Milk
¼ cup melted butter

Beat eggs and salt together in medium bowl with electric mixer. Add flour alternately with 2 cups milk, beating until smooth. Stir in melted butter. Allow crêpe batter to stand 1 hour or more in refrigerator before cooking. The batter should be the consistency of heavy cream. If the batter is too thick, add 1 to 2 tablespoons additional milk and stir well.

Cook crêpes in heated, nonstick pan over medium-high heat. With one hand, pour 3 tablespoons batter into pan; with other hand, lift pan off heat. Quickly rotate pan until batter covers bottom; return pan to heat. Cook until light brown; turn and brown other side for a few seconds. *Makes about 30 crêpes*

Favorite recipe from **Wisconsin Milk Marketing Board**

CHICKEN MARSALA

4 **BUTTERBALL**® Boneless Skinless Chicken
    Breast Fillets
3 cups sliced fresh mushrooms
2 tablespoons sliced green onion
2 tablespoons water
¼ teaspoon salt
¼ cup dry Marsala wine
1 teaspoon cornstarch

Flatten chicken fillets between two pieces of plastic wrap. Spray nonstick skillet with nonstick cooking spray; heat over medium heat until hot. Add chicken; cook 2 to 3 minutes on each side or until no longer pink in center. Transfer to platter; keep warm. Add mushrooms, onion, water and salt to skillet. Cook 3 minutes or until most of the liquid has evaporated. Combine wine and cornstarch in small bowl; add to skillet. Heat, stirring constantly, until thickened. Spoon over warm chicken.

Makes 4 servings

Preparation Time: 15 to 20 minutes

CHICKEN MARSALA

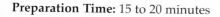

MEDITERRANEAN CORNISH HENS

1 cup **UNCLE BEN'S**® Instant Rice
¾ cup chopped fresh spinach
¼ cup chopped sun-dried tomatoes in oil, drained
2 Cornish hens, thawed (about 1 pound each)
1 tablespoon butter or margarine, melted
1 clove garlic, minced

1. Heat oven to 425°F. Cook rice according to package directions. Stir in spinach and sun-dried tomatoes; cool.

2. Spoon ½ rice mixture into cavity of each hen. Tie drumsticks together with cotton string. Place hens on rack in roasting pan. Combine butter and garlic; brush each hen with garlic butter.

3. Roast 45 to 50 minutes* or until juices run clear, basting occasionally with drippings.

Makes 2 servings

*If hens weigh over 18 ounces, roast 60 to 70 minutes.

Cook's Tip: Do not store garlic in the refrigerator. Garlic heads will keep up to two months if stored in an open container in a dark, cool place. Unpeeled cloves will keep for up to two weeks.

CLASSIC GRILLED CHICKEN

1 whole frying chicken* (3½ pounds), quartered
¼ cup lemon juice
¼ cup olive oil
2 tablespoons soy sauce
2 large cloves garlic, minced
½ teaspoon sugar
½ teaspoon ground cumin
¼ teaspoon black pepper

*Substitute 3½ pounds chicken parts for whole chicken, if desired. Grill legs and thighs about 35 minutes and breast halves about 25 minutes or until chicken is no longer pink in center, turning once.

Rinse chicken under cold running water; pat dry with paper towels. Arrange chicken in 13×9×2-inch glass baking dish. Combine remaining ingredients in small bowl; pour half of mixture over chicken. Cover and refrigerate chicken at least 1 hour or overnight. Cover and reserve remaining mixture in refrigerator to use for basting. Remove chicken from marinade; discard marinade. Arrange medium KINGSFORD® Briquets on each side of large rectangular metal or foil drip pan. Pour hot tap water into drip pan until half full. Place chicken on grid directly above drip pan. Grill chicken, skin side down, on covered grill 25 minutes. Baste with reserved baste. Turn chicken; cook 20 to 25 minutes or until juices run clear and chicken is no longer pink in center.

Makes 6 servings

ORIENTAL TURKEY TERRINE

2½ pounds ground turkey
2 eggs, beaten
¾ cup finely chopped onion
¼ cup chopped fresh cilantro or parsley
¼ cup KIKKOMAN® Soy Sauce
1½ cups dry bread crumbs
½ teaspoon ground ginger
¼ teaspoon fennel seed, crushed
¼ teaspoon pepper
⅛ teaspoon ground cloves
Dash ground cinnamon

Combine turkey, eggs, onion, cilantro and soy sauce in large bowl; set aside. Stir together bread crumbs, ginger, fennel, pepper, cloves and cinnamon. Add to turkey mixture and mix until thoroughly blended. Press firmly into greased 9¼×5¼-inch loaf pan. Bake in 375°F. oven 1 hour, or until top is lightly browned and starts to pull away from sides of pan. Turn out onto serving platter and let stand 5 minutes before serving.

Makes 6 to 8 servings

NOTE: If desired, press turkey mixture into greased 12-quart Bundt® or tube pan; bake in 375°F. oven 45 minutes.

CLASSIC GRILLED CHICKEN

SMOKED BARBECUED TURKEY

1 turkey (10 to 12 pounds)
1 quart water
1 quart orange juice
1 cup honey
½ cup LAWRY'S® Seasoned Salt
2 oranges, cut into quarters
2 limes, cut into quarters
2 tablespoons pickling spices
   Barbecue Sauce (recipe follows)

In large glass bowl, place turkey. In large saucepan, combine next 7 ingredients. Bring to a boil over medium-high heat, stirring occasionally; remove from heat and cool. Pour over turkey; cover. Marinate in refrigerator 4 to 6 hours. Remove turkey; discard used marinade. Secure wings behind back and tie legs and tail together with cotton string. Place turkey, breast side up, in center of smoker grill directly over drip pan. Grill, using indirect heat method, 13 to 15 minutes per pound (about 2 to 3 hours) or until internal temperature reaches 185°F. and juices run clear when cut. Remove from grill and place on rack in large pan; brush with warm Barbecue Sauce. Bake in 375°F oven 10 minutes.   *Makes 10 servings*

BARBECUE SAUCE

2 tablespoons vegetable oil
½ cup finely chopped onion
1 teaspoon LAWRY'S® Garlic Powder with Parsley
½ cup ketchup
½ cup white wine vinegar
½ cup lemon juice
½ cup honey
¼ cup Worcestershire sauce
2 teaspoons dry mustard
1½ teaspoons LAWRY'S® Seasoned Salt
½ teaspoon ground red pepper

In small saucepan, heat oil. Add onion and Garlic Powder with Parsley and cook over medium-high heat until tender. Add remaining ingredients and bring to a boil over medium-high heat; reduce heat to low and cook 10 to 15 minutes.   *Makes 2½ cups*

Serving Suggestion: Ladle Barbecue Sauce over sliced turkey.

SMOKED BARBECUED TURKEY

CHICKEN CAESAR TETRAZZINI

8 ounces uncooked spaghetti
2 cups shredded or cubed cooked chicken
1 cup chicken broth
1 cup HIDDEN VALLEY® Caesar Dressing
1 jar (4½ ounces) sliced mushrooms, drained
½ cup grated Parmesan cheese
2 tablespoons dry bread crumbs

Cook spaghetti according to package directions. Drain and combine with chicken, broth, dressing and mushrooms in a large mixing bowl. Place mixture in a 2-quart casserole. Mix together cheese and bread crumbs; sprinkle over spaghetti mixture. Bake at 350°F for 25 minutes or until casserole is hot and bubbly.

Makes 4 servings

CHICKEN CAESAR TETRAZZINI

CRANBERRY–GLAZED CORNISH HENS WITH WILD RICE

1 box UNCLE BEN'S® Long Grain & Wild Rice Fast Cook Recipe
½ cup sliced celery
⅓ cup slivered almonds (optional)
1 can (8 ounces) jellied cranberry sauce, divided
4 Cornish hens, thawed (about 1 pound each)
2 tablespoons olive oil, divided

1. Heat oven to 425°F. Prepare rice according to package directions. Stir in celery, almonds and ½ of cranberry sauce; cool.

2. Spoon about ¾ cup rice mixture into cavity of each hen. Tie drumsticks together with cotton string. Place hens on rack in roasting pan. Brush each hen with some of the oil. Roast 35 to 45 minutes or until juices run clear, basting occasionally with remaining oil.

3. Meanwhile, in small saucepan, heat remaining cranberry sauce until melted. Remove hens from oven; remove and discard string. Spoon cranberry sauce over hens.

Makes 4 servings

TURKEY CUTLETS WITH VICTORY GARDEN GRAVY

1 package BUTTERBALL® Fresh Boneless Turkey
    Breast Cutlets
½ cup milk
3 tablespoons flour
1 can (14½ ounces) chicken broth
2 cups broccoli florets
½ cup chopped plum tomatoes
1 tablespoon chopped fresh parsley
¼ teaspoon salt
¼ teaspoon black pepper
1 tablespoon vegetable oil
2 tablespoons grated Parmesan cheese

Whisk together milk and flour in small bowl. Combine milk mixture and chicken broth in large saucepan. Bring to a boil over medium-high heat, stirring constantly. Reduce heat to low; add broccoli. Simmer 5 minutes. Stir in tomatoes, parsley, salt and pepper. Heat oil in separate large skillet over medium heat until hot. Cook cutlets 2 to 2½ minutes on each side or until no longer pink in center. Serve with gravy. Sprinkle with Parmesan cheese.   *Makes 4 servings*

Preparation Time: 15 minutes

TURKEY CUTLETS WITH VICTORY GARDEN GRAVY

TURKEY WALDORF SALAD

⅔ cup HELLMANN'S® or BEST FOODS®
    Mayonnaise
2 tablespoons lemon juice
½ teaspoon salt
¼ teaspoon freshly ground pepper
2 cups diced cooked turkey or chicken
2 red apples, cored and diced
⅔ cup sliced celery
½ cup chopped walnuts

1. In large bowl combine mayonnaise, lemon juice, salt and pepper.

2. Add turkey, apples and celery; toss to coat well.

3. Cover; chill to blend flavors. Just before serving, sprinkle with walnuts.   *Makes 4 to 6 servings*

SOUTHWEST CHICKEN

2 tablespoons olive oil
1 clove garlic, pressed
1 teaspoon chili powder
1 teaspoon ground cumin
1 teaspoon dried oregano leaves
½ teaspoon salt
1 pound skinless boneless chicken breast halves
   or thighs

Combine oil, garlic, chili powder, cumin, oregano and salt; brush over both sides of chicken to coat. Grill chicken over medium-hot KINGSFORD® Briquets 8 to 10 minutes or until chicken is no longer pink, turning once. Serve immediately or use in Build a Burrito, Taco Salad or other favorite recipes.   *Makes 4 servings*

Note: Southwest Chicken can be grilled ahead and refrigerated for several days or frozen for longer storage.

Build a Burrito: Top warm large flour tortillas with strips of Southwest Chicken and your choice of drained canned black beans, cooked brown or white rice, shredded cheese, salsa verde, shredded lettuce, sliced black olives and chopped cilantro. Fold in sides and roll to enclose filling. Heat in microwave oven at HIGH until heated through. (Or, wrap in foil and heat in preheated 350°F oven.)

Taco Salad: For a quick one-dish meal, layer strips of Southwest Chicken with tomato wedges, blue or traditional corn tortilla chips, sliced black olives, shredded romaine or iceberg lettuce, shredded cheese and avocado slices. Serve with salsa, sour cream, guacamole or a favorite dressing.

GLAZED ORANGE DUCK

1 (5-pound) fresh or thawed duckling, cut up
½ cup KIKKOMAN® Teriyaki Baste & Glaze
¼ cup orange marmalade
1 tablespoon dry sherry
⅛ teaspoon ground red pepper

Trim excess fat from duckling pieces. Rinse pieces; dry thoroughly with paper towels. Score skin with diagonal slashes 1 inch apart. Place pieces, skin side up, on rack in shallow, foil-lined baking pan. Bake in 350°F oven

45 minutes. Meanwhile, combine teriyaki baste & glaze, marmalade, sherry and red pepper; remove and reserve ¼ cup glaze mixture. Pour off pan drippings. *Turn oven temperature to broil and raise oven rack 5 to 7 inches from heat.* Brush duckling pieces thoroughly with glaze mixture. Broil, skin side down, 5 minutes. Turn pieces over; brush again with glaze mixture. Broil 5 minutes longer, or until skin is crisp. Blend reserved glaze mixture with ¼ cup water in small saucepan; bring to boil. Serve duckling pieces with warm sauce.

Makes 4 servings

SOUTHWEST CHICKEN

CORNISH VERACRUZ

4 TYSON® Rock Cornish Game Hens (fresh or frozen, thawed)

1 cup UNCLE BEN'S® ORIGINAL CONVERTED® Brand Rice, cooked

Dried oregano, salt and black pepper to taste

½ cup olive oil

½ cup lime juice

1 onion, diced

1 can (8 ounces) tomatoes, drained

½ cup shredded Monterey Jack cheese

¼ cup sour cream

1 tablespoon each dried oregano leaves and capers

1 teaspoon each garlic powder and black pepper

½ teaspoon ground cumin

PREP: Preheat oven to 450°F. CLEAN: Wash hands. Sprinkle hens inside and out with oregano, salt and pepper. Combine oil and lime juice. Generously coat hens with mixture. Mix together remaining ingredients. Stuff into cavity of hens and truss. Place in greased roasting pan. CLEAN: Wash hands.

COOK: Bake 15 minutes. Reduce oven temperature to 375°F. Bake, basting occasionally with oil mixture, 30 to 45 minutes or until juices of hens runs clear. (Or insert instant-read meat thermometer in thickest part of hen. Temperature should read 180°F.)

SERVE: Serve with black beans, if desired.

CHILL: Refrigerate leftovers immediately.

Makes 8 servings

Prep Time: 15 minutes
Cook Time: 45 to 60 minutes

SOUTHERN FRIED CHICKEN

2½ to 3 pounds frying chicken pieces

WESSON® Vegetable Oil

2 cups self-rising flour

2 teaspoons salt

1 teaspoon pepper

1 teaspoon paprika

1 teaspoon onion powder

½ teaspoon ground sage

¼ teaspoon garlic powder

2 eggs beaten with 2 tablespoons water

Rinse chicken and pat dry; set aside. Fill a large deep-fry pot or electric skillet to no more than half its depth with Wesson® Oil. Heat oil to 325°F to 350°F. In bag, combine flour and seasonings. Shake chicken, one piece at a time, in flour mixture until coated. Dip in egg mixture, then shake again in flour mixture until completely coated. Fry chicken, a few pieces at a time, skin side down, for 10 to 14 minutes. Turn and fry chicken 10 minutes, covered, then 3 to 5 minutes, uncovered, or until chicken is tender and juices run clear. Drain on paper towels. Let stand 7 minutes before serving.

Makes 4 to 6 servings

Catch of the Day

SHRIMP CREOLE PRONTO

2 tablespoons oil
1 cup chopped onions
1 cup chopped celery
1 green bell pepper, chopped
2 garlic cloves, minced
2 cups chopped, peeled tomatoes
1 can (8 ounces) tomato sauce
½ cup HOLLAND HOUSE® Marsala Cooking Wine
¼ teaspoon freshly ground black pepper
1 pound fresh or frozen, thawed, uncooked shrimp, peeled, deveined
¼ to ½ teaspoon hot pepper sauce
4 cups hot cooked rice or 1 (10-ounce) package of egg noodles, cooked, drained

Heat oil in large saucepan over medium-high heat. Add onions, celery, bell pepper and garlic; cook 2 to 3 minutes. Add tomatoes; cook 2 to 3 minutes, stirring occasionally. Add remaining ingredients except rice; cook 2 to 3 minutes or until shrimp turn pink. Serve over hot cooked rice. *Makes 4 servings*

CREOLE SHRIMP

¼ cup CRISCO® Oil*
3 tablespoons all-purpose flour
⅓ cup chopped onion
¼ cup chopped celery
¼ cup chopped green bell pepper
1 can (14½ ounces) whole tomatoes, undrained and chopped
1 can (15 ounces) tomato sauce
1 package (10 ounces) frozen sliced okra, optional
1 thin slice lemon
2 teaspoons firmly packed light brown sugar
1 teaspoon chili powder
½ teaspoon salt
¼ teaspoon garlic powder
¼ teaspoon black pepper
¼ teaspoon dried basil leaves
¼ teaspoon dried thyme leaves
1 bay leaf
⅛ teaspoon cayenne pepper
1 pound fresh medium shrimp, peeled and deveined
4 cups hot cooked rice (cooked without salt or fat)

*Use your favorite Crisco Oil product.

1. Heat oil in large saucepan on medium heat. Add flour. Stir until smooth. Cook and stir 3 to 4 minutes or until lightly browned.

2. Add onion, celery and green pepper. Cook and stir 2 to 3 minutes or until tender.

3. Add tomatoes, tomato sauce, okra, if used, lemon, brown sugar, chili powder, salt, garlic powder, black pepper, basil, thyme, bay leaf and cayenne. Cover. Reduce heat to low. Simmer 45 minutes, stirring occasionally.

4. Stir in shrimp. Cover. Cook 3 minutes or until shrimp turn pink. Remove lemon slice and bay leaf before serving. Serve over hot rice. Garnish, if desired.

Makes 6 servings

HIDDEN VALLEY® BROILED FISH

1 packet (1 ounce) HIDDEN VALLEY® Original Ranch® Salad Dressing & Recipe Mix
⅓ cup lemon juice
3 tablespoons olive oil
3 tablespoons dry white wine or water
1½ to 2 pounds mild white fish fillets, such as red snapper or sole

Combine salad dressing & recipe mix, lemon juice, olive oil and wine in a shallow dish; mix well. Add fish and coat all sides with mixture. Cover and refrigerate for 15 to 30 minutes. Remove fish from marinade and place on broiler pan. Broil 9 to 12 minutes or until fish begins to flake when tested with a fork. *Makes 4 servings*

HIDDEN VALLEY® BROILED FISH

OLD NAPLES STYLE PENNE

1 dozen mussels, debearded and well scrubbed
1 dozen small clams, well scrubbed
¼ cup water
1 package (16 ounces) BARILLA® Penne
3 tablespoons olive oil
2 large cloves garlic, minced
8 ounces green beans, trimmed and cut into 1-inch pieces
2 large ripe tomatoes, seeded and diced
½ teaspoon salt
½ teaspoon pepper

1. Combine mussels, clams and water in large skillet with cover. Cover and cook 3 to 5 minutes over medium-high heat or until shells open. Remove shells and discard. Strain broth to remove sand. Place mussels, clams and strained broth in bowl; set aside. Clean and dry skillet.

2. Cook penne according to package directions; drain.

3. Meanwhile, heat olive oil in same skillet over medium-high heat. Add garlic; cook and stir 30 seconds. Add green beans and strained liquid from clams and mussels; cover and cook 5 minutes, stirring once. Add tomatoes, salt and pepper; cover and cook 6 to 8 minutes or until beans are tender. Add clams and mussels; heat through.

4. Place hot drained penne in serving bowl. Add clam and mussel sauce; toss to coat. Serve immediately.

Makes 6 servings

CRABMEAT WITH HERBS AND PASTA

1 small onion, minced
1 carrot, shredded
1 clove garlic, minced
⅓ cup olive oil
3 tablespoons butter or margarine
6 ounces canned crabmeat, drained and flaked
¼ cup chopped fresh basil *or* 1 teaspoon dried basil leaves, crushed
2 tablespoons chopped fresh parsley
1 tablespoon lemon juice
½ cup chopped pine nuts (optional)
½ teaspoon salt
½ package (8 ounces) uncooked vermicelli, hot cooked and drained

In large skillet over medium-high heat, cook and stir onion, carrot and garlic in hot oil and butter until vegetables are tender, but not brown. Reduce heat to medium. Stir in crabmeat, basil, parsley and lemon juice. Cook 4 minutes, stirring constantly. Stir in pine nuts and salt. Pour sauce over vermicelli in large bowl; toss gently to coat. Garnish as desired.

Makes 4 servings

*Favorite recipe from **New Jersey Department of Agriculture***

BAJA FISH TACOS

½ cup sour cream
½ cup mayonnaise
¼ cup chopped fresh cilantro
1 package (1½ ounces) ORTEGA® Taco Seasoning Mix, *divided*
1 pound (about 4) cod or other white fish fillets, cut into 1-inch pieces
2 tablespoons vegetable oil
2 tablespoons lemon juice

Toppings

Shredded cabbage, chopped tomato, lime juice, ORTEGA® Thick & Smooth Taco Sauce

COMBINE sour cream, mayonnaise, cilantro and 2 tablespoons taco seasoning mix in small bowl.

COMBINE cod, vegetable oil, lemon juice and remaining taco seasoning mix in medium bowl; pour into large skillet. Cook, stirring constantly, over medium-high heat for 4 to 5 minutes or until fish flakes easily when tested with fork.

FILL taco shells with fish mixture. Top with cabbage, tomato, sour cream mixture, lime juice and taco sauce.

Makes 6 servings

Tip: Try a variety of fish and seafood such as shark, shrimp, crab or lobster in these fresh-tasting tacos. Top with shredded cabbage.

BAKED SALMON IN FOIL

2 tablespoons FILIPPO BERIO® Olive Oil, divided
1 (10-ounce) package frozen chopped spinach, thawed
1 (8-ounce) can stewed tomatoes
1 onion, chopped
1 clove garlic, minced
4 salmon steaks, 1 inch thick (about 2 pounds)
4 pieces heavy-duty aluminum foil, each 12 inches square
4 thin lemon slices
1 tablespoon coarsely chopped fresh parsley
Salt and freshly ground black pepper

Preheat oven to 375°F. In medium saucepan, heat 1 tablespoon olive oil over medium heat until hot. Add spinach, tomatoes, onion and garlic. Cook, stirring occasionally, 5 minutes or until mixture is thick and onion is tender.

In medium skillet, heat remaining 1 tablespoon olive oil over medium-high heat until hot. Add salmon; cook 1 to 2 minutes on each side or until lightly browned. Remove from heat. Place one-fourth of spinach mixture in center of each piece of foil; top with one salmon steak. Drizzle liquid from skillet over salmon. Top each with lemon slice and parsley. Fold edges of each foil square together. Pinch well to seal, completely enclosing filling. Place on baking sheet. Bake 15 minutes or until salmon flakes easily when tested with fork. To serve, cut an "X" on top of each packet; carefully peel back foil. Season to taste with salt and pepper.

Makes 4 servings

SHRIMP & HAM JAMBALAYA

1 onion, cut into wedges

1 large green bell pepper, chopped

2 cloves garlic, minced

¼ teaspoon ground red pepper

2 tablespoons FLEISCHMANN'S® Original Margarine

3 cups cooked rice

2 cups large shrimp, cooked and cleaned (about 1 pound)

2 cups cubed cooked ham (about 1¼ pounds)

1 (16-ounce) can peeled tomatoes, chopped (undrained)

1 teaspoon natural hickory seasoning

1. Cook and stir onion, pepper, garlic and red pepper in margarine in large skillet over medium heat until vegetables are tender.

2. Stir in remaining ingredients. Cook for 10 to 15 minutes or until heated through, stirring occasionally. Serve immediately. *Makes 8 servings*

Preparation Time: 30 minutes
Cook Time: 20 minutes
Total Time: 50 minutes

SHRIMP & HAM JAMBALAYA

FISH VERACRUZ

FISH

  8 (about 1½ pounds *total*) red snapper or halibut fillets

  ½ cup (about 4) lime juice

  ½ teaspoon salt (optional)

SAUCE

  2 tablespoons vegetable oil

  1 cup (1 small) sliced onion

  1 cup (1 small) green bell pepper strips

  3 cloves garlic, finely chopped

  ⅓ cup dry white wine or chicken broth

  1¾ cups (16-ounce jar) ORTEGA® Thick & Chunky Salsa

  ½ cup tomato sauce

  ¼ cup ORTEGA® Sliced Jalapeños

  ¼ cup sliced ripe olives

  1 tablespoon capers (such as CROSSE & BLACKWELL®)

  Fresh cilantro sprigs (optional)

  Lime wedges (optional)

FOR FISH

ARRANGE fish in 13×9-inch baking pan. Sprinkle with lime juice and salt. Cover; refrigerate for at least 20 minutes.

FOR SAUCE

HEAT vegetable oil in large, nonstick skillet over medium-high heat. Add onion, bell pepper and garlic; cook for 1 to 2 minutes or until vegetables are crisp-tender. Add wine; cook for 1 minute.

STIR in salsa, tomato sauce, jalapeños, olives and capers. Bring to a boil. Place fish in sauce. Reduce heat to low. Cook, covered, for 8 to 10 minutes or until fish flakes when tested with fork. Serve with cilantro and lime.

Makes 8 servings

SHRIMP FETTUCCINE

  1½ cups prepared HIDDEN VALLEY® Original Ranch® Salad Dressing & Recipe Mix

  ¼ cup sour cream

  ¼ cup grated Parmesan cheese

  ½ pound fettuccine, cooked and drained

  ½ pound cooked shrimp, shelled and deveined

  ½ cup cooked peas

  Additional Parmesan cheese (optional)

In small bowl, combine salad dressing, sour cream and cheese. In large bowl, toss fettuccine with dressing mixture, shrimp and peas. Divide equally among 4 plates. Sprinkle with additional Parmesan cheese, if desired.

Makes 4 to 6 servings

SHRIMP FETTUCCINE

SEAFOOD PARMESAN

2 tablespoons margarine or butter
1 pound uncooked large shrimp, peeled and deveined
2 cloves garlic, minced
1 teaspoon paprika
⅛ to ¼ teaspoon cayenne pepper
1 (4.6-ounce) package PASTA RONI® Garlic & Olive Oil with Vermicelli
¾ cup frozen or canned peas, drained
¼ cup grated Parmesan cheese

1. In large saucepan over medium heat, melt margarine. Add shrimp, garlic, paprika and cayenne pepper; sauté 2 minutes. Remove from saucepan; set aside.

2. In same saucepan, bring 1¾ cups water to a boil. Slowly stir in pasta and Special Seasonings; reduce heat to medium. Gently boil uncovered, 6 minutes, stirring occasionally.

3. Stir in shrimp mixture and peas; boil 3 to 4 minutes or until pasta is tender, stirring frequently. Let stand 5 minutes before serving. Serve with cheese.

Makes 4 servings

Tip: To devein shrimp, make a small cut along the back of the shrimp; lift out the dark vein with the tip of a knife under cold running water.

Prep Time: 5 minutes
Cook Time: 20 minutes

FISH WITH HIDDEN VALLEY RANCH® TARTAR SAUCE

1 cup (½ pint) sour cream
¼ cup chopped sweet pickles
1 package (1 ounce) HIDDEN VALLEY® Milk Recipe Original Ranch® salad dressing mix
¾ cup dry bread crumbs
1½ pounds white fish fillets (sole, flounder, snapper or turbot)
1 egg, beaten
   Vegetable oil
   French fried shoestring potatoes (optional)
   Lemon wedges (optional)

To make sauce, in small bowl, combine sour cream, pickles and 2 tablespoons of the salad dressing mix; cover and refrigerate. On large plate, combine bread crumbs and remaining salad dressing mix. Dip fillets in egg, then coat with bread crumb mixture. Fry fillets in 3 tablespoons oil until golden. (Add more oil to pan if necessary to prevent sticking.) Serve with chilled sauce. Serve with French fries and lemon wedges, if desired.

Makes 4 servings

SEAFOOD PARMESAN

SCALLOPS IN ORANGE SAUCE

1 cup LAWRY'S® Citrus Grill Marinade with
    Orange Juice, divided
1½ pounds scallops
¼ cup all-purpose flour
½ teaspoon LAWRY'S® Garlic Salt, divided
½ teaspoon LAWRY'S® Seasoned Pepper
2 tablespoons butter
¼ cup half-and-half
2 egg yolks
⅓ cup dry white wine
½ teaspoon cornstarch blended with ½ teaspoon
    water
¼ teaspoon ground red pepper
2 tablespoons chopped fresh parsley

In large resealable plastic food storage bag, combine ½ cup Citrus Grill Marinade and scallops; seal bag.

Marinate in refrigerator at least 30 minutes. In medium bowl, combine flour, ¼ teaspoon Garlic Salt and Seasoned Pepper. Remove scallops; discard used marinade. Coat scallops in flour mixture, shaking off excess. In large skillet, heat butter. Add scallops and cook over medium heat 10 minutes or until golden brown. Drain scallops on paper towels. In top of double boiler, whisk together half-and-half, egg yolks, wine, cornstarch mixture and additional ½ cup marinade, stirring constantly over medium heat 2 to 3 minutes or until thickened. Remove from heat and add remaining ¼ teaspoon Garlic Salt and red pepper. Arrange scallops on warm platter; pour sauce over scallops and sprinkle parsley on top. *Makes 6 servings*

Serving Suggestion: Serve over hot cooked linguine.

• Classic Tip •

When purchasing scallops, select those with a creamy white color, a shiny texture and a sweet smell. Scallops should be used within one day of purchase to guarantee freshness.

CHILI GARLIC PRAWNS

2 tablespoons vegetable oil
1 pound prawns, peeled and deveined
3 tablespoons LEE KUM KEE® Chili Garlic Sauce
1 green onion, cut into slices

1. Heat oil in wok or skillet.

2. Add prawns and stir-fry until just pink.

3. Add chili garlic sauce and stir-fry until prawns are completely cooked.

4. Sprinkle with green onion and serve.

Makes 4 servings

MEDITERRANEAN–STYLE HERBED CATFISH

Nonstick cooking spray
1 cup FIBER ONE® cereal
2 tablespoons grated Parmesan cheese
1½ teaspoons dried oregano leaves
1½ teaspoons dried thyme leaves
¾ teaspoon lemon pepper
6 catfish fillets* (4 ounces each)
1 teaspoon paprika
Tomato-Olive Sauce (recipe follows)
⅓ to ½ cup feta cheese, crumbled

Any whitefish, such as sole or pollock, can be used.

1. Heat oven to 400°F. Spray 11×7×1½-inch baking dish with cooking spray.

2. Place cereal, Parmesan cheese, oregano, thyme and lemon pepper in blender or food processor. Cover and blend on low speed 30 to 45 seconds or until cereal is finely crushed. Coat fillets with cereal mixture; place in baking dish. Sprinkle with paprika. Spray tops of fillets lightly with cooking spray.

3. Bake 20 minutes. Meanwhile, prepare Tomato-Olive Sauce. Reduce oven temperature to 350°F; bake 5 minutes longer or until crust is golden and fish flakes easily with fork. Arrange fillets on serving plate; top with sauce. Sprinkle with feta cheese.

Makes 6 servings

Prep Time: 15 minutes
Bake Time: 25 minutes

**MEDITERRANEAN-STYLE
HERBED CATFISH**

TOMATO-OLIVE SAUCE

1 can (8 ounces) stewed tomatoes
½ cup Kalamata olives, pitted and thinly sliced
2 cloves garlic, finely chopped
1 teaspoon dried oregano leaves
1 teaspoon dried thyme leaves
2 tablespoons white wine or water
1 teaspoon cornstarch

Stir tomatoes, olives, garlic, oregano and thyme in 2-quart saucepan. Stir together wine and cornstarch; stir into tomato mixture. Cook over medium-high heat, stirring occasionally, until mixture thickens and boils.

SNAPPER WITH PESTO BUTTER

½ cup butter or margarine, softened
1 cup packed fresh basil leaves, coarsely chopped
   or ½ cup chopped fresh parsley plus
   2 tablespoons dried basil leaves, crushed
3 tablespoons finely grated fresh Parmesan cheese
1 clove garlic, minced
   Olive oil
2 to 3 teaspoons lemon juice
4 to 6 red snapper, rock cod, salmon or other
   medium-firm fish fillets (at least ½ inch thick)
   Salt and black pepper
   Lemon wedges
   Fresh basil or parsley sprigs and lemon strips for
   garnish

To make Pesto Butter, place butter, basil, cheese, garlic and 1 tablespoon oil in blender or food processor; process until blended. Stir in lemon juice to taste. Rinse fish; pat dry with paper towels. Brush one side of fish lightly with oil; season with salt and pepper.

Oil hot grid to help prevent sticking. Grill fillets, oil sides down, on a covered grill, over medium KINGSFORD® Briquets, 5 to 9 minutes. Halfway through cooking time, brush tops with oil; season with salt and pepper. Turn and continue grilling until fish turns opaque throughout. (Allow 3 to 5 minutes for each ½ inch of thickness.) Serve each fillet with a spoonful of Pesto Butter and a wedge of lemon. Garnish with basil sprigs and lemon strips.

Makes 4 to 6 servings

MAGIC FRIED OYSTERS

6 dozen medium to large shucked oysters in their
   liquor (about 3 pounds)
3 tablespoons Chef Paul Prudhomme's Seafood
   Magic®, divided
1 cup all-purpose flour
1 cup corn flour
1 cup cornmeal
   Vegetable oil for deep-frying

Place oysters and oyster liquor in large bowl. Add 2 tablespoons of the Seafood Magic® to oysters, stirring well. In medium bowl, combine flour, corn flour,

cornmeal and the remaining Seafood Magic®. Heat 2 inches or more of oil in deep-fryer or large saucepan to 375°F. Drain oysters and then use a slotted spoon to toss them lightly and quickly in seasoned flour mixture (so oysters do not produce excess moisture, which cakes the flour); shake off excess flour and carefully slip each oyster into hot oil. Fry in single layer in batches just until crispy and golden brown, 1 to 1½ minutes; do not overcook. (Adjust heat as needed to maintain temperature at about 375°F.) Drain on paper towels and serve.

Makes 6 servings

SNAPPER WITH PESTO BUTTER

"GRILLED" TUNA WITH VEGETABLES IN HERB BUTTER

4 pieces heavy-duty aluminum foil, each
    12×18 inches
1 can (12 ounces) STARKIST® Tuna, drained and
    broken into chunks
1 cup slivered red or green bell pepper
1 cup slivered yellow squash or zucchini
1 cup pea pods, cut crosswise into halves
1 cup slivered carrots
4 green onions, cut into 2-inch slices
    Salt and black pepper to taste (optional)

Herb Butter

3 tablespoons butter or margarine, melted
1 tablespoon lemon or lime juice
1 clove garlic, minced
2 teaspoons dried tarragon leaves, crushed
1 teaspoon dried dill weed

On each piece of foil, mound tuna, bell pepper, squash, pea pods, carrots and onions. Sprinkle with salt and black pepper.

For Herb Butter, in small bowl stir together butter, lemon juice, garlic, tarragon and dill. Drizzle over tuna and vegetables. Fold edges of each foil square together to make packets.

To grill

Place foil packets about 4 inches above hot coals. Grill for 10 to 12 minutes or until heated through, turning packets over halfway through grill time.

To bake

Place foil packets on baking sheet. Bake in preheated 450°F oven for 15 to 20 minutes or until heated through.

To serve

Cut an "X" on top of each packet; peel back foil.

Makes 4 servings

• Classic Tip •

To easily juice a lemon or lime, be sure it is at room temperature. Roll it around on the counter under the flat of your hand before cutting them in half. This releases the juice from the small sacs of the lemon or lime. A reamer or juicer can be used to extract the juice.

FISHERMAN'S SOUP

⅛ teaspoon dried thyme, crushed
½ pound halibut or other firm whitefish
2 tablespoons vegetable oil
1 medium onion, chopped
1 clove garlic, crushed
3 tablespoons all-purpose flour
2 cans (14 ounces each) low-salt chicken broth
1 can (15¼ ounces) DEL MONTE® Whole Kernel
    Golden Sweet Corn, No Salt Added, undrained
1 can (14½ ounces) DEL MONTE® Whole New
    Potatoes, drained and chopped

1. Sprinkle thyme over both sides of fish. In large saucepan, cook fish in 1 tablespoon hot oil over medium-high heat until fish flakes easily when tested with a fork. Remove fish from saucepan; set aside.

2. Heat remaining 1 tablespoon oil in same saucepan over medium heat. Add onion and garlic; cook until onion is tender. Stir in flour; cook 1 minute. Stir in broth; cook until thickened, stirring occasionally. Stir in corn and potatoes.

3. Discard skin and bones from fish; cut fish into bite-sized pieces.

4. Add fish to soup just before serving; heat through. Stir in chopped parsley or sliced green onions, if desired.   *Makes 4 to 6 servings*

Prep Time: 5 minutes
Cook Time: 12 minutes

CAJUN GRILLED SHRIMP

3 green onions, minced
2 tablespoons lemon juice
3 cloves garlic, minced
2 teaspoons paprika
1 teaspoon salt
¼ to ½ teaspoon black pepper
¼ to ½ teaspoon cayenne pepper
1 tablespoon olive oil
1½ pounds shrimp, shelled with tails intact,
    deveined
    Lemon wedges

Combine onions, lemon juice, garlic, paprika, salt and peppers in 2-quart glass dish; stir in oil. Add shrimp; turn to coat. Cover and refrigerate at least 15 minutes. Thread shrimp onto metal or wooden skewers. (Soak wooden skewers in hot water 30 minutes to prevent burning.) Grill shrimp over medium-hot KINGSFORD® Briquets about 2 minutes per side until opaque. Serve immediately with lemon wedges.   *Makes 4 servings*

STEWED CATFISH AND BELL PEPPERS

1½ pounds catfish fillets or other firm
    white-fleshed fish
1 onion, chopped
1 *each* green and red bell pepper, cut into 1-inch
    pieces
1 clove garlic, minced
1 cup clam juice
1 tomato, chopped
¼ cup *Frank's® RedHot®* Cayenne Pepper Sauce
2 tablespoons minced parsley

1. On sheet of waxed paper, mix *2 tablespoons flour* with
½ teaspoon salt. Lightly coat fillets with flour mixture;
set aside.

2. Heat *1 tablespoon oil* in large nonstick skillet until hot.
Add onion, peppers and garlic. Cook and stir 3 minutes
or until crisp-tender; transfer to dish.

3. Heat *1 tablespoon oil* in same skillet until hot. Cook
fillets 5 minutes or until golden brown, turning once.
Return vegetables to skillet. Add clam juice, tomato,
Frank's RedHot and parsley. Heat to boiling. Reduce
heat to medium-low. Cook, covered, 8 to 10 minutes or
until fish flakes with fork. Serve with hot cooked rice, if
desired.   *Makes 6 servings*

Prep Time: 15 minutes
Cook Time: 20 minutes

**STEWED CATFISH
AND BELL PEPPERS**

WISCONSIN TUNA CAKES WITH LEMON–DILL SAUCE

1 can (12 ounces) STARKIST® Tuna, drained and finely flaked
¾ cup seasoned bread crumbs
¼ cup minced green onions
2 tablespoons chopped drained pimentos
1 egg
½ cup low-fat milk
½ teaspoon grated lemon peel
2 tablespoons margarine or butter

Lemon-Dill Sauce
¼ cup chicken broth
1 tablespoon lemon juice
¼ teaspoon dried dill weed
  Hot steamed shredded zucchini and carrots
  Lemon slices

In large bowl, toss together tuna, bread crumbs, onions and pimentos. In small bowl, beat together egg and milk; stir in lemon peel. Stir into tuna mixture; toss until moistened. With lightly floured hands, shape into eight 4-inch patties.

In large nonstick skillet, melt margarine. Fry patties, a few at a time, until golden brown on both sides, about 3 minutes per side. Place on ovenproof platter in 300°F oven until ready to serve.

For Lemon-Dill Sauce, in small saucepan, heat broth, lemon juice and dill. Serve tuna cakes with zucchini and carrots; spoon sauce over cakes. Garnish with lemon slices.   *Makes 4 servings*

QUICK MEDITERRANEAN FISH

1 medium onion, sliced
2 tablespoons olive oil
1 clove garlic, crushed
1 can (14½ ounces) DEL MONTE® Italian Recipe Stewed Tomatoes
3 to 4 tablespoons medium salsa
¼ teaspoon ground cinnamon
1½ pounds firm fish (such as halibut, red snapper or sea bass)
12 stuffed green olives, halved crosswise

Microwave Directions

1. Combine onion, oil and garlic in 1½-quart microwavable dish. Cover and microwave on HIGH 3 minutes; drain.

2. Stir in tomatoes, salsa and cinnamon. Top with fish and olives.

3. Cover and microwave on HIGH 3 to 4 minutes or until fish flakes easily with fork. Garnish with chopped parsley, if desired.   *Makes 4 to 6 servings*

Prep Time: 7 minutes
Microwave Cook Time: 7 minutes

WISCONSIN TUNA CAKES WITH LEMON-DILL SAUCE

CATFISH WITH FRESH CORN RELISH

4 catfish fillets (each about 6 ounces and at least ½ inch thick)
2 tablespoons paprika
½ teaspoon ground red pepper
½ teaspoon salt
　Fresh Corn Relish (recipe follows)
　Lime wedges
　Grilled baking potatoes (optional)
　Tarragon sprigs for garnish

Rinse fish; pat dry with paper towels. Combine paprika, red pepper and salt in cup; lightly sprinkle on both sides of fish.

Oil hot grid to help prevent sticking. Grill fish, on a covered grill, over medium KINGSFORD® Briquets, 5 to 9 minutes. Halfway through cooking time, turn fish over and continue grilling until fish turns from translucent to opaque throughout. (Grilling time depends on the thickness of fish; allow 3 to 5 minutes for each ½ inch of thickness.) Serve with Fresh Corn Relish, lime wedges and potatoes, if desired. Garnish with tarragon sprigs. *Makes 4 servings*

FRESH CORN RELISH

¼ cup cooked fresh corn or thawed frozen corn
¼ cup finely diced green bell pepper
¼ cup finely slivered red onion
1 tablespoon vegetable oil
2 tablespoons seasoned (sweet) rice vinegar
　Salt and black pepper
½ cup cherry tomatoes, cut into quarters

Toss together corn, green pepper, onion, oil and vinegar in a medium bowl. Season with salt and pepper. Cover and refrigerate until ready to serve. Just before serving, gently mix in tomatoes. *Makes about 1½ cups*

• Classic Tip •

Tarragon is a perennial aromatic herb with a distintive aniselike flavor. This herb can be found fresh in the summer and early fall.

CATFISH WITH FRESH CORN RELISH

SALMON LINGUINI SUPPER

8 ounces linguini, cooked in unsalted water and
    drained
1 package (10 ounces) frozen peas
1 cup milk
1 can (10¾ ounces) condensed cream of celery
    soup
¼ cup (1 ounce) grated Parmesan cheese
⅛ teaspoon dried tarragon, crumbled (optional)
1 can (15½ ounces) salmon, drained and flaked
1 egg, slightly beaten
¼ teaspoon salt
¼ teaspoon pepper
1⅓ cups *French's® Taste Toppers™* French Fried
    Onions, divided

Preheat oven to 375°F. Return hot pasta to saucepan;
stir in peas, milk, soup, cheese and tarragon; spoon into
12×8-inch baking dish. In medium bowl, using fork,
combine salmon, egg, salt, pepper and ⅔ cup *Taste
Toppers*. Shape salmon mixture into 4 oval patties.
Place patties on pasta mixture. Bake, covered, at 375°F
for 40 minutes or until patties are done. Top patties
with remaining ⅔ *cup Taste Toppers*; bake, uncovered,
3 minutes or until *Taste Toppers* are golden brown.

Makes 4 servings

Microwave Directions

Prepare pasta mixture as above, except increase milk to
1¼ cups; spoon into 12×8-inch microwave-safe dish.
Cook, covered, on HIGH 3 minutes; stir. Prepare
salmon patties as above using 2 eggs. Place patties on
pasta mixture. Cook, covered, 10 to 12 minutes or until
patties are done. Rotate dish halfway through cooking
time. Top patties with remaining onions; cook,
uncovered, 1 minute. Let stand 5 minutes.

CRUSTY HOT PAN-FRIED FISH

1½ cups all-purpose flour
1 tablespoon plus ½ teaspoon Chef Paul
    Prudhomme's Seafood Magic®, divided
1 large egg, beaten
1 cup milk
6 fish fillets (4 ounces each), speckled trout or
    drum or your favorite fish
Vegetable oil for frying

In flat pan, combine flour and 2 teaspoons of the
Seafood Magic®. In separate pan, combine egg and
milk until well blended. Season fillets by sprinkling
about ¼ teaspoon of the Seafood Magic® on each. In
large skillet, heat about ¼ inch oil over medium heat
until hot. Meanwhile, coat each fillet with seasoned
flour, shake off excess and coat well with milk mixture;
then, just before frying, coat fillets once more with
flour, shaking off excess. Fry fillets in hot oil until
golden brown, 1 to 2 minutes per side. Drain on paper
towels and serve immediately on heated serving plates.

Makes 6 servings

SEAFOOD GUMBO

1 bag SUCCESS® Rice
1 tablespoon reduced-calorie margarine
¼ cup chopped onion
¼ cup chopped green bell pepper
2 cloves garlic, minced
1 can (28 ounces) whole tomatoes, cut up, undrained
2 cups chicken broth
½ teaspoon ground red pepper
½ teaspoon dried thyme leaves, crushed
½ teaspoon dried basil leaves, crushed
¾ pound whitefish, cut into 1-inch pieces
1 package (10 ounces) frozen cut okra, thawed and drained
½ pound shrimp, peeled and deveined

Prepare rice according to package directions.

Melt margarine in large saucepan over medium-high heat. Add onion, green pepper and garlic; cook and stir until crisp-tender. Stir in tomatoes, broth, red pepper, thyme and basil. Bring to a boil. Reduce heat to low; simmer, uncovered, until thoroughly heated, 10 to 15 minutes. Stir in fish, okra and shrimp; simmer until fish flakes easily with fork and shrimp curl and turn pink. Add rice; heat thoroughly, stirring occasionally, 5 to 8 minutes.   *Makes 4 servings*

SEAFOOD GUMBO

Catch of the Day

CREAMY ALFREDO SEAFOOD NEWBURG

2 tablespoons margarine or butter
¼ cup finely chopped onion
1 pound uncooked medium shrimp, peeled, deveined and coarsely chopped
1 jar (16 ounces) RAGÚ® Cheese Creations!® Classic Alfredo Sauce
¼ teaspoon ground white pepper
4 croissants or crescent rolls

1. In 12-inch nonstick skillet, melt margarine over medium-high heat and cook onion, stirring occasionally, 2 minutes or until tender.

2. Stir in shrimp and cook, stirring constantly, 2 minutes or until shrimp are almost pink. Stir in Ragú Cheese Creations! Sauce and pepper. Bring to a boil over high heat.

3. Reduce heat to low and simmer uncovered, stirring occasionally, 5 minutes or until shrimp turn pink. To serve, spoon shrimp mixture onto bottom of croissants and sprinkle, if desired, with chopped fresh parsley. Top with remaining croissant halves.

Makes 4 servings

Variation: For a light dish, substitute Ragú Cheese Creations! Light Parmesan Alfredo Sauce.

Tip: Substitute 1 pound imitation crabmeat for shrimp.

Prep Time: 5 minutes
Cook Time: 15 minutes

GARLIC SHRIMP WITH NOODLES

4 tablespoons margarine or butter, divided
¼ cup finely chopped onion
2 cups water
1 package LIPTON® Noodles & Sauce—Butter & Herb
2 tablespoons olive oil
1 tablespoon finely chopped garlic
1 pound uncooked medium shrimp, cleaned
1 can (14 ounces) artichoke hearts, drained and halved
¼ cup finely chopped fresh parsley
Pepper to taste

In medium saucepan, melt 2 tablespoons butter; cook onion until tender. Add water; bring to a boil. Stir in Noodles & Sauce—Butter & Herb and continue boiling over medium heat, stirring occasionally, 8 minutes or until noodles are tender.

Meanwhile, in large skillet, heat remaining 2 tablespoons butter with olive oil. Add garlic; cook over medium-high heat 30 seconds. Add shrimp and artichokes; cook, stirring occasionally, 3 minutes or until shrimp turn pink. Stir in parsley and pepper. To serve, combine shrimp mixture with hot noodles. Garnish, if desired, with watercress.

Makes about 4 servings

LEMON–PARSLEY SALMON STEAKS

½ cup A.1.® Steak Sauce
½ cup parsley sprigs, finely chopped
¼ cup lemon juice
¼ cup finely chopped green onions
2 teaspoons sugar
2 cloves garlic, minced
½ teaspoon ground black pepper
4 (6- to 8-ounce) salmon steaks, about 1 inch thick

Blend steak sauce, parsley, lemon juice, onions, sugar, garlic and pepper. Place salmon steaks in glass dish; coat with ½ cup parsley mixture. Cover; refrigerate 1 hour, turning occasionally.

Remove steaks from marinade; discard marinade. Grill for 4 to 6 minutes on each side or until fish flakes easily when tested with fork, brushing often with reserved parsley mixture. *Makes 4 servings*

EASY PAELLA

1 medium onion, cut into halves and chopped
1 large red or green bell pepper, sliced
1 clove garlic, minced
2 tablespoons vegetable oil
1 can (16 ounces) tomatoes with juice, cut up
1 package (9 ounces) frozen artichoke hearts, cut into quarters
½ cup dry white wine
½ teaspoon dried thyme, crushed
¼ teaspoon salt
⅛ teaspoon saffron or turmeric
2 cups cooked rice
1 cup frozen peas
½ pound large shrimp, peeled and deveined
1 (3-ounce) pouch of STARKIST® Tuna, drained and broken into chunks

In a large skillet sauté onion, bell pepper and garlic in oil for 3 minutes. Stir in tomatoes with juice, artichoke hearts, wine and seasonings. Bring to a boil; reduce heat. Simmer for 10 minutes. Stir in rice, peas, shrimp and tuna. Cook for 3 to 5 minutes more or until shrimp turn pink and mixture is heated. *Makes 4 servings*

Prep Time: 30 minutes

• Classic Tip •

Turmeric is a spice that is related to ginger. Because of its intense golden mustard color, it is also used as a dye. Use it sparingly—a little goes a long way.

EASY PAELLA

GRILLED FISH FLORENTINE

MARINADE
- ¼ cup oil
- 2 tablespoons lemon juice
- 2 tablespoons soy sauce
- 1 teaspoon grated lemon peel
- 1 garlic clove, minced
- 4 fresh or frozen red snapper or swordfish steaks, thawed

FLORENTINE SAUCE
- 1 tablespoon butter
- ½ cup chopped scallions
- ¼ cup chopped fresh mushrooms
- 1 cup chicken broth
- ⅓ cup HOLLAND HOUSE® White Cooking Wine
- ½ cup whipping cream
- 4 cups chopped fresh spinach
- ¼ teaspoon pepper

1. In large plastic bowl, combine oil, lemon juice, soy sauce, lemon peel and garlic; mix well. Add fish, turning to coat all sides. Cover; refrigerate 2 hours. Prepare barbecue grill. Meanwhile, melt butter in large skillet over medium heat. Add scallions and mushrooms; cook until softened, about 3 minutes, stirring occasionally. Stir in chicken broth and cooking wine. Bring to a boil; boil until sauce is reduced by half, about 10 minutes. Add whipping cream; simmer over medium heat until sauce is reduced to about ½ cup, about 10 minutes. Strain into food processor bowl. Add spinach; process until smooth. Add pepper, keep warm.

2. Drain fish, reserving lemon-soy sauce mixture. Place fish on grill over medium-hot coals. Cook 10 minutes or until fish flakes easily with a fork, turning once and brushing frequently with lemon-soy sauce.* Discard any leftover marinade. Serve fish with spinach sauce.

Makes 4 servings

*Do not marinate during last 5 minutes of cooking.

POACHED SEAFOOD ITALIANO

- 1 tablespoon olive or vegetable oil
- 1 large clove garlic, minced
- ¼ cup dry white wine or chicken broth
- 4 (6 ounce) salmon steaks or fillets
- 1 can (14.5 ounces) CONTADINA® Recipe Ready Diced Tomatoes with Italian Herbs, undrained
- 2 tablespoons chopped fresh basil (optional)

1. Heat oil in large skillet. Add garlic; sauté 30 seconds. Add wine. Bring to boil.

2. Add salmon; cover. Reduce heat to medium; simmer 6 minutes.

3. Add undrained tomatoes; simmer 2 minutes or until salmon flakes easily when tested with fork. Sprinkle with basil just before serving, if desired.

Makes 4 servings

GRILLED FISH FLORENTINE

Meatless Entrées

FLORENTINE STRATA

8 ounces BARILLA® Spaghetti or Linguine
1 jar (26 ounces) BARILLA® Roasted Garlic and Onion Pasta Sauce, divided
1 package (12 ounces) frozen spinach soufflé, thawed
2 cups (8 ounces) shredded mozzarella cheese, divided
¼ cup (1 ounce) grated Parmesan cheese, divided

1. Cook spaghetti according to package directions until partially done but still firm, 5 to 8 minutes. Drain.

2. Meanwhile, coat microwave-safe 13×9×2-inch baking dish with nonstick cooking spray. Pour 1½ cups pasta sauce into baking dish; top with half of drained spaghetti, half of spinach soufflé, 1 cup mozzarella cheese and 2 tablespoons Parmesan. Repeat layers of spaghetti, pasta sauce and cheeses.

3. Cover with plastic wrap and microwave on HIGH, turning every 4 minutes, until strata is bubbly and cheese is melted, 8 to 10 minutes. Let stand 3 minutes before serving.   *Makes 8 servings*

Tip: When preparing pasta that will be used in a casserole, it's important to reduce the suggested cooking time on the package by about one third. The pasta will continue to cook and absorb liquid while the casserole is cooking.

BAKED CUT ZITI

1 package (16 ounces) BARILLA® Cut Ziti
3 tablespoons butter
3 tablespoons all-purpose flour
½ teaspoon *each* salt, pepper and dried oregano
1½ cups milk
4 ripe tomatoes (about 2 pounds), divided
¼ cup Italian-flavored bread crumbs
1 tablespoon olive oil
½ cup grated Parmesan cheese
¼ cup fresh basil, chopped

1. Cook ziti according to package directions; drain and set aside.

2. To prepare white sauce, melt butter in small saucepan over medium heat. Add flour, salt, pepper and oregano; cook and stir 1 minute or until bubbly. Gradually stir in milk; cook 2 to 3 minutes or until thickened, stirring constantly. Remove from heat.

3. Preheat oven to 350°F. Peel, seed and chop 3 tomatoes. Slice remaining tomato. Combine bread crumbs and olive oil in small cup.

4. Combine cooked ziti, white sauce, chopped tomatoes, cheese and basil in large bowl. Transfer to 2-quart baking dish; arrange tomato slices on top and sprinkle with bread crumbs. Bake 30 minutes. Cool slightly before serving. *Makes 6 to 8 servings*

CHEESE ENCHILADAS WITH GREEN CHILES

1¼ cups (10-ounce can) ORTEGA® Enchilada Sauce
1 cup ORTEGA® Garden Style Salsa
15 (6-inch) corn tortillas
1 pound Monterey Jack cheese, sliced into 15 strips
1 can (7 ounces) ORTEGA® Whole Green Chiles, sliced into 3 strips
1 cup (4 ounces) shredded Monterey Jack cheese

PREHEAT oven to 350°F.

COMBINE enchilada sauce and salsa in medium bowl; mix well. Pour *1½ cups* sauce mixture onto bottom of ungreased 13×9-inch baking pan.

HEAT tortillas, one at a time, in lightly greased medium skillet over medium-high heat for 20 seconds on each side or until soft. Place 1 strip cheese and 1 strip chile in center of each tortilla; roll up. Place seam-side down in baking pan. Repeat with remaining tortillas, cheese and chiles. Ladle *remaining* sauce mixture over enchiladas; sprinkle with shredded cheese.

BAKE, covered, for 20 minutes. Remove cover; bake for additional 5 minutes or until heated through and cheese is melted. *Makes 6 to 8 servings*

BROCCOLI–STUFFED SHELLS

1 tablespoon butter or margarine
¼ cup chopped onion
1 cup ricotta cheese
1 egg
2 cups chopped cooked broccoli *or* 1 package
    (10 ounces) frozen chopped broccoli, thawed
    and well drained
1 cup (4 ounces) shredded Monterey Jack cheese
20 jumbo pasta shells
1 can (28 ounces) crushed tomatoes with added
    purée
1 package (1 ounce) HIDDEN VALLEY® Milk
    Recipe Original Ranch® salad dressing mix
¼ cup grated Parmesan cheese

Preheat oven to 350°F. In small skillet, melt butter over medium heat. Add onion; cook until onion is tender but not browned. Remove from heat; cool. In large bowl, stir ricotta cheese and egg until well-blended. Add broccoli and Jack cheese; mix well. In large pot of boiling water, cook pasta shells 8 to 10 minutes or just until tender; drain. Rinse under cold running water; drain again. Stuff each shell with about 2 tablespoons broccoli-cheese mixture.

In medium bowl, combine tomatoes, sautéed onion and salad dressing mix; mix well. Pour one third of the tomato mixture into 13×9-inch baking dish. Arrange filled shells in dish. Spoon remaining tomato mixture over top. Sprinkle with Parmesan cheese. Bake, covered, until hot and bubbly, about 30 minutes.

Makes 4 servings

CHEESY RATATOUILLE

1 pound eggplant, peeled and cut into ½-inch
    cubes
6 plum tomatoes, coarsely chopped
1 medium zucchini, cut into ½-inch chunks
1⅓ cups *French's® Taste Toppers™* French Fried
    Onions, divided
3 tablespoons olive oil
2 cloves garlic, minced
1½ cups (6 ounces) shredded mozzarella cheese

1. Preheat oven to 400°F. Combine eggplant, tomatoes, zucchini, ⅔ *cup Taste Toppers*, oil, garlic, ⅛ *teaspoon salt* and ⅛ *teaspoon pepper* in 3-quart shallow baking dish. Bake 40 minutes or until vegetables are tender, stirring occasionally.

2. Sprinkle cheese and remaining ⅔ *cup Taste Toppers* over vegetables. Bake 3 minutes or until *Taste Toppers* are golden. *Makes 6 servings*

Prep Time: 15 minutes
Cook Time: 45 minutes

Meatless Entrées

LASAGNA FLORENTINE

2 tablespoons olive or vegetable oil

3 medium carrots, finely chopped

1 package (8 to 10 ounces) sliced mushrooms

1 medium onion, finely chopped

2 cloves garlic, finely chopped

1 jar (28 ounces) RAGÚ® Hearty Robusto! Pasta Sauce

1 container (15 ounces) ricotta cheese

2 cups shredded mozzarella cheese, divided

1 box (10 ounces) frozen chopped spinach, thawed and squeezed dry

¼ cup grated Parmesan cheese

2 eggs

1 teaspoon salt

1 teaspoon dried Italian seasoning

16 lasagna noodles, cooked and drained

Preheat oven to 375°F. In 12-inch skillet, heat oil over medium heat and cook carrots, mushrooms, onion and garlic until carrots are almost tender, about 5 minutes. Stir in Ragú® Hearty Robusto! Pasta Sauce; heat through.

Meanwhile, in medium bowl, combine ricotta cheese, 1½ cups mozzarella cheese, spinach, Parmesan cheese, eggs, salt and Italian seasoning; set aside.

In 13×9-inch baking dish, evenly spread ½ cup sauce mixture. Arrange 4 lasagna noodles, lengthwise over sauce, overlapping edges slightly. Spread ⅓ of the ricotta mixture over noodles; repeat layers, ending with noodles. Top with remaining sauce and ½ cup mozzarella cheese. Cover with foil and bake 40 minutes. Remove foil and continue baking 10 minutes or until bubbling. *Makes 8 servings*

LASAGNA FLORENTINE

ANGEL HAIR WITH ROASTED RED PEPPER SAUCE

1 package (16 ounces) BARILLA® Angel Hair
1 jar (12 ounces) roasted red peppers with juice, divided
1 tablespoon olive or vegetable oil
3 cloves garlic, minced
2 cups heavy cream
1½ teaspoons salt
1 teaspoon pepper
½ cup (2 ounces) grated Romano cheese, divided
3 tablespoons fresh basil leaves, cut into thin strips (optional)

1. Cook angel hair according to package directions; drain.

2. Meanwhile, chop ¼ cup roasted peppers; set aside. Purée remaining peppers and juice in food processor or blender.

3. Heat oil in large nonstick skillet. Add garlic; cook and stir 2 minutes over medium-low heat. Add pepper purée, cream, salt and pepper; cook over medium heat, stirring frequently, about 6 minutes or until hot and bubbly. Stir in ¼ cup cheese.

4. Combine hot drained angel hair with pepper mixture. Top with reserved chopped peppers, ¼ cup cheese and basil, if desired. *Makes 6 to 8 servings*

· *Classic Tip* ·

Serve this hearty bowl of soup with a loaf of crusty bread and a tossed green salad for a complete meal everyone will love.

BLACK BEAN SOUP

¼ cup mild salsa
1 can (16 ounces) black beans
2 cups water
1 cup cherry tomatoes, tops removed
1½ teaspoons ground cumin
1 teaspoon sugar

Strain salsa, discarding chunks. Drain and rinse black beans; reserve 1 tablespoon. Place remaining beans with all ingredients in food processor or blender; process until smooth. Stir in reserved black beans and refrigerate until ready to serve. *Makes 4 servings*

Favorite recipe from **The Sugar Association, Inc**

ANGEL HAIR WITH ROASTED RED PEPPER SAUCE

GRILLED VEGETABLE FETTUCCINE

1 large zucchini
1 large yellow squash
1 medium red bell pepper
1 medium yellow or green bell pepper
¼ cup non-creamy Italian salad dressing
⅔ cup milk
1 tablespoon margarine or butter
1 (4.7-ounce) package PASTA RONI® Fettuccine Alfredo
¾ cup (3 ounces) crumbled goat cheese or feta cheese
¼ cup julienned fresh basil leaves

1. Preheat grill or broiler. Cut zucchini and squash lengthwise into quarters. Cut bell peppers lengthwise into quarters; discard stems and seeds. Brush dressing over all surfaces of vegetables. Grill over medium coals 10 to 12 minutes or broil on top rack 10 to 12 minutes or until vegetables are tender, turning occasionally.

2. Meanwhile, in medium saucepan, bring 1¼ cups water, milk, margarine, pasta and Special Seasonings to a boil. Reduce heat to medium-low. Gently boil uncovered, 5 to 6 minutes or until pasta is slightly firm, stirring occasionally.

3. Cut grilled vegetables into ½-inch chunks; stir into pasta mixture. Let stand 3 minutes. Top with cheese and basil.   *Makes 4 servings*

Tip: Speed up the preparation by using leftover grilled veggies from your weekend barbecue.

Prep Time: 15 minutes
Cook Time: 20 minutes

ITALIAN BAKED FRITTATA

1 cup broccoli flowerettes
½ cup sliced mushrooms
½ red pepper, cut into rings
2 green onions, sliced into 1-inch pieces
1 tablespoon margarine
8 eggs
¼ cup GREY POUPON® Dijon or COUNTRY DIJON® Mustard
¼ cup water
½ teaspoon Italian seasoning
1 cup (4 ounces) shredded Swiss cheese

1. Cook broccoli, mushrooms, red pepper and green onions in margarine or butter in 10-inch ovenproof skillet over medium-high heat until tender-crisp, about 5 minutes. Remove from heat.

2. Beat eggs, mustard, water and Italian seasoning in small bowl with electric mixer at medium speed until foamy; stir in cheese. Pour mixture into skillet over vegetables.

3. Bake at 375°F for 20 to 25 minutes or until set. Serve immediately.   *Makes 4 servings*

GRILLED VEGETABLE FETTUCCINE

146

EASY CHEESE & TOMATO MACARONI

2 packages (7 ounces each) macaroni and cheese dinner
1 tablespoon olive or vegetable oil
1 cup finely chopped onion
1 cup thinly sliced celery
1 can (28 ounces) CONTADINA® Recipe Ready Crushed Tomatoes
Grated Parmesan cheese (optional)
Sliced green onion or celery leaves (optional)

1. Cook macaroni (from macaroni and cheese dinner) according to package directions; drain.

2. Heat oil in large skillet. Add chopped onion and celery; sauté for 3 minutes or until vegetables are tender.

3. Combine tomatoes and cheese mix from dinner in small bowl. Stir into vegetable mixture.

4. Simmer for 3 to 4 minutes or until mixture is thickened and heated through. Add macaroni to skillet; stir until well coated with sauce. Heat thoroughly, stirring occasionally. Sprinkle with Parmesan cheese and sliced green onion, if desired.

Makes 6 to 8 servings

Prep Time: 5 minutes
Cook Time: 15 minutes

MUSHROOM FRITTATA

1 teaspoon butter or margarine
1 medium zucchini, shredded
1 medium tomato, chopped
1 can (4 ounces) sliced mushrooms, drained
6 eggs, beaten
2 cups (8 ounces) shredded Swiss cheese
¼ cup milk
2 teaspoons Dijon mustard
½ teaspoon LAWRY'S® Seasoned Salt
½ teaspoon LAWRY'S® Seasoned Pepper

In large, ovenproof skillet, melt butter. Cook zucchini, tomato and mushrooms over medium high heat 1 minute. In large bowl, combine remaining ingredients; mix well. Pour egg mixture into skillet; cook 10 minutes over low heat. To brown top, place skillet under broiler 2 to 3 minutes.

Makes 4 servings

Serving Suggestion: Serve directly from skillet or remove frittata to serving dish. Serve with additional Swiss cheese and fresh fruit.

Hint: Try serving frittata with prepared LAWRY'S® Spaghetti Sauce Seasoning Blend with Imported Mushrooms.

PASTA WITH ZESTY TOMATO PESTO

1 jar (8 ounces) sun-dried tomatoes, in oil,
   undrained
⅓ cup *French's*® Hearty Deli Brown Mustard
¼ cup grated Parmesan cheese
2 tablespoons pine nuts or slivered almonds
1 tablespoon *Frank's*® *RedHot*® Cayenne Pepper
   Sauce
1 clove garlic, coarsely chopped
1 box (16 ounces) uncooked bow-tie pasta

1. Combine sun-dried tomatoes with oil, 1 cup water,
mustard, Parmesan, pine nuts, *Frank's RedHot* Sauce
and garlic in blender or food processor. Cover; process
until well blended.

2. Cook pasta according to package directions; drain
well. Place in large bowl. Pour sauce over pasta; toss
well to coat evenly. Serve warm or at room temperature.

Makes 6 side-dish servings (2 cups pesto)

Note: If you enjoy the taste of pesto sauce, try adding
¼ cup *French's*® Dijon Mustard to 1 cup prepared pesto
to make a spicy pesto dip or spread.

Prep Time: 15 minutes
Cook Time: 10 minutes

PASTA WITH ZESTY TOMATO PESTO

CHUNKY GARDEN STEW

Spicy Hot Sauce (recipe follows)
1 tablespoon olive or canola oil
3 medium Colorado Sangre red potatoes, cut into chunks
1 large carrot, sliced diagonally
1 medium onion, quartered
1 large yellow squash or zucchini, sliced
1 Japanese eggplant *or* ½ regular eggplant, cut into cubes
2 celery stalks, sliced
1 small red or green bell pepper, cut into chunks
1 teaspoon ground cinnamon
1 teaspoon coriander
1 teaspoon turmeric
½ teaspoon ground cumin
½ teaspoon ground cardamom
½ teaspoon salt
2 cans (14½ ounces each) vegetable broth *or* 1½ cups water
1 can (15 ounces) chick-peas, drained
⅔ cup raisins
6 cups hot cooked rice

Prepare Spicy Hot Sauce; set aside. Heat oil in Dutch oven over medium-high heat. Add potatoes and carrot; cook and stir 5 minutes. Add onion, squash, eggplant, celery, bell pepper, spices and salt; cook and stir 3 to 5 minutes. Add broth, chick-peas and raisins; bring to a simmer. Simmer, covered, about 15 minutes or until potatoes are tender. Serve vegetable stew over rice. Serve with Spicy Hot Sauce. *Makes 5 to 6 servings*

SPICY HOT SAUCE

⅓ cup coarsely chopped cilantro
¼ cup water
1 tablespoon olive or canola oil
2 cloves garlic
½ teaspoon salt
½ teaspoon turmeric
¼ to ½ teaspoon ground red pepper
¼ teaspoon sugar
¼ teaspoon ground cumin
¼ teaspoon ground cardamom
¼ teaspoon ground coriander

Combine all ingredients in blender; process until smooth. Adjust flavors to taste.

Makes about ½ cup sauce

Favorite recipe from **Colorado Potato Administrative Committee**

MEXICAN–STYLE STUFFED PEPPERS

6 medium red or green bell peppers, halved, seeded
3 tablespoons water
2 cups cooked long-grain white rice
1¾ cups (1-pound jar) ORTEGA® Garden Style Salsa, *divided*
1½ cups (6 ounces) shredded Cheddar cheese, *divided*
¾ cup frozen peas and carrots
¾ cup whole-kernel corn
½ cup (about 3) chopped green onions
½ teaspoon garlic salt

PREHEAT oven to 375°F.

PLACE bell peppers and water in microwave-safe dish; cover with plastic wrap. Microwave on HIGH (100%) power for 4 to 5 minutes or until slightly tender; drain.

COMBINE rice, ¾ *cup* salsa, *1 cup* cheese, peas and carrots, corn, green onions and garlic salt in large bowl. Fill peppers with mixture, mounding slightly. Place peppers in ungreased 13×9-inch baking pan; top with *remaining* cheese. Cover.

BAKE for 35 to 40 minutes. Uncover; bake for additional 5 minutes or until heated through and cheese is melted.   *Makes 6 servings*

For Freeze Ahead: PREPARE as above; do not bake. Cover; freeze for up to 2 months. Thaw overnight in refrigerator. **PREHEAT** oven to 375°F. **BAKE** for 40 to 45 minutes. Uncover, bake for additional 5 minutes or until heated through and cheese is melted.

7 VEGGIE MAC 'N CHEESE

1 can (15 ounces) VEG•ALL® Original Mixed Vegetables, drained
1 box (7¼ ounces) macaroni and cheese mix, prepared
1 teaspoon onion powder
1 teaspoon prepared mustard
1 tomato, sliced
1 teaspoon dried parsley

1. Preheat oven to 350°F. Combine Veg•All, prepared macaroni and cheese, onion powder, and mustard; mix

well. Pour into greased 1-quart casserole. Bake for 20 to 25 minutes. Garnish with tomato slices and dried parsley. Serve hot.   *Makes 6 servings*

Prep Time: 7 minutes
Cook Time: 20 minutes

SAVORY ROASTED VEGETABLES & PASTA

4 carrots, thinly sliced
2 red bell peppers, cut into strips
2 zucchini, cut into ½-inch chunks
2 yellow squash, cut into ½-inch chunks
4 cloves garlic, peeled
½ cup half-and-half
3 tablespoons *French's®* Dijon Mustard
8 ounces penne pasta, cooked
   Shaved Parmesan cheese

1. Preheat oven to 425°F. In roasting pan, toss vegetables and garlic with *2 tablespoons olive oil, 1 teaspoon salt* and *¼ teaspoon black pepper.* Bake, uncovered, 20 minutes or until tender, stirring occasionally.

2. Spoon half of vegetables into blender or food processor. Add half-and-half, mustard and *2 tablespoons water.* Process until mixture is smooth.

3. Toss pasta with vegetable purée in large serving bowl. Spoon remaining vegetables on top. Sprinkle with Parmesan cheese.   *Makes 4 servings*

Prep Time: 20 minutes
Cook Time: 20 minutes

QUICK FRIED RICE

1 cup UNCLE BEN'S® Instant Brown Rice
1 tablespoon margarine
½ cup sliced yellow summer squash
½ cup diced red bell pepper
½ cup chopped green onions with tops
2 eggs, lightly beaten
2 teaspoons soy sauce

1. Cook rice according to package directions.

2. Melt margarine in medium nonstick skillet. Add squash, bell pepper and green onions; cook and stir over medium-low heat 5 minutes. Add eggs; cook and stir 2 minutes just until eggs are cooked.

3. Add rice to vegetable mixture; sprinkle with soy sauce. Cover skillet and cook over low heat 5 minutes or until rice is hot.   *Makes 4 servings*

• Classic Tip •

Boost your daily fiber intake with the delicious Quick Fried Rice recipe. The brown rice in this recipe is high in fiber with a nutlike flavor and chewy texture.

SOUTHWESTERN CHILIES RELLENOS

  2 tablespoons olive oil
½ teaspoon white pepper
½ teaspoon salt
½ teaspoon ground red pepper
¼ teaspoon ground cloves
  4 cans (4 ounces each) whole green chilies,
     drained, seeded
1½ cups (6 ounces) shredded Wisconsin Cheddar
     cheese
1½ cups (6 ounces) shredded Wisconsin Monterey
     Jack cheese
  1 package (16 ounces) egg roll wrappers
  1 egg yolk plus 1 teaspoon water
     Vegetable oil

Combine olive oil and seasonings in small bowl. Add chilies; toss to coat. Let stand 1 hour. Combine cheeses in separate small bowl.

For each chili relleno, place 1 chili in center of 1 egg roll wrapper; top with ¼ cup cheese mixture. Brush edges of egg roll wrapper with combined egg yolk and water. Fold lengthwise edges over filling, overlapping edges; press together. Seal ends, enclosing filling.

Heat vegetable oil in heavy saucepan over medium-high heat until oil reaches 375°F; adjust heat to maintain temperature. Fry chilies rellenos, a few at a time, in hot oil 2 to 3 minutes or until golden brown. Drain on paper towels.   *Makes 6 servings*

Favorite recipe from **Wisconsin Milk Marketing Board**

**SOUTHWESTERN CHILIES
RELLENOS**

RIGATONI CON RICOTTA

1 package (16 ounces) BARILLA® Rigatoni
2 eggs
1 container (15 ounces) ricotta cheese
¾ cup (3 ounces) grated Parmesan cheese
1 tablespoon dried parsley
2 jars (26 ounces each) BARILLA® Lasagna & Casserole Sauce or Marinara Pasta Sauce, divided
3 cups (12 ounces) shredded mozzarella cheese, divided

1. Preheat oven to 375°F. Spray 13×9×2-inch baking pan with nonstick cooking spray. Cook rigatoni according to package directions: drain.

2. Beat eggs in small bowl. Stir in ricotta, Parmesan and parsley.

3. To assemble casserole, spread 2 cups lasagna sauce to cover bottom of pan. Place half of cooked rigatoni over sauce; top with half of ricotta mixture, dropped by spoonfuls. Layer with 1 cup mozzarella, 2 cups lasagna sauce, remaining rigatoni and ricotta mixture. Top with 1 cup mozzarella, remaining lasagna sauce and remaining 1 cup mozzarella.

4. Cover with foil and bake 60 to 70 minutes or until bubbly. Uncover and continue cooking about 5 minutes or until cheese is melted. Let stand 15 minutes before serving.

Makes 12 servings

HERBED VEGGIE CHEESE AND RICE

1 bag (16 ounces) BIRDS EYE® frozen Farm Fresh Mixtures Broccoli, Green Beans, Pearl Onions & Red Peppers
2 cups cooked white rice
2 tablespoons grated Parmesan cheese
1 teaspoon dried basil
1 teaspoon dill weed
½ cup reduced-fat shredded Cheddar cheese
½ cup reduced-fat shredded Monterey Jack cheese

• In large saucepan, cook vegetables according to package directions; drain and return to saucepan.

• Add rice, using fork to keep rice fluffy.

• Add Parmesan cheese, basil, dill and salt and pepper to taste.

• Add Cheddar and Monterey Jack cheeses; toss together. Cook over medium heat until heated through.

Makes 4 servings

Prep Time: 6 minutes
Cook Time: 12 to 15 minutes

RIGATONI CON RICOTTA

SPAGHETTI WITH TOMATOES AND OLIVES

2 tablespoons extra-virgin olive oil
3 cloves garlic, finely chopped
1½ pounds fresh ripe tomatoes, seeded and chopped (about 3 cups)
1 tablespoon tomato paste
1 teaspoon dried oregano
⅛ teaspoon ground red pepper
½ cup pitted brine-cured black olives, coarsely chopped
2 tablespoons capers
Salt and pepper
1 package (16 ounces) BARILLA® Thin Spaghetti
Grated Parmesan cheese

1. Heat olive oil and garlic in large skillet over low heat until garlic begins to sizzle. Add tomatoes, tomato paste, oregano and red pepper; simmer, uncovered, until sauce is thickened, about 15 minutes. Add olives, capers and salt and pepper to taste.

2. Meanwhile, cook spaghetti according to package directions; drain.

3. Toss spaghetti with sauce. Sprinkle with cheese before serving.

Makes 6 to 8 servings

HEARTY MEATLESS CHILI

1 envelope LIPTON® RECIPE SECRETS® Onion or Onion-Mushroom Soup Mix
4 cups water
1 can (16 ounces) chick-peas or garbanzo beans, rinsed and drained
1 can (16 ounces) red kidney beans, rinsed and drained
1 can (14½ ounces) whole peeled tomatoes, undrained and chopped
1 cup lentils, rinsed and drained
1 large rib celery, coarsely chopped
1 tablespoon chili powder
2 teaspoons ground cumin (optional)
1 medium clove garlic, finely chopped

In 4-quart saucepan or stockpot, combine all ingredients. Bring to a boil over high heat. Reduce heat to low and simmer covered, stirring occasionally, 20 minutes or until lentils are almost tender. Remove cover and simmer, stirring occasionally, an additional 20 minutes or until liquid is almost absorbed and lentils are tender.

Makes about 4 (2-cup) servings

Note: For spicier chili, add ¼ teaspoon crushed red pepper flakes.

Serving Suggestion: Serve over hot cooked brown or white rice and top with shredded Cheddar cheese.

SPAGHETTI WITH TOMATOES AND OLIVES

BAKED EGGPLANT PARMESAN

2 cups seasoned dry bread crumbs

1½ cups grated Parmesan cheese, divided

2 medium eggplants (about 2 pounds), peeled and cut into ¼-inch round slices

4 eggs, beaten with 3 tablespoons water

1 jar (26 to 28 ounces) RAGÚ® Hearty Robusto! Pasta Sauce

1½ cups shredded mozzarella cheese (about 6 ounces)

Preheat oven to 350°F. In medium bowl, combine bread crumbs and ½ cup Parmesan cheese. Dip eggplant slices in egg mixture, then bread crumb mixture. On lightly oiled baking sheets, arrange eggplant slices in single layer; bake 25 minutes or until golden.

In 13×9-inch baking dish, evenly spread 1 cup Ragú® Hearty Robusto! Pasta Sauce. Layer ½ of the baked eggplant slices, then 1 cup sauce and ½ cup Parmesan cheese; repeat. Cover with aluminum foil and bake 45 minutes. Remove foil and sprinkle with mozzarella cheese. Bake uncovered an additional 10 minutes or until cheese is melted. *Makes 6 servings*

LOUISIANA RED BEANS & RICE

1 package (7.2 ounces) RICE-A-RONI® Herb & Butter

1 cup chopped green or yellow bell pepper

¾ cup chopped onion

2 cloves garlic, minced

2 tablespoons vegetable oil or olive oil

1 can (15 or 16 ounces) red beans or kidney beans, rinsed and drained

1 can (14½ or 16 ounces) tomatoes or stewed tomatoes, undrained

1 teaspoon dried thyme leaves or dried oregano leaves

⅛ teaspoon hot pepper sauce or black pepper

2 tablespoons chopped parsley (optional)

1. Prepare Rice-A-Roni® Mix as package directs.

2. While Rice-A-Roni® is simmering, in second large skillet, sauté green pepper, onion and garlic in oil 5 minutes.

3. Stir in beans, tomatoes, thyme and hot pepper sauce. Simmer, uncovered, 10 minutes, stirring occasionally. Stir in parsley. Serve over rice. *Makes 5 servings*

Serving Suggestion: Serve with one 8-ounce glass of milk per serving.

VEGGIE CALZONES

1½ cups BIRDS EYE® frozen Farm Fresh Mixtures
    Broccoli, Red Peppers, Onions & Mushrooms
½ cup ricotta cheese
½ cup shredded mozzarella cheese
¼ cup grated Parmesan cheese
1 teaspoon dried Italian seasoning
¼ teaspoon pepper
1 pound fresh pizza dough or thawed frozen
    bread dough
1 egg, beaten

• Preheat oven to 425°F.

• Rinse vegetables under warm water to thaw; drain well and pat gently with paper towel.

• In medium bowl, combine vegetables, cheeses, Italian seasoning and pepper.

• Divide dough into 4 pieces. Roll out each piece into 6-inch circle.* Spoon ¼ of vegetable mixture over ½ of each circle, leaving ½-inch border. Moisten edge of dough with water; fold dough over filling to form half circle. Pinch edges well to seal. Cut several slits in top of dough; brush with egg.

• Place on greased baking sheet and bake 12 to 14 minutes or until golden brown.　　*Makes 4 servings*

Dough is easier to work with on nonfloured surface.

Prep Time: 10 minutes
Cook Time: 15 minutes

VEGGIE CALZONE

VIKING VEGETABLE CASSOULET

4 cups sliced mushrooms

2 tablespoons Lucini Premium Select Extra Virgin Olive Oil

2 large onions, thickly sliced

1 large clove garlic, minced

2 medium zucchini, cut into 1-inch pieces

1½ cups sliced yellow squash

2 cans (16 ounces each) white beans, drained

1 can (14½ ounces) plum tomatoes, cut up, with juice

⅓ cup chopped parsley

1 teaspoon dried basil, crushed

½ teaspoon dried oregano, crushed

½ cup bread crumbs

1 teaspoon butter, melted

2 cups (8 ounces) shredded JARLSBERG Cheese

In large, deep skillet, brown mushrooms in oil. Add onions and garlic; sauté 5 minutes. Add zucchini and squash; sauté until vegetables are crisp-tender. Blend in beans, tomatoes, parsley, basil and oregano.

Spoon into 2-quart baking dish. Combine bread crumbs and butter in small bowl. Sprinkle bread crumbs around edge. Bake at 350°F 20 minutes. Top with cheese and bake 20 minutes longer.

Makes 6 to 8 servings

VEGETABLE BOW TIE PASTA

1 box (16 ounces) bow tie pasta

1 cup chopped fresh broccoli

1 cup shredded carrots

1 small red bell pepper, diced

1 small zucchini or yellow squash, diced

1 jar (26 to 28 ounces) RAGÚ® Light Pasta Sauce

Cook pasta according to package directions, stirring in vegetables during last 5 minutes of boiling; drain.

In 2-quart saucepan, heat Ragú® Light Pasta Sauce. Toss sauce with hot pasta and sprinkle, if desired, with grated Parmesan cheese.

Makes 6 servings

> ## • Classic Tip •
>
>
>
> *Don't pitch those last few slices of bread in the garbage when they dry out. Simply tear into small pieces and place in a food processor and blend. Process a few seconds until fine crumbs form. Store in the freezer to have bread crumbs on hand anytime.*

VEGETABLE BOW TIE PASTA

VEGETABLE PARMESAN BAKE

1 envelope LIPTON® RECIPE SECRETS® Garlic
   Mushroom Soup Mix
¼ cup grated Parmesan cheese
1 large baking potato, cut into ¼-inch-thick slices
1 medium zucchini, diagonally cut into ¼-inch-thick slices
1 large tomato, cut into ¼-inch-thick slices
1 tablespoon margarine or butter, cut into small
   pieces

1. Preheat oven to 375°F. In small bowl, combine soup mix and Parmesan cheese; set aside.

2. In shallow 1-quart casserole sprayed with nonstick cooking spray, arrange potato slices, overlapping slightly. Sprinkle with ⅓ of the soup mixture. Top with zucchini slices, overlapping slightly. Sprinkle with ⅓ of the soup mixture. Top with tomato slices, overlapping slightly. Sprinkle with remaining soup mixture. Top with margarine.

3. Bake covered 40 minutes. Remove cover and bake an additional 10 minutes or until vegetables are tender.

Makes 4 servings

Recipe Tip: For delicious tomatoes any time of the year, store them on your kitchen counter out of direct sunlight as sunlight can change their color without ripening the flavor or texture. And never store them in the refrigerator as this can spoil their flavor and texture.

OLD MEXICO BLACK BEANS & RICE

2 tablespoons vegetable oil
1 package (6.8 ounces) RICE-A-RONI® Spanish
   Rice
½ cup chopped green bell pepper
½ cup chopped onion
2 cloves garlic, minced
1 can (14½ ounces) tomatoes, undrained, chopped
¼ to ½ teaspoon hot pepper sauce
1 can (16 ounces) black beans, rinsed, drained
1 can (16 ounces) pinto beans, rinsed, drained
½ cup (2 ounces) shredded Cheddar cheese or
   Monterey Jack cheese
2 tablespoons chopped parsley or cilantro
   (optional)

1. In large skillet, heat oil over medium heat. Add rice-vermicelli mix, green pepper, onion and garlic; sauté, stirring frequently, until vermicelli is golden brown.

2. Stir in 2 cups water, tomatoes, hot pepper sauce and Special Seasonings; bring to a boil over high heat.

3. Cover; reduce heat. Simmer 15 minutes.

4. Stir in black and pinto beans.

5. Cover; continue to simmer 5 minutes or until liquid is absorbed and rice is tender. Serve topped with cheese; sprinkle with parsley, if desired.

Makes 4 servings

PASTA E FAGIOLI

10 ounces (1¼ cups) dry Navy or Cranberry Beans, sorted and rinsed
3¾ cups cold water
1½ teaspoons salt
⅔ cup plus 3 tablespoons vegetable oil
1 bay leaf
2 to 3 cloves garlic
3 carrots, diced
2 ribs celery, sliced
1 large onion, chopped
1 to 2 cloves garlic, crushed
1 teaspoon dried oregano leaves
½ teaspoon dried basil leaves
   Black pepper
6 to 7 tomatoes, peeled, coarsely chopped
8 ounces shell-shaped pasta

1. Place beans in Dutch oven; add cold water. Soak beans at room temperature 6 to 8 hours or overnight.

2. Add salt, ⅔ cup oil, bay leaf and whole garlic cloves to soaked beans. Simmer gently until beans are tender, 2 to 3 hours, stirring occasionally. Drain beans; reserve 1½ cups cooking liquid. Remove and discard bay leaf and garlic.

3. Heat 3 tablespoons oil in large skillet. Add carrots, celery and onion; cook until soft. Add crushed garlic and seasonings; simmer 30 minutes. Add tomatoes; cook 10 minutes.

4. Cook pasta in boiling water until just tender; drain. Combine beans, vegetables, pasta and reserved cooking liquid. Cover; simmer 10 minutes, stirring occasionally.

5. Garnish with chopped fresh parsley; serve with grated Parmesan cheese. *Makes 6 to 8 servings*

Favorite recipe from **Michigan Bean Commission**

DOWN HOME MACARONI & CHEESE

¼ cup (4 tablespoons) butter or margarine, divided
¼ cup flour
1 teaspoon salt
1 cup milk
¼ pound (4 ounces) VELVEETA® Pasteurized Prepared Cheese Product, cut up
1 package (8 ounces) KRAFT® Shredded Cheddar Cheese, divided
2 cups (8 ounces) elbow macaroni, cooked, drained
2 tablespoons seasoned dry bread crumbs

MELT 3 tablespoons of the butter in saucepan on low heat. Blend in flour and salt; cook and stir 1 minute.

Gradually add milk; cook, stirring constantly, until thickened. Add Velveeta and 1½ cups of the Cheddar cheese; stir until melted. Stir in macaroni.

POUR into 1½-quart casserole. Melt remaining 1 tablespoon butter; mix with bread crumbs. Sprinkle casserole with remaining ½ cup Cheddar cheese and bread crumb mixture.

BAKE at 350°F for 20 minutes or until thoroughly heated. *Makes 6 to 8 servings*

Prep Time: 10 minutes

SPICY THAI NOODLES

1¼ cups water
2½ teaspoons brown sugar
2 teaspoons soy sauce
1 teaspoon LAWRY'S® Garlic Powder with Parsley
¾ teaspoon LAWRY'S® Seasoned Salt
½ teaspoon cornstarch
⅛ to ¼ teaspoon hot pepper flakes
¼ cup chunky peanut butter
¼ cup sliced green onion
1 tablespoon chopped fresh cilantro
8 ounces linguine, cooked, drained and kept hot
1½ cups shredded red cabbage

In large skillet, combine first seven ingredients. Bring to a boil over medium-high heat; reduce heat to low and cook, uncovered, 5 minutes. Cool 10 minutes. Stir in peanut butter, green onion and cilantro. Add hot linguine and cabbage; toss lightly to coat. Serve immediately. *Makes 4 servings*

Serving Suggestion: Great served with a marinated cucumber salad.

SPICY THAI NOODLES

HARVEST CASSEROLE

2 cups USA lentils, rinsed and cooked
2 cups fresh or frozen broccoli, chopped
1½ cups cooked rice
1¼ cups (6 ounces) shredded Cheddar cheese
1 tablespoon soy sauce
½ teaspoon salt (optional)
¼ teaspoon dried thyme
¼ teaspoon dried marjoram
¼ teaspoon dried rosemary
4 eggs
1 cup milk

Preheat oven to 350°F.

Mix lentils, broccoli, rice, cheese, soy sauce, salt, thyme, marjoram and rosemary in large bowl. Place mixture in greased 9-inch casserole dish.

Stir together eggs and milk in medium bowl. Pour egg mixture over lentil mixture. Bake 45 minutes or until lightly browned. Top with additional shredded Cheddar cheese, if desired. *Makes 8 servings*

Favorite recipe from **USA Dry Pea & Lentil Council**

VEGETABLE CHOW MEIN

Chinese Noodle Cakes (recipe follows)
¾ **cup water**
3 **tablespoons KIKKOMAN® Soy Sauce**
4 **teaspoons cornstarch**
2 **tablespoons vegetable oil**
2 **medium carrots, cut into julienne strips**
1 **medium onion, thinly sliced**
2 **teaspoons minced fresh gingerroot**
1 **clove garlic, minced**
6 **ounces fresh bean sprouts**
1 **large stalk celery, thinly sliced**
¼ **pound fresh mushrooms, sliced**

Prepare Chinese Noodle Cakes. Combine water, soy sauce and cornstarch in small bowl; set aside. Heat oil in hot wok or large skillet over high heat. Add carrots, onion, ginger and garlic; stir-fry 1 minute. Add bean sprouts, celery and mushrooms; stir-fry 2 minutes longer. Stir in soy sauce mixture; cook and stir until sauce boils and thickens. Serve over noodle cakes.

Makes 4 to 6 servings

CHINESE NOODLE CAKES

8 **ounces uncooked capellini (angel hair pasta)**
4 **tablespoons vegetable oil, divided**

Cook capellini according to package directions. Drain, rinse under cold water and drain thoroughly. Heat 1 tablespoon oil in large nonstick skillet over medium-high heat. Add half of the capellini; spread slightly to fill bottom of skillet to form noodle cake. Cook 5 minutes, without stirring, or until golden on bottom. Lift cake with wide spatula; add 1 tablespoon oil to skillet and turn cake over. Cook 5 minutes longer, or until golden brown, shaking skillet occasionally to brown evenly; remove to rack and keep warm in 200°F oven. Repeat with remaining capellini and oil.

Makes 4 to 6 servings

*Favorite recipe from **Kikkoman International Inc.***

• *Classic Tip* •

Julienne means to cut into long very thin strips. To julienne a carrot, cut into ⅛-inch-thick slices. Stack the slices and then cut into ⅛-inch-thick strips.

VEGETABLE CHOW MEIN

CREAMY SHELLS WITH SPINACH AND MUSHROOMS

1 package (16 ounces) BARILLA® Medium or Large Shells
1 can (12 ounces) evaporated milk
1 cup (4 ounces) grated Parmesan cheese, divided
4 ounces brick cheese, cubed (about ¾ cup)
4 tablespoons butter or margarine
2 tablespoons olive or vegetable oil
1 small onion, chopped
3 cloves garlic, minced
2 packages (10 ounces each) frozen chopped spinach, thawed and well drained
1½ cups (4 ounces) sliced mushrooms

1. Cook pasta shells according to package directions; drain.

2. Meanwhile, heat evaporated milk, Parmesan (reserving 2 tablespoons for topping) and brick cheese in small saucepan over medium heat until cheeses melt, stirring frequently. Set aside.

3. Heat butter and oil in large skillet over medium-high heat. Add onion and garlic; cook about 5 minutes, stirring occasionally, until onion is transparent. Add spinach and mushrooms; cook 5 minutes, stirring occasionally.

4. Stir cheese mixture into skillet; mix well. Pour over hot drained pasta shells on platter; sprinkle with reserved Parmesan. *Makes 8 servings*

SPINACH ZITI CASSEROLE

1 pound ziti or other pasta
2 teaspoons vegetable oil
1 medium onion, chopped
1 (16-ounce) can tomato sauce
2 teaspoons sugar
2 tablespoons dried oregano leaves
½ teaspoon black pepper
½ teaspoon chili powder
1 (10-ounce) package frozen spinach, thawed and squeezed dry
1 (16-ounce) container non-fat cottage cheese
1 (15-ounce) can kidney beans, drained and rinsed

Cook pasta according to directions in large saucepan. Drain and return to saucepan. Meanwhile, heat oil in medium saucepan over low heat. Add onion; cook and stir 5 minutes.

Add tomato sauce, sugar, oregano, pepper, chili powder and spinach. Cook over low heat 15 minutes. Add tomato sauce mixture, cottage cheese and kidney beans to pasta; mix well. Pour into 2-quart baking dish. Cover and bake in 350°F oven 20 minutes.

Makes 6 servings

Note: If desired, recipe can be heated just on the stovetop. Do not remove pasta mixture from saucepan; heat thoroughly, over medium heat, stirring occasionally.

Favorite recipe from **The Sugar Association, Inc.**

Soups & Salads

2 pieces bacon, diced
1 large red bell pepper, diced
1 large green bell pepper, diced
1 celery stalk, chopped
1 carrot, peeled and chopped
1 small onion, chopped
1 clove garlic, finely chopped
2 cups bottled clam juice
1 cup CLAMATO® Tomato Cocktail
2 medium potatoes, peeled and diced
1 large tomato, chopped
1 teaspoon oregano
½ teaspoon black pepper
2 cups fresh or canned clams, chopped (about 24 shucked clams)

In heavy 4-quart saucepan, sauté bacon, peppers, celery, carrot, onion and garlic over medium heat until tender, about 10 minutes. (Do not brown bacon.) Add clam juice, Clamato, potatoes, tomato, oregano and pepper. Simmer 35 minutes or until potatoes are tender. Add clams; cook 5 minutes more.   *Makes 8 servings*

HEARTY ONE–POT CHICKEN STEW

12 TYSON® Individually Fresh Frozen® Boneless, Skinless Chicken Tenderloins
1 box UNCLE BEN'S CHEF'S RECIPE™ Traditional Red Beans & Rice
1 can (14½ ounces) diced tomatoes, undrained
3 new red potatoes, unpeeled, cut into 1-inch pieces
2 carrots, sliced ½ inch thick
1 onion, cut into 1-inch pieces

PREP: CLEAN: Wash hands. Remove protective ice glaze from frozen chicken by holding under cool running water 1 to 2 minutes. Cut into 1-inch pieces. CLEAN: Wash hands.

COOK: In large saucepan, combine chicken, beans and rice, contents of seasoning packet, 2¼ cups water, tomatoes, potatoes, carrots and onion. Bring to a boil. Cover, reduce heat; simmer 20 minutes or until internal juices of chicken run clear. (Or insert instant-read meat thermometer in thickest part of chicken. Temperature should read 170°F.)

SERVE: Serve with hot rolls, if desired.

CHILL: Refrigerate leftovers immediately.

Makes 4 servings

Prep Time: 10 minutes
Cook Time: 20 to 25 minutes

HEARTY POTATO–HAM CHOWDER

5 pounds COLORADO potatoes, peeled and cubed (about 15 cups)
3 large onions, finely chopped (about 1 pound)
3 tablespoons instant chicken bouillon granules
2 tablespoons dried marjoram leaves
1 tablespoon dry mustard
1 teaspoon ground black pepper
4 quarts milk, divided
1¼ cups all-purpose flour
1 pound process Swiss cheese, shredded
1½ pounds sodium-reduced ham, diced
½ cup snipped fresh parsley

Steam potatoes and onions in 1 quart water 20 to 30 minutes or until tender. *Do not drain.* Mash slightly. Stir in bouillon granules, marjoram, mustard and pepper. Combine about 1 quart milk with flour; whisk to blend until smooth. Add remaining milk, cheese and milk/flour mixture to potato mixture. Cook and stir over medium high heat until slightly thickened and bubbly. Cook and stir 2 minutes longer. Stir in ham and parsley; return to near boiling. Reduce heat; serve hot.

Makes 24 servings

Favorite recipe from **Colorado Potato Administrative Committee**

HEARTY ONE-POT CHICKEN STEW

ZESTY NOODLE SOUP

1 pound BOB EVANS® Zesty Hot Roll Sausage
1 (16-ounce) can whole tomatoes, undrained
½ pound fresh mushrooms, sliced
1 large onion, chopped
1 small green bell pepper, chopped
2½ cups tomato juice
2½ cups water
¼ cup chopped fresh parsley
1 teaspoon lemon juice
1 teaspoon Worcestershire sauce
1 teaspoon celery seeds
½ teaspoon salt
½ teaspoon dried thyme leaves
1 cup uncooked egg noodles

Crumble sausage into 3-quart saucepan. Cook over medium-high heat until browned, stirring occasionally. Drain off any drippings. Add tomatoes with juice, mushrooms, onion and pepper; cook until vegetables are tender, stirring well to break up tomatoes. Stir in all remaining ingredients except noodles. Bring to a boil over high heat. Reduce heat to low; simmer, covered, 30 minutes. Add noodles; simmer just until noodles are tender, yet firm. Serve hot. Refrigerate leftovers.

Makes 6 servings

Serving Suggestion: Serve with crusty French bread.

ZESTY NOODLE SOUP

CHUNKY POTATO BACON SOUP

1 package (32 ounces) frozen Southern-style hash brown potatoes, thawed
1 quart milk
1 can (10¾ ounces) condensed cream of celery soup
1 cup (6 ounces) cubed processed cheese
⅓ cup cooked chopped bacon (4 slices uncooked)
1 tablespoon *French's®* Worcestershire Sauce
1⅓ cups *French's® Taste Toppers™* French Fried Onions

1. Combine potatoes, milk, soup, cheese, bacon and Worcestershire in large saucepot. Heat to boiling over medium-high heat, stirring often.

2. Heat *Taste Toppers* in microwave on HIGH 2 minutes or until golden. Ladle soup into bowls. Sprinkle with *Taste Toppers*. Garnish with fresh minced parsley if desired.   *Makes 6 servings*

Prep Time: 5 minutes
Cook Time: 10 minutes

CHEDDAR BROCCOLI SOUP

1 tablespoon olive or vegetable oil
1 rib celery, chopped (about ½ cup)
1 carrot, chopped (about ½ cup)
1 small onion, chopped (about ½ cup)
½ teaspoon dried thyme leaves, crushed (optional)
2 cans (13¾ ounces each) chicken broth
1 jar (16 ounces) RAGÚ® Cheese Creations!® Double Cheddar Sauce
1 box (10 ounces) frozen chopped broccoli, thawed and drained

In 3-quart saucepan, heat oil over medium heat and cook celery, carrot, onion and thyme 3 minutes or until vegetables are almost tender. Add chicken broth and bring to a boil over high heat. Reduce heat to medium and simmer uncovered 10 minutes.

In food processor or blender, purée vegetable mixture until smooth; return to saucepan. Stir in Ragú Cheese Creations! Sauce and broccoli. Cook 10 minutes or until heated through.   *Makes 6 (1-cup) servings*

CHEDDAR BROCCOLI SOUP

COUNTRY CHICKEN STEW WITH DUMPLINGS

1 tablespoon olive or vegetable oil
1 chicken (3 to 3½ pounds), cut into serving pieces
   (with or without skin)
4 large carrots, cut into 2-inch pieces
3 ribs celery, cut into 1-inch pieces
1 large onion, cut into 1-inch wedges
1 envelope LIPTON® RECIPE SECRETS® Savory
   Herb with Garlic Soup Mix*
1½ cups water
½ cup apple juice
   Parsley Dumplings, optional (recipe follows)

Also terrific with LIPTON® RECIPE SECRETS® Golden Onion Soup Mix.

In 6-quart Dutch oven or heavy saucepot, heat oil over medium-high heat and brown ½ of the chicken; remove and set aside. Repeat with remaining chicken. Return chicken to Dutch oven. Stir in carrots, celery, onion and savory herb with garlic soup mix blended with water and apple juice. Bring to a boil over high heat. Reduce heat to low and simmer covered 25 minutes or until chicken is done and vegetables are tender.

Meanwhile, prepare Parsley Dumplings. Drop 12 rounded tablespoonfuls of batter into simmering broth around chicken. Continue simmering covered 10 minutes or until toothpick inserted in center of dumpling comes out clean. Season stew, if desired, with salt and pepper.   *Makes about 6 servings*

Parsley Dumplings: In medium bowl, combine 1⅓ cups all-purpose flour, 2 teaspoons baking powder, 1 tablespoon chopped fresh parsley and ½ teaspoon salt; set aside. In measuring cup, blend ⅔ cup milk, 2 tablespoons melted butter or margarine and 1 egg. Stir milk mixture into flour mixture just until blended.

Variation: Add 1 pound quartered red potatoes to stew with carrots; eliminate dumplings.

Menu Suggestion: Serve this as a meal-in-one!

CHILE CON CARNE

2 tablespoons vegetable oil
2 pounds ground beef
2 cups (2 small) chopped onions
4 cloves garlic, finely chopped
3½ cups (two 15-ounce cans) kidney, pinto or black
   beans, drained
3½ cups (29-ounce can) crushed tomatoes
1¾ cups (16-ounce jar) ORTEGA® Thick & Chunky
   Salsa
½ cup dry white wine
½ cup (4-ounce can) ORTEGA® Diced Green Chiles
3 tablespoons chili powder
1 to 2 tablespoons ORTEGA® Diced Jalapeños
1 tablespoon ground cumin
1 tablespoon dried oregano, crushed
2 teaspoons salt

HEAT vegetable oil in large saucepan over medium-high heat. Add beef, onions and garlic; cook for 4 to 5 minutes or until no longer pink; drain.

STIR in beans, crushed tomatoes, salsa, wine, chiles, chili powder, jalapeños, cumin, oregano and salt. Bring to a boil. Reduce heat to low; cover. Cook, stirring frequently, for 1 hour.   *Makes 10 to 12 servings*

CLASSIC MATZOH BALL SOUP

1 whole chicken (about 3½ pounds), cut into
    serving pieces
7 cups plus 2 tablespoons water, divided
3 carrots, cut into 1-inch pieces
3 ribs celery, cut into 1-inch pieces
1 medium onion, unpeeled, quartered
1 large parsnip, cut into 1-inch pieces (optional)
1 head garlic, separated into cloves, unpeeled
3 sprigs parsley
8 to 10 whole black peppercorns
4 eggs
1 cup matzoh meal
¼ cup parve margarine, melted, cooled
1 tablespoon grated onion
½ teaspoon salt
⅛ teaspoon ground white pepper *or* ¼ teaspoon
    freshly ground black pepper
    Chopped fresh parsley, for garnish

Combine chicken and 7 cups water in Dutch oven.
Bring to a boil over medium heat. Remove any foam
from surface of water with large metal spoon; discard.
Add carrots, celery, unpeeled onion, parsnip, garlic,
parsley and whole peppercorns. Cover; simmer 3 hours
or until chicken is no longer pink in center. Remove
from heat; cool 30 minutes. Strain soup; reserve chicken
and broth separately. Discard vegetables. Remove skin
and bones from chicken; discard.* Reserve chicken for
another use.

Beat eggs in large bowl on medium speed of electric
mixer. Add matzoh meal, margarine, remaining
2 tablespoons water, grated onion, salt and ground
pepper. Mix at low speed until well blended. Let stand
15 to 30 minutes. With wet hands, form matzoh mixture
into 12 (2-inch) balls.

Bring 8 cups water to a boil in Dutch oven. Drop
matzoh balls, one at a time, into boiling water. Reduce
heat. Cover; simmer 35 to 40 minutes or until matzoh
balls are cooked through. Drain well.

Add reserved broth to Dutch oven. Bring to a boil over
high heat. Add salt to taste. Reduce heat; cover. Simmer
5 minutes or until matzoh balls are heated through.
Garnish with parsley, if desired.   *Makes 6 servings*

**Chicken and broth may be covered and refrigerated up to 3 days or
frozen up to 3 months.*

Favorite recipe from **Hebrew National**®

• Classic Tip •

*Matzoh meal can be found in Jewish
markets and most supermarkets. It is
available in a fine texture or a medium
texture. Matzoh meal is used in a variety
of foods and can also be used to thicken
soups and for breading food to be fried.*

SPICY SOUTHWEST CORN CHEESE SOUP

1 package (10 ounces) frozen sweet corn, thawed, drained
1 clove garlic, minced
1 tablespoon butter or margarine
¾ pound (12 ounces) VELVEETA® Pasteurized Prepared Cheese Product, cut up
1 can (4 ounces) chopped green chilies
¾ cup chicken broth
¾ cup milk
2 tablespoons chopped fresh cilantro

1. Cook and stir corn and garlic in butter in large saucepan on medium-high heat until tender. Reduce heat to medium.

2. Stir in remaining ingredients; cook until Velveeta is melted and soup is thoroughly heated. Top each serving with crushed tortilla chips, if desired.

Makes 4 (1-cup) servings

A Taste of Nutrition: A serving of Spicy Southwest Corn Cheese Soup is high in calcium. In addition, it is also an excellent source of vitamins A and C.

Prep Time: 15 minutes
Cook Time: 10 minutes

HEARTY SAUSAGE STEW

¼ cup olive oil
4 carrots, chopped
1 onion, cut into quarters
1 cup chopped celery
2 cloves garlic, finely chopped
1 teaspoon finely chopped fennel
   Salt and black pepper to taste
12 small new potatoes
1 pound mushrooms, cut into halves
2 cans (12 ounces each) diced tomatoes, undrained
1 can (8 ounces) tomato sauce
1 tablespoon dried oregano leaves
1 pound HILLSHIRE FARM® Polska Kielbasa,* sliced

Or use any variety Hillshire Farm® Smoked Sausage.

Heat oil in heavy skillet over medium-high heat; add carrots, onion, celery, garlic, fennel, salt and pepper. Sauté until vegetables are soft. Add potatoes, mushrooms, tomatoes with liquid, tomato sauce and oregano; cook 20 minutes over low heat. Add Polska Kielbasa; simmer 15 minutes or until heated through.

Makes 6 servings

Farm Fresh Tip: Did you know?—If you don't have 2 cups of tomato sauce, you can substitute with ¾ cup of tomato paste mixed into 1 cup of water.

SPICY SOUTHWEST CORN CHEESE SOUP

KIELBASA & CHICKEN GUMBO

6 slices bacon

1 pound BOB EVANS® Kielbasa Sausage, cut into 1-inch pieces

½ pound boneless skinless chicken breasts, cut into 1-inch chunks

¼ cup all-purpose flour

1 can (12 ounces) tomato juice

1 cup water

1 can (28 ounces) whole tomatoes, undrained

2 cubes chicken bouillon

1 can (8 ounces) tomato sauce

1½ cups sliced fresh okra *or* 1 package (10 ounces) frozen cut okra, thawed

1 medium onion, coarsely chopped

1 medium green bell pepper, coarsely chopped

2 bay leaves

½ teaspoon salt

½ teaspoon ground red pepper

⅛ teaspoon ground allspice

1 pound uncooked medium shrimp, peeled and deveined

Hot cooked rice (optional)

KIELBASA & CHICKEN GUMBO

Cook bacon in large Dutch oven over medium-high heat until crisp. Remove bacon; drain and crumble on paper towel. Set aside. Cook and stir kielbasa and chicken in drippings over medium heat until chicken is lightly browned. Remove kielbasa and chicken; set aside. Drain off all but 3 tablespoons drippings from Dutch oven. Add flour to drippings; cook over medium heat 12 to 15 minutes or until a reddish-brown roux forms, stirring constantly. Gradually stir in tomato juice and water until smooth. Add tomatoes with juice and bouillon, stirring well to break up tomatoes. Add reserved kielbasa, chicken, tomato sauce, okra, onion, green pepper, bay leaves, salt, red pepper and allspice; mix well. Bring to a boil over high heat. Reduce heat to low; simmer, covered, 1 hour, stirring occasionally. Add shrimp and simmer, covered, 10 minutes more or until shrimp turn pink and opaque. Remove and discard bay leaves. Stir in reserved bacon. Serve hot over rice and with cornbread, if desired. Refrigerate leftovers.

Makes 10 servings

RED AND GREEN CABBAGE SLAW

2½ cups thinly sliced red cabbage
2½ cups thinly sliced green cabbage
 ½ cup chopped yellow or red bell pepper
 ½ cup chopped carrot
 ⅓ cup chopped red onion
 8 ounces reduced-fat Cheddar cheese, cubed
 ½ cup fat-free mayonnaise
 1 tablespoon red wine vinegar
2½ teaspoons EQUAL® FOR RECIPES *or* 8 packets
    EQUAL® sweetener *or* ⅓ cup EQUAL®
    SPOONFUL™
 ¼ teaspoon celery seed
    Salt and pepper
    Lettuce leaves (optional)

• Combine vegetables and cheese in bowl. Mix mayonnaise, vinegar, Equal® and celery seed; stir into cabbage mixture. Season to taste with salt and pepper.

• Spoon mixture onto lettuce-lined plates, if desired.

Makes 8 servings

Tip: Packaged cole slaw vegetables can be used; use 6 cups vegetables and add onion, cheese and mayonnaise dressing as above. Any desired flavor of reduced-fat cheese can be substituted for the Cheddar cheese.

RED AND GREEN CABBAGE SLAW

TORTILLA SOUP

1 tablespoon butter or margarine
½ cup chopped green bell pepper
½ cup chopped onion
½ teaspoon ground cumin
3½ cups (two 14½-ounce cans) chicken broth
1¾ cups (16-ounce jar) ORTEGA® Thick & Chunky
    Salsa or Garden Style Salsa
1 cup whole-kernel corn
1 tablespoon vegetable oil
6 corn tortillas, cut into ½-inch strips
¾ cup (3 ounces) shredded 4 cheese Mexican blend
    Sour cream (optional)

MELT butter in medium saucepan over medium heat. Add bell pepper, onion and cumin; cook for 3 to 4 minutes or until tender. Stir in broth, salsa and corn. Bring to a boil. Reduce heat to low; cook for 5 minutes.

HEAT vegetable oil in medium skillet over medium-high heat. Add tortilla strips; cook for 3 to 4 minutes or until tender. Stir in broth, salsa and corn. Bring to a boil. Reduce heat to low; cook for 5 minutes.

SERVE in soup bowls. Top with tortilla strips, cheese and a dollop of sour cream.

Makes 6 servings

NITA LOU'S CREAM OF BROCCOLI SOUP

⅓ cup plus 1 tablespoon WESSON® Vegetable Oil
3 cups coarsely chopped broccoli florets and stems
1 cup diced carrots
1½ cups fresh chopped leeks
3 tablespoons all-purpose flour
1½ teaspoons minced fresh garlic
2 (12-ounce) cans evaporated milk
1½ cups homemade chicken stock or canned
    chicken broth
½ teaspoon garlic salt
¼ teaspoon ground nutmeg
⅛ teaspoon pepper
3 tablespoons chopped fresh parsley
    Salt to taste

In a large saucepan, heat *3 tablespoons* Wesson® Oil. Add broccoli and carrots; sauté until tender. Remove vegetables; set aside. Add *remaining* oil, leeks, flour and garlic; sauté until leeks are limp and flour is lightly browned, about 2 minutes, stirring constantly. Whisk in the evaporated milk and stock. Continue to cook, whisking constantly until the flour has dissolved and the mixture is smooth. *Do not bring mixture to a boil.* Reduce heat to LOW. Add cooked vegetables along with any juices, garlic salt, nutmeg and pepper. Simmer 5 minutes longer, being careful not to bring soup to a boil. Remove the pan from the heat; stir in parsley. Let soup stand 5 minutes before serving. Salt to taste.

Makes 6 servings

TORTILLA SOUP

VEGETABLE SOUP

2 tablespoons FILIPPO BERIO® Olive Oil
2 medium potatoes, peeled and quartered
2 medium onions, sliced
3 cups beef broth
8 ounces fresh green beans, trimmed and cut into
   1-inch pieces
3 carrots, peeled and chopped
8 ounces fresh spinach, washed, drained, stemmed
   and chopped
1 green pepper, diced
2 tablespoons chopped fresh parsley
1 tablespoon chopped fresh basil *or* 1 teaspoon
   dried basil leaves
½ teaspoon ground cumin
1 clove garlic, finely minced
   Salt and freshly ground black pepper

In Dutch oven, heat olive oil over medium-high heat until hot. Add potatoes and onions; cook and stir 5 minutes. Add beef broth, green beans and carrots. Bring mixture to a boil. Cover; reduce heat to low and simmer 10 minutes, stirring occasionally. Add spinach, bell pepper, parsley, basil, cumin and garlic. Cover; simmer an additional 15 to 20 minutes or until potatoes are tender. Season to taste with salt and black pepper. Serve hot. *Makes 6 to 8 servings*

SASSY SAUSAGE AND BLACK BEAN SOUP

1 tablespoon vegetable oil
1 medium onion, chopped
2 cloves garlic, minced
1 can (16 ounces) black beans, rinsed and drained
1 can (14½ ounces) stewed tomatoes, undrained
1 can (10½ ounces) kosher condensed beef broth
½ cup prepared chunky salsa
½ cup water
1 package (12 ounces) HEBREW NATIONAL® Beef
   Polish Sausage
¼ cup chopped cilantro
   Lime wedges, for garnish

Heat oil in large saucepan over medium heat. Add onion and garlic; cook 8 minutes or until tender. Stir in beans, tomatoes with liquid, broth, salsa and water. Bring to a boil over high heat.

Cut sausage into ½-inch pieces; stir into soup. Reduce heat. Cover; simmer 15 minutes, stirring occasionally. Ladle into soup bowls; sprinkle with cilantro. Garnish with lime wedges, if desired. *Makes 4 to 5 servings*

VEGETABLE SOUP

FARMERS' MARKET SALAD

Dressing

- ½ cup chopped peperoncini
- ⅓ cup seasoned rice vinegar
- 3 tablespoons country Dijon mustard
- 2 tablespoons chopped fresh dill
- 1½ teaspoons sugar
- 1½ teaspoons garlic salt
- 1½ teaspoons fresh lemon juice
- 1½ teaspoons grated fresh lemon peel
- ½ teaspoon coarsely ground pepper
- ⅔ cup WESSON® Best Blend Oil

Salad

- 1 pound baby red potatoes, unpeeled
- 1 pound baby asparagus
- 1 pound mixed salad greens or spinach leaves, washed and drained
- 1 basket cherry tomatoes, halved or baby teardrop yellow tomatoes
- 1 large orange bell pepper, thinly sliced
- 4 hard boiled eggs, quartered

Dressing

In blender or food processor, add *all dressing* ingredients *except* Wesson® Oil. Pulse ingredients and slowly add Wesson® Oil until dressing is partially smooth; refrigerate.

Salad

In a saucepan of water, cook potatoes until tender. Drain potatoes; immerse in ice water for 5 minutes to stop cooking process. Cool completely; drain well. In large pot of boiling water, cook asparagus until crisp-tender. Repeat cooling procedure with asparagus. In a large bowl, toss salad greens with ⅓ dressing. Evenly divide salad greens among 4 plates. Arrange potatoes, asparagus, tomatoes, bell pepper and eggs in sections over salad greens. Drizzle half the remaining dressing over arranged vegetables and eggs. Serve salad with remaining dressing, if desired.

Makes 4 servings

SPINACH & ORANGE SALAD

- 10 cups torn spinach
- 2 cups fresh orange sections
- ½ cup sliced red onion
- 1 package (4 ounces) ATHENOS® Crumbled Feta Cheese
- 1 cup prepared GOOD SEASONS® Italian Salad Dressing for Fat Free Dressing

TOSS spinach, oranges, onion and cheese in large bowl.

ADD dressing; toss lightly.   *Makes 10 servings*

Variation: Prepare as directed, substituting 2 cans (11 ounces each) mandarin orange segments, drained, for fresh orange sections.

Variation: Prepare as directed, adding ¼ cup toasted slivered almonds.

Prep: 20 minutes

TANGY GARLIC TORTELLINI SALAD

¼ cup mayonnaise

¼ cup plain yogurt

1 tablespoon plus 1½ teaspoons lemon juice

1 tablespoon olive oil

2 teaspoons chopped fresh chives or ¼ cup chopped green onion

1 teaspoon LAWRY'S® Seasoned Pepper

1 to 1¼ teaspoons LAWRY'S® Garlic Salt

9 ounces fresh cheese-filled tortellini or 8 ounces spiral pasta, cooked and drained

1 medium-sized red bell pepper, cut into thin strips

1 medium zucchini, cut into julienne strips

2 medium carrots, cut into julienne strips

In small bowl, combine all ingredients except pasta and vegetables. In medium bowl, combine pasta and vegetables; mix lightly. Add dressing; toss lightly to coat. Refrigerate at least 30 minutes. Garnish as desired.

Makes 4 to 6 servings

Serving Suggestion: Serve with crusty French or sourdough bread.

TANGY GARLIC TORTELLINI SALAD

GINGER PINEAPPLE MOLD

1 can (20 ounces) crushed pineapple in juice, undrained

1½ cups boiling water

1 package (8-serving size) or 2 packages (4-serving size) JELL-O® Brand Lime Flavor Gelatin Dessert

1 cup cold ginger ale or water

¼ teaspoon ground ginger

DRAIN pineapple, reserving juice. Stir boiling water into gelatin in large bowl at least 2 minutes until completely dissolved. Stir in reserved juice, ginger ale and ginger. Refrigerate about 1¼ hours or until slightly thickened (consistency of unbeaten egg whites).

STIR in pineapple. Pour into 5-cup mold.

REFRIGERATE 4 hours or until firm. Unmold.

Makes 10 servings

FRESH & FANCY CUCUMBER SALAD

2 medium cucumbers, unpeeled (about 1½ to 1¾ pounds)
⅔ cup seasoned rice vinegar
⅓ cup WESSON® Canola Oil
1½ tablespoons chopped fresh dill *or* 1 teaspoon dried dill weed
½ teaspoon salt
½ teaspoon sugar
Pinch pepper
1½ cups red onion wedges (⅛ inch thick)

Slightly piercing cucumbers, run fork tines down length of cucumbers on *all* sides; thinly slice. In medium bowl, combine vinegar, Wesson® Oil, dill, salt, sugar and pepper; mix until sugar is dissolved. Toss in cucumbers and onions; mix until vegetables are well coated with dressing. Refrigerate 15 minutes. Toss salad before serving. Serve with slotted spoon.

Makes 4 to 6 servings

FRESH & FANCY CUCUMBER SALAD

SPARKLING BERRY SALAD

2 cups boiling diet cranberry juice cocktail

1 package (8-serving size) or 2 packages (4-serving size) JELL-O® Brand Sugar Free Low Calorie Gelatin Dessert or JELL-O® Brand Gelatin Dessert, any red flavor

1½ cups cold seltzer or club soda

¼ cup crème de cassis liqueur (optional)

1 teaspoon lemon juice

3 cups assorted berries (blueberries, raspberries and sliced strawberries), divided

STIR boiling cranberry juice into gelatin in large bowl at least 2 minutes until completely dissolved. Stir in cold seltzer, liqueur and lemon juice. Refrigerate about 1½ hours or until slightly thickened (consistency of unbeaten egg whites).

STIR in 2 cups of the berries. Spoon into 5-cup mold.

REFRIGERATE 4 hours or until firm. Unmold. Top with remaining 1 cup berries.   *Makes 8 servings*

Preparation Time: 15 minutes
Refrigerating Time: 5½ hours

ANTIPASTO SALAD

1 cup MIRACLE WHIP® Salad Dressing

½ cup milk

2 packages GOOD SEASONS® Italian Salad Dressing Mix

1 package (16 ounces) uncooked mostaccioli, cooked, drained

1 package (8 ounces) OSCAR MAYER® Cotto Salami Slices, cut into strips

1 package (8 ounces) KRAFT® Low-Moisture Part-Skim Mozzarella Cheese, cubed

¾ cup *each* thin red bell pepper strips and thin zucchini strips

½ cup pitted ripe olives, drained, halved

• MIX salad dressing, milk, and salad dressing mix in large bowl.

• ADD pasta; mix lightly.

• ARRANGE remaining ingredients over pasta mixture; cover. Refrigerate several hours or overnight until chilled.   *Makes 10 to 12 servings*

Prep Time: 15 minutes plus refrigerating

SPARKLING BERRY SALAD

POTATO & PROSCIUTTO SALAD

3 medium Colorado Sangre red potatoes, unpeeled
½ pound green beans, trimmed and cut into
  2½-inch pieces
1 red bell pepper, thinly sliced
1½ cups frozen corn, thawed
6 ounces mozzarella cheese, cut into ½-inch cubes
3 ounces thinly sliced prosciutto or ham, cut into
  strips
3 green onions, sliced
⅓ cup olive oil
¼ cup lemon juice
2 tablespoons water
1 to 2 cloves garlic, minced
1 tablespoon chopped fresh thyme *or* 1½ teaspoon
  dried thyme leaves
  Salt and black pepper

Cook potatoes in boiling water 25 minutes until tender. Drain; cool. Cut into ½-inch-thick slices; cut into quarters. Cook green beans in boiling water until tender. Drain; cool. Combine potatoes, beans, bell pepper, corn, cheese, prosciutto and onions in large bowl. Whisk together oil, lemon juice, water, garlic and thyme. Pour dressing over potato mixture; toss to coat. Season to taste with salt and pepper.

Makes 6 to 8 servings

*Favorite recipe from **Colorado Potato Administrative Committee***

POTATO & PROSCIUTTO SALAD

MEDITERRANEAN PASTA SALAD

1 package (8 ounces) refrigerated or frozen cheese tortellini
1½ cups broccoli or cauliflower florets
1 can (8 ounces) DOLE® Pineapple Chunks
2 tablespoons balsamic or red wine vinegar
1 tablespoon olive or vegetable oil
¼ pound fresh link turkey sausage, cooked, drained and sliced
1 medium DOLE® Red, Yellow or Green Bell Pepper, cubed

• Prepare tortellini according to package directions, adding Italian Style Vegetables (reserve seasoning packet) during last 2 minutes of cooking. Meanwhile, prepare dressing.

• Drain pineapple; reserve ¼ cup juice.

• Combine reserved juice, vinegar, oil and tomato basil seasoning packet from vegetable package in large serving bowl.

• Drain tortellini and vegetables. Add tortellini, vegetables, sausage, bell pepper and pineapple to dressing; toss well to evenly coat. Serve at room temperature or chilled. Toss before serving.

Makes 6 servings

Prep Time: 10 minutes
Cook Time: 20 minutes

SPINACH, BACON AND MUSHROOM SALAD

1 large bunch (12 ounces) fresh spinach leaves, washed, drained and torn
¾ cup sliced fresh mushrooms
4 slices bacon, cooked and crumbled
¾ cup croutons
4 hard-cooked eggs, finely chopped
    Black pepper, to taste
¾ cup prepared HIDDEN VALLEY® Original Ranch® Salad Dressing & Recipe Mix

In medium salad bowl, combine spinach, mushrooms and bacon; toss. Top with croutons and eggs; season with pepper. Pour salad dressing over all.

Makes 6 servings

SPINACH, BACON AND MUSHROOM SALAD

FRUIT SALAD WITH HONEY–ORANGE DRESSING

½ cup low-fat plain yogurt
¼ cup nonfat mayonnaise
¼ cup honey
¾ teaspoon grated orange peel
¼ teaspoon dry mustard
3 tablespoons orange juice
1½ teaspoons vinegar
4 cups assorted fruit

Whisk together yogurt, mayonnaise, honey, orange peel and mustard in small bowl until blended. Gradually mix in orange juice and vinegar. Toss fruit gently with dressing. Cover and refrigerate until ready to serve.

Makes 4 servings

Favorite recipe from **National Honey Board**

COBB SALAD

4 skinless boneless chicken breast halves, cooked, cooled
⅔ cup vegetable oil
⅓ cup **HEINZ**® Distilled White or Apple Cider Vinegar
1 clove garlic, minced
2 teaspoons dried dill weed
1½ teaspoons granulated sugar
½ teaspoon salt
¼ teaspoon pepper
8 cups torn salad greens, chilled
1 large tomato, diced
1 medium green bell pepper, diced
1 small red onion, chopped
¾ cup crumbled blue cheese
6 slices bacon, cooked, crumbled
1 hard-cooked egg, chopped

Shred chicken into bite-size pieces. For dressing, in jar, combine oil, vinegar, garlic, dill, sugar, salt and pepper; cover and shake vigorously. Pour ½ cup dressing over chicken; toss well to coat. Toss greens with remaining dressing. Line each of 4 large individual salad bowls with greens; mound chicken mixture in center. Arrange mounds of tomato, green pepper, onion, cheese, bacon and egg around chicken.

Makes 4 servings

FRUIT SALAD WITH HONEY-ORANGE DRESSING

Soups & Salads

MIXED SALAD WITH RASPBERRY HONEY DIJON DRESSING

⅓ cup GREY POUPON® COUNTRY DIJON® Mustard*
⅓ cup dairy sour cream**
¼ cup raspberry-flavored vinegar
2 tablespoons honey
4 cups mixed salad greens
1 cup cut green beans, steamed
1 cup cooked sliced beets
½ cup sliced mushrooms
½ cup shredded carrots
8 ounces turkey, cut into julienne strips

*⅓ cup GREY POUPON® Honey Mustard may be substituted for Country Dijon® Mustard; omit honey.

**Lowfat sour cream may be substituted for regular sour cream.

1. Blend mustard, sour cream, vinegar and honey in small bowl; refrigerate dressing until serving time.

2. Arrange vegetables and turkey on large serving platter lined with salad greens. Drizzle with prepared dressing just before serving.   *Makes 6 servings*

CUCUMBER SOUR CREAM MOLD

1½ cups boiling water
1 package (8-serving size) or 2 packages (4-serving size) JELL-O® Brand Lime Flavor Gelatin Dessert
¼ teaspoon salt
1½ cups cold water
1 tablespoon lemon juice
½ cup MIRACLE WHIP® Salad Dressing
½ cup BREAKSTONE'S® Sour Cream
1½ cups chopped seeded peeled cucumber
2 tablespoons minced onion
1 teaspoon dill weed

STIR boiling water into gelatin and salt in large bowl at least 2 minutes until completely dissolved. Stir in cold water and lemon juice. Refrigerate about 1¼ hours or until slightly thickened (consistency of unbeaten egg whites).

MIX salad dressing and sour cream in small bowl until well blended. Stir into thickened gelatin. Refrigerate about 15 minutes or until thickened (spoon drawn through leaves definite impression). Stir in cucumber, onion and dill weed. Pour into 5-cup mold.

REFRIGERATE 4 hours or until firm. Unmold. Garnish as desired.   *Makes 10 servings*

Preparation Time: 15 minutes
Refrigerating Time: 5½ hours

SMUCKER'S® THREE BEAN SALAD WITH SWEET AND SOUR APRICOT DRESSING

½ cup SMUCKER'S® Apricot Preserves
¼ cup red wine vinegar
1 teaspoon celery seeds
1 (16-ounce) can kidney beans, rinsed and drained
1 cup cooked fresh or frozen green beans, cut into 2-inch pieces
¼ pound (1 cup) cooked fresh or frozen yellow wax beans, cut into 2-inch pieces
1 small red onion, thinly sliced
Salt and pepper to taste

Combine Smucker's® Apricot Preserves, vinegar and celery seeds in medium salad bowl. Add kidney beans, green and yellow beans and onion. Toss well to combine. Season with salt and freshly ground pepper.

Makes 6 servings

SMUCKER'S® THREE BEAN SALAD WITH SWEET AND SOUR APRICOT DRESSING

CARAMELIZED APPLE & ONION SALAD

¼ cup I CAN'T BELIEVE IT'S NOT BUTTER!® Spread
1 large Granny Smith or other tart apple, peeled, cored and thinly sliced
1 large onion, sliced
4 cups mixed salad greens or mesclun WISH-BONE® Balsamic Vinaigrette Dressing
½ cup toasted chopped walnuts or pecans (optional)

In 12-inch skillet, melt I Can't Believe It's Not Butter! Spread over medium-high heat and cook apple and onion, stirring occasionally, 4 minutes or until tender. Reduce heat to medium and cook uncovered, stirring occasionally, 20 minutes or until apple and onion are golden brown. Serve warm apple mixture over greens. Drizzle with dressing and garnish with walnuts.

Makes 2 servings

APPLE BLOSSOM MOLD

1½ cups boiling water
1 package (8-serving size) or 2 packages (4-serving size each) JELL-O® Brand Lemon Flavor Gelatin
2 cups cold apple juice
1 cup diced red and green apples

STIR boiling water into gelatin in large bowl at least 2 minutes until completely dissolved. Stir in cold juice. Refrigerate about 1½ hours or until thickened (spoon drawn through leaves definite impression). Stir in apples. Pour into 6-cup mold which has been sprayed with no stick cooking spray.

REFRIGERATE 4 hours or until firm. Unmold. Garnish as desired. *Makes 10 servings*

Variation: Sugar Free Low Calorie Gelatin may be substituted.

Prep Time: 15 minutes
Refrigerate Time: 5½ hours

Accompaniments

ITALIAN VEGETABLES WITH GARLIC BUTTER RICE

1 package UNCLE BEN'S NATURAL SELECT™ Garlic & Butter Rice
1 yellow squash, sliced
1 zucchini, sliced
1 cup diced red bell pepper
1 cup sliced eggplant
⅓ cup balsamic vinaigrette
1 tablespoon chopped fresh rosemary

PREP: CLEAN: Wash hands. In large bowl, combine vegetables, vinaigrette and rosemary; set aside 15 minutes.

COOK: Meanwhile, prepare rice according to package directions; set aside. Sauté vegetables in marinade until crisp-tender.

SERVE: Serve vegetable mixture over rice.

CHILL: Refrigerate leftovers immediately.   *Makes 4 servings*

Prep Time: 5 minutes
Cook Time: 15 minutes

GOURMET GRITS

½ pound BOB EVANS® Italian Roll Sausage
3 cups water
1 cup uncooked white grits
½ (10-ounce) package frozen chopped spinach, thawed and squeezed dry
¼ cup grated Parmesan cheese
¼ cup chopped sun-dried tomatoes
¼ cup olive oil
1 clove garlic, chopped

Crumble sausage into medium skillet. Cook over medium heat until browned, stirring occasionally. Drain off any drippings; set aside. Bring water to a rapid boil in large saucepan. While stirring, add grits in steady stream until mixture thickens into smooth paste.

Reduce heat to low; simmer 5 to 7 minutes, stirring frequently to prevent sticking. Stir in sausage, spinach, cheese and tomatoes. Pour into greased 9×5-inch loaf pan. Refrigerate until cool and firm.

Unmold. Slice into ½-inch-thick slices. Heat oil in large skillet over medium-high heat until hot. Add garlic; cook and stir 30 seconds or until soft. Add grit slices, 4 to 5 at a time, and cook until golden brown on both sides. Repeat until all slices are cooked. Serve hot. Refrigerate leftovers.   *Makes 4 to 6 side-dish servings*

Serving Suggestion: Melt thin slice of mozzarella cheese on top of each browned slice. This also makes a wonderful side dish for chicken, topped with warmed seasoned tomato or spaghetti sauce.

• Classic Tip •

To easily chop sun-dried tomatoes, soften them first. To soften them, cover with hot water for 30 minutes or boiling water for 5 minutes. Drain before using.

ORIGINAL RANCH® ROASTED POTATOES

2 pounds small red potatoes, quartered
¼ cup vegetable oil
1 packet (1 ounce) HIDDEN VALLEY® Original Ranch® Salad Dressing & Recipe Mix

Place potatoes in a gallon-size Glad® Zipper Storage Bag. Pour oil over potatoes. Seal bag and toss to coat. Add salad dressing & recipe mix; seal bag and toss again until coated. Bake in ungreased baking pan at 450°F. for 30 to 35 minutes or until potatoes are brown and crisp.   *Makes 4 to 6 servings*

ORIGINAL RANCH® ROASTED POTATOES

MARINATED TOMATOES & MOZZARELLA

**MARINATED TOMATOES &
MOZZARELLA**

1 cup chopped fresh basil leaves
1 pound Italian tomatoes, sliced
½ pound fresh packed buffalo mozzarella cheese,
    sliced
¼ cup olive oil
3 tablespoons chopped fresh chives
2 tablespoons red wine vinegar
2 teaspoons sugar
½ teaspoon dried oregano
½ teaspoon LAWRY'S® Seasoned Pepper
½ teaspoon LAWRY'S® Garlic Powder with Parsley
    Fresh basil leaves (optional)

In large resealable plastic food storage bag, combine all
ingredients except whole basil leaves; mix well.
Marinate in refrigerator at least 30 minutes. To serve,
arrange tomato and cheese slices on serving plate.
Garnish with whole basil leaves, if desired.

Makes 4 to 6 servings

Serving Suggestion: Serve with grilled chicken
sandwiches or as a zesty Italian appetizer.

GLAZED ACORN SQUASH

2 medium acorn squash, halved and seeded
1½ cups water
⅓ cup KARO® Light or Dark Corn Syrup
1 tablespoon margarine or butter, melted
½ teaspoon ground cinnamon
¼ teaspoon salt

1. Place squash cut-side down in 13×9×2-inch baking
dish; add water. Bake in 400°F oven 30 minutes or until
squash is nearly fork tender.

2. Turn squash cut-side up. In small bowl combine corn
syrup, margarine, cinnamon and salt. Spoon corn syrup
mixture into squash cavities.

3. Bake in 350°F oven 15 minutes or until fork tender,
basting occasionally.   *Makes 4 servings*

Prep Time: 5 minutes
Bake Time: 45 minutes

SAUTÉED SNOW PEAS & BABY CARROTS

1 tablespoon I CAN'T BELIEVE IT'S NOT
  BUTTER!® Spread
2 tablespoons chopped shallots or onion
5 ounces frozen whole baby carrots, partially
  thawed
4 ounces snow peas (about 1 cup)
2 teaspoons chopped fresh parsley (optional)

In 12-inch nonstick skillet, melt I Can't Believe It's Not Butter! Spread over medium heat and cook shallots, stirring occasionally, 1 minute or until almost tender. Add carrots and snow peas and cook, stirring occasionally, 4 minutes or until crisp-tender. Stir in parsley and heat through.   *Makes 2 servings*

Note: Recipe can be doubled.

SAUTÉED SNOW PEAS & BABY CARROTS

GREEN BEANS WITH TOASTED PECANS

**3 tablespoons I CAN'T BELIEVE IT'S NOT
  BUTTER!® Spread, melted**
1 teaspoon sugar
¼ teaspoon garlic powder
  Pinch ground red pepper
  Salt to taste
⅓ cup chopped pecans
1 pound green beans

In small bowl, blend I Can't Believe It's Not Butter!
Spread, sugar, garlic powder, pepper and salt.

In 12-inch nonstick skillet, heat 2 teaspoons garlic mixture over medium-high heat and cook pecans, stirring frequently, 2 minutes or until pecans are golden. Remove pecans and set aside.

In same skillet, heat remaining garlic mixture and stir in green beans. Cook covered over medium heat, stirring occasionally, 6 minutes or until green beans are tender. Stir in pecans.

Makes 4 servings

BROCCOLI WITH SESAME VINAIGRETTE

1 pound broccoli, cut into bite-sized pieces
1 to 2 teaspoons sesame seeds, toasted
**2 tablespoons plus 1½ teaspoons white wine
  vinegar**
1 tablespoon water
2 teaspoons olive or sesame oil
½ teaspoon LAWRY'S® Seasoned Salt
½ teaspoon LAWRY'S® Seasoned Pepper

In large saucepan, place broccoli. Add about 1 inch water. Cook over medium-high heat until crisp-tender,

about 3 to 5 minutes; drain any excess liquid. In small bowl, combine sesame seeds, vinegar, water, oil, Seasoned Salt and Seasoned Pepper; drizzle over broccoli. Garnish as desired.

Makes 4 servings

Serving Suggestion: Serve with any grilled meat or poultry.

Hint: To toast sesame seeds in microwave, on shallow microwave-safe plate, place butter and sesame seeds. Cover with plastic wrap. Microwave on HIGH 1 minute or until seeds are toasted; set aside.

GREEN BEANS WITH TOASTED PECANS

RAINBOW RIBBON MOLD

6¼ cups boiling water
  5 packages (4-serving size) JELL-O® Brand Gelatin
    Dessert, any 5 different flavors
  1 cup (½ pint) BREAKSTONE'S® Sour Cream or
    BREYERS® Vanilla Lowfat Yogurt

STIR 1¼ cups boiling water into 1 flavor of gelatin in small bowl at least 2 minutes until completely dissolved. Pour ¾ cup of the dissolved gelatin into 6-cup ring mold. Refrigerate about 15 minutes until set but not firm (gelatin should stick to finger when touched and should mound). Refrigerate remaining gelatin in bowl about 5 minutes until slightly thickened (consistency of unbeaten egg whites). Gradually stir in 3 tablespoons of the sour cream. Spoon over gelatin in pan. Refrigerate about 15 minutes or until set but not firm (gelatin should stick to finger when touched and should mound).

MEANWHILE, repeat process with each remaining gelatin flavor. (Be sure to cool dissolved gelatin to room temperature before pouring into mold.) Refrigerate gelatin as directed to create a total of 10 alternating clear and creamy gelatin layers.

REFRIGERATE 2 hours or until firm. Unmold. Garnish as desired.

Makes 12 servings

JELL-O® Fun Facts: JELL-O gelatin is the largest-selling prepared dessert in America.

Preparation Time: 1 hour
Refrigerating Time: 4½ hours

SCALLOPED GARLIC POTATOES

3 medium all-purpose potatoes, peeled and thinly
  sliced (about 1½ pounds)
1 envelope LIPTON® RECIPE SECRETS® Garlic
  Mushroom Soup Mix*
1 cup (½ pint) whipping or heavy cream
½ cup water

*Also terrific with LIPTON® RECIPE SECRETS® Savory Herb with Garlic Soup Mix.

1. Preheat oven to 375°F. In lightly greased 2-quart shallow baking dish, arrange potatoes. In medium bowl, blend remaining ingredients; pour over potatoes.

2. Bake uncovered 45 minutes or until potatoes are tender.

Makes 4 servings

BUFFALO POTATOES

1 envelope LIPTON® RECIPE SECRETS® Savory
    Herb with Garlic Soup Mix*
⅓ cup margarine or butter, melted
1 to 2 tablespoons cayenne pepper sauce
4 medium baking potatoes, sliced lengthwise into
    wedges (about 2 pounds)
    WISH-BONE® Chunky Blue Cheese Dressing

Also terrific with LIPTON® RECIPES® SECRETS Onion Soup Mix.

1. Preheat oven to 450°F. In large plastic bag or bowl,
add all ingredients except Wish-Bone Dressing. Close
bag and shake, or toss in bowl, until potatoes are
evenly coated.

2. In 13×9-inch baking or roasting pan, arrange
potatoes; discard bag.

3. Bake uncovered, stirring occasionally, 45 minutes or
until potatoes are crisp. Serve with Wish-Bone
Dressing.   *Makes 4 servings*

MEXICAN RICE

MEXICAN RICE

2 tablespoons butter or margarine
1 cup long-grain white rice*
½ cup chopped onion
2 cloves garlic, finely chopped
1 jar (16 ounces) ORTEGA® Salsa Prima-Thick &
    Chunky
1¼ cups water*
¾ cup (1 large) peeled, shredded carrot
½ cup frozen peas, thawed (optional)

*For a quick-cook Mexican Rice, use 4 cups instant rice instead of
1 cup long-grain white rice, and 2½ cups water instead of 1¼ cups
water. After salsa mixture comes to a boil, cook for a length of time
recommended on instant rice package.*

MELT butter in large saucepan over medium heat. Add
rice, onion and garlic; cook, stirring occasionally, for
3 to 4 minutes or until rice is golden. Stir in salsa, water,
carrot and peas. Bring to a boil. Reduce heat to low;
cook, covered, for 25 to 30 minutes or until liquid is
absorbed and rice is tender.   *Makes 8 servings*

Tip: Serve this traditional side dish to complete any
Mexican meal.

TOMATO–BREAD CASSEROLE

½ pound loaf French bread, sliced
3 tablespoons butter or margarine, softened
1 can (14½ ounces) whole peeled tomatoes, cut up
1½ pounds fresh tomatoes, thinly sliced
1 cup lowfat cottage or ricotta cheese
¼ cup olive or vegetable oil
¾ teaspoon LAWRY'S® Seasoned Salt
½ teaspoon dried oregano, crushed
½ teaspoon LAWRY'S® Garlic Powder with Parsley
½ cup Parmesan cheese

Spread bread slices with butter; cut into large cubes. Arrange on jelly-roll pan. Toast in 350°F oven about 7 minutes. Place ½ of cubes in greased 13×9×2-inch baking dish. Drain canned tomatoes, reserving liquid. Top bread cubes with ½ of fresh tomato slices, ½ reserved tomato liquid, ½ of cottage cheese, ½ of oil, ½ of canned tomatoes, ½ of Seasoned Salt, ½ of oregano and ½ of Garlic Powder with Parsley. Repeat layers. Sprinkle with Parmesan cheese. Bake, covered, in 350°F oven 40 minutes. Uncover and bake 5 minutes longer to brown top.   *Makes 8 to 10 servings*

Serving Suggestion: Sprinkle with parsley. Serve with any grilled or baked meat, fish or poultry entrée.

TOMATO-BREAD CASSEROLE

CHEESY RICE & BROCCOLI

1 package (10 ounces) frozen chopped broccoli, thawed, drained
1 cup water
1½ cups MINUTE® White Rice, uncooked
½ pound (8 ounces) VELVEETA® Pasteurized Prepared Cheese Product, cut up

1. Bring broccoli and water to full boil in medium saucepan over medium-high heat.

2. Stir in rice; cover. Remove from heat. Let stand 5 minutes.

3. Add Velveeta; stir until Velveeta is melted.

Makes 6 servings

Prep Time: 5 minutes
Cook Time: 10 minutes plus standing

Accompaniments

GARBANZO BEAN ROUND–UP

1 can (16 ounces) cut green beans, drained
1 can (15½ ounces) garbanzo beans, drained
1 can (2¼ ounces) sliced black olives, drained
1 medium tomato, chopped
½ cup chopped red onion
3 tablespoons red wine vinegar
1½ tablespoons vegetable oil
1 teaspoon LAWRY'S® Lemon Pepper
¾ teaspoon LAWRY'S® Seasoned Salt

In medium bowl, combine all ingredients; mix well. Refrigerate at least 1 hour before serving.

Makes 6 servings

Serving Suggestion: Served with grilled chicken breasts or fish steaks.

Hint: One can (15¼ ounces) kidney beans can be substituted for the green beans or can be added for additional color and flavor.

• *Classic Tip* •

Garbanzo beans are also commonly referred to as chickpeas. They are a buff colored legume with a firm texture and a mild, nut-like flavor.

OVEN–ROASTED VEGETABLES

1½ pounds assorted cut-up fresh vegetables*
3 tablespoons I CAN'T BELIEVE IT'S NOT BUTTER!® Spread, melted
2 cloves garlic, finely chopped
1 tablespoon chopped fresh oregano leaves *or* 1 teaspoon dried oregano leaves, crushed
Salt and ground black pepper to taste

*Use any combination of the following: zucchini, red, green or yellow bell peppers, Spanish or red onions, white or portobello mushrooms and carrots.

Preheat oven to 450°F.

In bottom of broiler pan, without rack, combine all ingredients. Roast 20 minutes or until vegetables are tender, stirring once.

Makes 4 servings

OVEN-ROASTED VEGETABLES

CHEESY POTATO PANCAKES

1½ quarts prepared instant mashed potatoes, cooked dry and cooled
1½ cups (6 ounces) shredded Wisconsin Colby or Muenster cheese
4 eggs, lightly beaten
1½ cups all-purpose flour, divided
¾ cup chopped fresh parsley
⅓ cup chopped fresh chives
1½ teaspoons dried thyme, rosemary or sage leaves
2 eggs, lightly beaten

1. In large bowl, combine potatoes, cheese, 4 beaten eggs, ¾ cup flour and herbs; mix well. Cover and refrigerate at least 4 hours before molding and preparing.

2. To prepare, form 18 (3-inch) patties. Dip in 2 beaten eggs and dredge in remaining ¾ cup flour. Cook each patty in nonstick skillet over medium heat 3 minutes per side or until crisp, golden brown and heated through.

3. Serve warm with eggs or omelets, or serve with sour cream and sliced pan-fried apples or applesauce.

Makes 4 to 6 servings

Variation: Substitute Wisconsin Cheddar or Smoked Cheddar for Colby or Muenster.

*Favorite recipe from **Wisconsin Milk Marketing Board***

HARVEST VEGETABLE SCALLOP

4 medium carrots, thinly sliced
1 package (10 ounces) frozen chopped broccoli, thawed and drained
1⅓ cups *French's® Taste Toppers™* French Fried Onions, divided
5 small red potatoes, sliced ⅛ inch thick
1 jar (8 ounces) pasteurized processed cheese spread
¼ cup milk
    Freshly ground black pepper
    Seasoned salt

Preheat oven to 375°F. In 12×8-inch baking dish, combine carrots, broccoli and ⅔ *cup Taste Toppers*. Tuck potato slices into vegetable mixture at an angle. Dot vegetables evenly with cheese spread. Pour milk over vegetables; sprinkle with seasonings as desired. Bake, covered, at 375°F for 30 minutes or until vegetables are tender. Top with remaining ⅔ *cup Taste Toppers*; bake, uncovered, 3 minutes or until *Taste Toppers* are golden brown.

Makes 6 servings

Microwave Directions: In 12×8-inch microwavable dish, prepare vegetables as above. Top with cheese spread, milk and seasonings as above. Cook, covered, at HIGH 12 to 14 minutes or until vegetables are tender, rotating dish halfway through cooking time. Top with remaining onions; cook, uncovered, 1 minute. Let stand 5 minutes.

GEORGIA–STYLE LEMON PILAF

GEORGIA-STYLE LEMON PILAF

¼ cup WESSON® Vegetable Oil
½ cup minced sweet onion
½ cup diced celery
1 cup uncooked long-grain rice
1 (14½-ounce) can chicken broth
½ cup water
⅓ cup dried currants
2 tablespoons fresh lemon juice
2 teaspoons grated fresh lemon peel
¼ cup sliced almonds, toasted
1 tablespoon fresh chopped parsley

In a large saucepan, heat Wesson® Oil until hot. Add onion and celery; sauté until crisp-tender. Add rice; continue sautéing an additional 3 minutes. Mix in *remaining* ingredients *except* almonds and parsley. Bring mixture to a boil, stirring occasionally. Cover, reduce heat to medium-low and cook until liquid is absorbed and rice is tender, about 20 minutes. Mix in almonds and parsley; cover and let stand 5 minutes. Fluff with fork before serving. *Makes 4 servings*

PORK FRIED RICE

2½ cups uncooked long-grain white rice
4 pork chops, diced
2 tablespoons vegetable oil
1 medium onion, finely chopped
1 can (14½ ounces) DEL MONTE® Peas and
   Carrots, drained
3 green onions, sliced
3 to 4 tablespoons soy sauce

1. Cook rice according to package directions.

2. Cook meat in hot oil in large skillet or wok until no longer pink in center, stirring occasionally. Add chopped onion; cook until tender.

3. Stir in rice, peas and carrots, green onions and soy sauce; heat through, stirring frequently. Season with pepper, if desired. *Makes 4 servings*

Prep and Cook Time: 30 minutes

GREEN BEAN CASSEROLE

1 envelope LIPTON® RECIPE SECRETS® Onion Mushroom Soup Mix
1 tablespoon all-purpose flour
1 cup milk
2 packages (10 ounces each) frozen cut green beans, thawed
1 cup shredded Cheddar cheese (about 4 ounces), divided
¼ cup plain dry bread crumbs

1. Preheat oven to 350°F. In 1½-quart casserole, combine soup mix, flour and milk; stir in green beans and ½ cup cheese.

2. Bake uncovered 25 minutes.

3. Sprinkle with bread crumbs and remaining ½ cup cheese. Bake an additional 5 minutes or until cheese is melted.   *Makes 8 servings*

Prep Time: 5 minutes
Cook Time: 30 minutes

CHEESY BROCCOLI 'N MUSHROOM BAKE

2 packages (10 ounces each) frozen broccoli spears, thawed
1 can (10¾ ounces) condensed cream of mushroom soup
½ cup MIRACLE WHIP® Salad Dressing
½ cup milk
1 cup KRAFT® Shredded Cheddar Cheese
½ cup coarsely crushed croutons

• ARRANGE broccoli in 12×8-inch baking dish.

• WHISK together soup, salad dressing and milk. Pour over broccoli. Sprinkle with cheese and croutons.

• Bake at 350°F for 30 to 35 minutes or until thoroughly heated.   *Makes 6 to 8 servings*

Prep Time: 10 minutes
Bake Time: 35 minutes

CHEESY BROCCOLI 'N MUSHROOM BAKE

PUFFY POTATOES

4 slices bacon, diced
5 medium baking potatoes (about 3 pounds)
⅓ cup milk
¾ cup prepared HIDDEN VALLEY® Original
   Ranch® Salad Dressing & Recipe Mix
3 teaspoons chopped parsley, divided

Preheat oven to 400°F. In skillet, cook bacon until crisp; drain on paper towels. Crumble bacon and set aside. Pierce potatoes with fork; bake until tender, about 45 minutes. Cut slits lengthwise, then crosswise in top of each potato. Scoop out centers of potatoes and place in large bowl; reserve 4 potato skins. Mash potatoes. Add milk and salad dressing; beat until smooth. Stir in bacon and 2 teaspoons of the parsley. Fill skins with potato mixture. Bake at 400°F until puffy and golden, about 15 minutes. Sprinkle with remaining 1 teaspoon parsley.

Makes 4 servings

Note: If desired, beat potatoes with ½ cup milk and bake in casserole dish instead of potato skins.

NUTTY VEGETABLE PILAF

1 tablespoon vegetable oil
2 cups coarsely chopped broccoli
2 medium carrots, julienned
1 medium onion, chopped
1 cup sliced fresh mushrooms
2 cloves garlic, minced
½ teaspoon dried thyme leaves
½ teaspoon dried basil leaves
½ teaspoon salt
¼ teaspoon ground black pepper
3 cups cooked brown rice (cooked in low-sodium
   chicken broth*)
½ cup chopped pecans, toasted**
½ cup shredded Parmesan cheese (optional)

Heat oil in large skillet over medium-high heat until hot. Add broccoli, carrots and onion. Cook and stir 5 to 7 minutes or until broccoli and carrots are tender and onion is beginning to brown. Add mushrooms, garlic, thyme, basil, salt and pepper. Cook and stir 2 to 3 minutes or until mushrooms are tender. Add rice and pecans; cook 1 to 2 minutes, stirring, until well blended and thoroughly heated. Just before serving sprinkle with cheese, if desired.

Makes 6 servings

Favorite recipe from **USA Rice Federation**

*For a vegetarian entrée, cook brown rice in vegetable broth.

**To toast pecans, place on baking sheet; bake 5 to 7 minutes in 350°F oven, or until nuts are just beginning to darken and are fragrant.

NUTTY VEGETABLE PILAF

RITZ® CRACKER STUFFING

1 cup coarsely chopped mushrooms or broccoli
½ cup chopped onion
½ cup chopped celery
¼ cup margarine or butter
4 Stay Fresh Packs RITZ® Crackers, coarsely
   crushed (about 7 cups crumbs)
2 cups PLANTERS® Walnuts, Pecans or Almonds,
   coarsely chopped
¼ cup chopped parsley
1 tablespoon poultry seasoning
½ teaspoon ground black pepper
1 (14½-ounce) can chicken broth
2 eggs, beaten

1. Cook mushrooms or broccoli, onion and celery in margarine or butter in skillet over medium heat until tender.

2. Mix cracker crumbs, nuts, parsley, poultry seasoning, pepper and vegetable mixture in large bowl.

Add broth and eggs, tossing until well combined. Spoon into 2-quart baking dish or pan; cover.

3. Bake at 325°F for 30 to 40 minutes or until heated through. Or use as stuffing for turkey, chicken or pork.

Makes about 6 cups

Note: For fewer servings, recipe can be halved. Spoon into 1-quart baking dish. Cover; bake at 325°F for 25 to 30 minutes, or microwave at HIGH for 6 to 8 minutes.

Microwave Directions: Combine mushrooms or broccoli, onion, celery and margarine or butter in 2½-quart microwave-proof bowl; cover. Microwave at HIGH (100%) power for 3 to 4 minutes or until tender. Stir in remaining ingredients as above; cover. Microwave at HIGH for 10 to 12 minutes or until hot, stirring after 6 minutes.

Preparation Time: 20 minutes
Cook Time: 35 minutes
Total Time: 55 minutes

GARLIC FRIES

1 envelope LIPTON® RECIPE SECRETS® Savory
   Herb with Garlic Soup Mix*
1 cup plain dry bread crumbs
2 pounds large red or all-purpose potatoes, cut
   lengthwise into wedges
⅓ cup margarine or butter, melted

Also terrific with LIPTON® RECIPE SECRETS® Onion Soup Mix.

1. Preheat oven to 400°F. In large bowl, blend soup mix with bread crumbs. Dip potatoes in margarine, then soup mixture, until evenly coated.

2. In 15½×10½×1-inch jelly-roll pan sprayed with nonstick cooking spray, arrange potatoes in single layer.

3. Bake uncovered 40 minutes or until potatoes are tender and golden brown. *Makes 4 servings*

HOME–STYLE BAKED BEANS

HOME-STYLE BAKED BEANS

2 strips bacon, finely chopped
1 large green or red bell pepper, seeded and chopped
1 small onion, chopped
3 cans (1 pound each) pork and beans
½ cup *French's*® Worcestershire Sauce
½ cup *French's*® Hearty Deli Brown Mustard
½ cup packed brown sugar
　Additional chopped bell pepper
　Shredded cheese

Microwave Directions:

Place bacon, pepper and onion in microwave-safe 3-quart bowl. Cover loosely with waxed paper. Microwave on HIGH 5 minutes or until bacon is partially cooked. Stir in beans, Worcestershire, mustard and sugar. Microwave, uncovered, on HIGH 20 minutes or until heated through and mixture is slightly thickened, stirring twice. Garnish with additional pepper and cheese. Serve warm.

Makes 8 to 10 side-dish servings

Conventional Oven Directions:

Preheat oven to 400°F. Cook and stir bacon, pepper and onion in large skillet over medium heat until bacon is crisp; transfer to 3-quart casserole dish. Stir in remaining ingredients except additional pepper and cheese. Bake 45 to 50 minutes, stirring occasionally. Garnish as directed.

Prep Time: 10 minutes
Cook Time: 25 minutes

GREEN BEANS WITH BLUE CHEESE

1 box (9 ounces) BIRDS EYE® frozen Cut Green Beans

2 tablespoons walnut pieces (toasted, if desired)

1 heaping tablespoon Roquefort or other blue cheese

1 tablespoon butter or margarine, melted (optional)

- Cook beans according to package directions; drain.

- Combine with remaining ingredients; mix well.

- Serve hot.   *Makes 3 servings*

Prep Time: 2 to 3 minutes
Cook Time: 4 to 6 minutes

KIELBASA TOMATO SALAD

1 pound BOB EVANS FARMS® Kielbasa Sausage

1 pound tomatoes, cut into wedges

1 large red onion, chopped

1 red bell pepper, chopped

1 yellow bell pepper, chopped

3 green onions with tops, cut into ½-inch pieces

½ cup chopped fresh parsley

⅓ cup balsamic vinegar

2 teaspoons salt

1 teaspoon chopped fresh rosemary

1 teaspoon chopped fresh thyme

1 teaspoon black pepper

½ cup olive oil

   Fresh rosemary sprig (optional)

Cut sausage kielbasa into ½-inch rounds; place in medium skillet. Cook over medium heat until browned, turning occasionally. Remove sausage to large glass bowl. Add tomatoes, red onion, bell peppers and green onions to sausage; toss lightly. Combine all remaining ingredients except oil and rosemary sprig in small bowl. Whisk in oil gradually until well blended. Pour over sausage mixture; cover and refrigerate 2 hours or until chilled. Garnish with rosemary sprig, if desired. Serve cold. Refrigerate leftovers.

Makes 8 side-dish servings

KIELBASA TOMATO SALAD

SOUTHWEST STUFFED POTATOES

 4 large (or 8 small) baking potatoes
½ cup milk
¼ cup butter, softened
¼ teaspoon salt
 2 teaspoons chili powder
¼ teaspoon pepper
 1 can (15 ounce) VEG•ALL® Original Mixed
    Vegetables, drained
¼ cup shredded cheddar cheese

1. Preheat oven to 400°F.

2. Bake potatoes in oven until tender.

3. Slice top of each potato lengthwise.

4. Scoop out potato pulp, leaving a thin shell.

5. Mash potato pulp until smooth; add milk, butter, salt, chili powder, and pepper; beat until fluffy.

6. Fold in Veg•All.

7. Divide mixture among shells; sprinkle with cheese.

8. Place on baking sheet.

9. Bake 10 minutes or until cheese has melted and tops are golden brown.

10. Serve hot.   *Makes 4 to 8 servings*

• Classic Tip •

Before baking potatoes, be sure to scrub them with a vegetable brush under running water to remove any embedded dirt. Pat them dry and pierce several times with the tines of a fork to allow steam to escape.

BEST PICKLED BEETS

 2 cans (15 ounces each) small, whole or sliced
    beets
½ cup white vinegar
5½ to 7¼ teaspoons EQUAL® FOR RECIPES *or* 18 to
    24 packets EQUAL® sweetener *or* ¾ to 1 cup
    EQUAL® SPOONFUL™

• Combine beets, beet juice, vinegar and Equal® in medium bowl; cover tightly.

• Chill at least 8 hours before serving. Drain before serving.   *Makes 16 servings*

GRILLED ASPARAGUS AND NEW POTATOES

1 pound small red potatoes, scrubbed and quartered
¼ cup *French's*® Classic Yellow® or Dijon Mustard
3 tablespoons minced fresh dill *or* 2 teaspoons dried dill weed
3 tablespoons olive oil
3 tablespoons lemon juice
1 tablespoon grated lemon peel
⅛ teaspoon black pepper
1 pound asparagus, washed and trimmed

1. Place potatoes and ¼ cup water in shallow microwavable dish. Cover and microwave on HIGH (100%) 8 minutes or until potatoes are crisp-tender, turning once. Drain.

2. Combine mustard, dill, oil, lemon juice, lemon peel and pepper in small bowl. Brush mixture on potatoes and asparagus. Place vegetables in grilling basket. Grill over medium-high heat 8 minutes or until potatoes and asparagus are fork-tender, turning and basting often with mustard mixture. *Makes 4 servings*

Prep Time: 15 minutes
Cook Time: 16 minutes

CONFETTI SCALLOPED CORN

1 egg, beaten
1 cup skim milk
1 cup coarsely crushed saltine crackers (about 22 two-inch square crackers), divided
¼ teaspoon salt
⅛ teaspoon pepper
1 can (16½ ounces) cream-style corn
¼ cup finely chopped onion
1 jar (2 ounces) chopped pimiento, drained
1 tablespoon CRISCO® Oil*
1 tablespoon chopped fresh parsley

Use your favorite Crisco Oil product.

1. Heat oven to 350°F.

2. Combine egg, milk, ⅔ cup cracker crumbs, salt and pepper in medium bowl. Stir in corn, onion and pimiento. Pour into ungreased one-quart casserole.

3. Combine remaining ⅓ cup cracker crumbs with oil in small bowl. Toss to coat. Sprinkle over corn mixture.

4. Bake at 350°F for one hour or until knife inserted in center comes out clean. *Do not overbake.* Sprinkle with parsley. Let stand 5 to 10 minutes before serving. Garnish, if desired. *Makes 6 servings*

BROCCOLI & RED PEPPER SAUTÉ

BROCCOLI & RED PEPPER SAUTÉ

2 tablespoons olive or vegetable oil
4 cups small broccoli florets
1 large red bell pepper, cut into thin strips
1 medium onion, sliced
1 clove garlic, finely chopped
1 envelope LIPTON® RECIPE SECRETS® Golden
    Herb with Lemon Soup Mix*
1 cup water
¼ cup sliced almonds, toasted (optional)

*Also terrific with LIPTON® RECIPE SECRETS® Savory Herb
with Garlic Soup Mix.

In 12-inch skillet, heat oil over medium heat and cook
broccoli, red pepper, onion and garlic, stirring
occasionally, 5 minutes or until onion is tender. Add
Golden Herb with Lemon Soup Mix with water.
Simmer covered 5 minutes or until broccoli is tender.
Sprinkle with almonds.   *Makes about 6 servings*

MALLOW TOPPED SWEET POTATOES

3 (15-ounce) cans sweet potatoes, drained
2 tablespoons margarine or butter, melted
2 tablespoons orange juice
2 tablespoons packed brown sugar
1 teaspoon ground cinnamon
¼ teaspoon ground nutmeg
3 cups JET-PUFFED® Marshmallows (about 25)

1. Place sweet potatoes into greased 9×9×2-inch
baking pan.

2. Blend margarine or butter, orange juice, brown
sugar, cinnamon and nutmeg; pour over potatoes. Bake
at 350°F for 15 minutes.

3. Top potatoes with marshmallows. Bake 10 minutes
more or until marshmallows are golden brown.

Makes 8 servings

Tip: 10 miniature marshmallows = 1 large
marshmallow.

Cook Time: 25 minutes
Total Time: 35 minutes

CALIFORNIA BAKED POTATOES

3 cold baked Idaho potatoes, cut into spears
½ cup KRAFT FREE CATALINA® Fat Free Dressing
1 tablespoon garlic powder
1 tablespoon parsley flakes

HEAT oven to 375°F.

TOSS potato spears with dressing.

SPRINKLE each spear with garlic powder and parsley. Place on cookie sheet.

BAKE 20 minutes or until crispy.　　*Makes 6 servings*

Prep Time: 10 minutes
Bake Time: 20 minutes

CALIFORNIA BAKED POTATOES

RISOTTO–STYLE PRIMAVERA

1 tablespoon FILIPPO BERIO® Olive Oil
1 small zucchini, sliced
1 medium onion, sliced
½ red bell pepper, seeded and cut into thin strips
3 mushrooms, sliced
½ cup uncooked long grain rice
¼ cup dry white wine
1 cup chicken broth
1¾ cups water, divided
2 tablespoons grated Parmesan cheese
Salt and freshly ground black pepper

In large saucepan or skillet, heat olive oil over medium heat until hot. Add zucchini, onion, bell pepper and mushrooms. Cook and stir 5 to 7 minutes or until zucchini is tender-crisp. Remove vegetables; set aside. Add rice and wine; stir until wine is absorbed. Add chicken broth. Cook, uncovered, stirring frequently, until absorbed. Add 1 cup water. Cook, uncovered, stirring frequently, until absorbed. Add remaining ¾ cup water. Cook, uncovered, stirring frequently, until absorbed. (Total cook time will be about 25 minutes until rice is tender and mixture is creamy.) Stir in vegetables and Parmesan cheese. Season to taste with salt and black pepper.　　*Makes 4 servings*

CONFETTI CORN

6 medium tomatoes
2 tablespoons butter or margarine
⅓ cup chopped green onions
⅓ cup chopped red bell pepper
1 package (10 ounces) frozen corn, thawed
2 tablespoons vinegar
2 tablespoons chopped fresh cilantro
1 teaspoon LAWRY'S® Garlic Salt

Cut ¼ inch off top of tomatoes. Hollow out, reserving pulp. Chop pulp into chunks; set aside. In medium skillet, heat butter. Add green onions and bell pepper and cook over medium-high heat until tender. Add corn, vinegar, tomato pulp, cilantro and Garlic Salt; mix well. Heat 5 minutes or until flavors are blended. Place tomato shells in baking dish and heat in 350°F oven 5 minutes. Spoon tomato-corn mixture into shells.

Makes 6 servings

Serving Suggestion: Serve on a lettuce-lined platter as a side dish with grilled chicken, fish or beef entrées.

• *Classic Tip* •

When choosing peppers for these recipes, be sure to select ones that are firm, crisp and feel heavy for their size. They should be shiny and brightly colored and their stems should be green and hard. Avoid peppers that have wrinkles, soft spots or bruises.

SPANISH RICE

1 bag SUCCESS® Rice
1 tablespoon reduced-calorie margarine
½ cup chopped onion
½ cup chopped green bell pepper
½ cup chopped red bell pepper
1 can (8 ounces) tomato sauce
1 chicken bouillon cube, crushed
2 teaspoons chili powder
1 teaspoon ground paprika
½ teaspoon garlic powder
¼ teaspoon ground cumin

Prepare rice according to package directions.

Melt margarine in medium skillet over medium-high heat. Add onion and bell peppers; cook and stir until crisp-tender. Stir in tomato sauce, bouillon and seasonings. Bring to a boil. Reduce heat to low; simmer 5 minutes. Add rice; heat thoroughly, stirring occasionally.

Makes 4 servings

CONFETTI CORN

Accompaniments

VEGETABLES & WILD RICE

1 box UNCLE BEN'S® Long Grain & Wild Rice
   Roasted Garlic
2⅓ cups water
2 tablespoons butter or margarine
1 cup corn, fresh or frozen
1 medium tomato, chopped
4 strips bacon, cooked and crumbled
3 tablespoons chopped green onions

COOK: CLEAN: Wash hands. In medium skillet, combine water, butter, rice and contents of seasoning packet. Bring to a boil. Cover tightly and simmer 15 minutes. Add corn and simmer 15 minutes or until water is absorbed. Stir in tomato and bacon. Sprinkle with green onions.

SERVE: Serve with garlic toast, if desired.

CHILL: Refrigerate leftovers immediately.

Makes 6 servings

Prep Time: none
Cook Time: 30 minutes

NORSE SKILLET POTATOES

1½ pounds new potatoes, scrubbed
1½ teaspoons fresh rosemary leaves
⅓ cup Lucini Premium Select Extra Virgin Olive
   Oil
1 to 2 tablespoons dried mustard
½ teaspoon freshly ground black pepper
1 pound JARLSBERG cheese, grated

Slice potatoes wafer thin, using vegetable slicer or food processor, dropping them into cold water to avoid discoloration. Rub rosemary between fingers to break leaves and reserve.

Preheat oven 425°F. Heat oil in 12-inch cast iron skillet. Add potatoes; cook over medium-high heat, shaking pan gently to toss but not break potatoes. When potatoes are slightly limp, sprinkle with rosemary, mustard to taste and pepper. Shake well to mix. Press with spatula. Cook until brown and crisp on bottom, lifting carefully to check.

Sprinkle with cheese. Immediately place skillet in oven. Bake 2 to 3 minutes until cheese starts to bubble and brown.

Makes 8 to 10 servings

*Favorite recipe from **Norseland, Inc.***

Bread Basket

APPLE CRUMB COFFEECAKE

2¼ cups all-purpose flour, divided
½ cup sugar
1 envelope FLEISCHMANN'S® RapidRise™ Yeast
½ teaspoon salt
¼ cup water
¼ cup milk
⅓ cup butter or margarine
2 large eggs
2 cooking apples, cored and sliced
Crumb Topping (recipe follows)

In large bowl, combine 1 cup flour, sugar, undissolved yeast, and salt. Heat water, milk and butter until very warm (120° to 130°F). Gradually add to dry ingredients. Beat 2 minutes at medium speed of electric mixer, scraping bowl occasionally. Add eggs and ½ cup flour. Beat 2 minutes at high speed, scraping bowl occasionally. Stir in remaining flour to make stiff batter. Spread evenly in greased 9-inch square pan. Arrange apple slices evenly over batter. Sprinkle Crumb Topping over apples. Cover; let rise in warm, draft-free place until doubled in size, about 1 hour.

Bake at 375°F for 35 to 40 minutes or until done. Cool in pan 10 minutes. Remove from pan; cool on wire rack.

Makes 1 (9-inch) cake

Crumb Topping: Combine ⅓ cup sugar, ¼ cup all-purpose flour, 1 teaspoon ground cinnamon, and 3 tablespoons cold butter or margarine. Mix until crumbly.

MINIATURE ORANGE COCONUT ROLLS

Dough
- ¼ cup water
- ½ cup milk
- 1 egg
- ¼ cup soft butter
- ½ teaspoon salt
- ¼ cup sugar
- 1 teaspoon orange zest
- 2¾ cups bread flour
- 2¼ teaspoons RED STAR® Active Dry Yeast or QUICK•RISE™ Yeast

Filling
- ¼ cup sugar
- 2 teaspoons orange zest
- 2 tablespoons butter, melted
- ½ cup coconut
- **Orange Glaze (recipe follows)**

Bread Machine Method

Have liquid ingredients at 80°F and all others at room temperature. Place ingredients in pan in order specified by owner's manual. Select dough/manual cycle. Do not use delay timer. At end of last kneading cycle, press STOP/CLEAR; remove dough and proceed with shaping and baking instructions.

Mixer Methods

Combine yeast, 1 cup flour, and other dry ingredients. Combine water and milk; heat to 120° to 130°F.

Hand-Held Mixer Method

Combine dry mixture, liquid ingredients, and butter in mixing bowl on low speed. Beat 2 to 3 minutes on medium speed. Add egg; beat 1 minute. By hand, stir in enough remaining flour to make a firm dough.

Knead on floured surface 3 to 5 minutes or until smooth and elastic.

Stand Mixer Method

Combine dry mixture, liquid ingredients and butter in mixing bowl with paddle or beaters for 4 minutes on medium speed. Add egg; beat 1 minute. Gradually add remaining flour and knead with dough hook(s) 5 to 7 minutes until smooth and elastic.

Food Processor Method

Put dry mixture in processing bowl with steel blade. While motor is running, add butter, egg, and liquid ingredients. Process until mixed. Continue processing, adding remaining flour until dough forms a ball.

Shaping and Baking

To prepare filling, combine ¼ cup sugar and 2 teaspoons orange zest. Divide dough into 2 parts. On lightly floured surface, roll or pat each half into 12×6-inch rectangle. Spread half of melted butter over each rectangle. Sprinkle with half of filling and ¼ cup coconut. Starting with longer side, roll up tightly. Pinch edge to seal. Cut each roll into 12 slices. Place in greased miniature muffin pan cups. Cover; let rise in warm place about 40 minutes (30 minutes for Quick•Rise™ Yeast). Bake in preheated 375°F oven for 25 to 30 minutes until golden brown. Remove from pans; cool 5 to 10 minutes. Brush rolls with Orange Glaze.   *Makes 24 miniature rolls*

Orange Glaze: Combine ¼ cup sugar, ¼ cup orange juice, and 2 tablespoons light corn syrup in small saucepan. Bring to a boil and simmer 3 minutes. Remove from heat; cool.

Bread Basket

POTATO ROSEMARY ROLLS

Dough
- 1 cup plus 2 tablespoons water (70 to 80°F)
- 2 tablespoons olive oil
- 1 teaspoon salt
- 3 cups bread flour
- ½ cup instant potato flakes or buds
- 2 tablespoons nonfat dry milk powder
- 1 tablespoon sugar
- 1 teaspoon SPICE ISLANDS® Rosemary, crushed
- 1½ teaspoons FLEISCHMANN'S® Bread Machine Yeast

Topping
- 1 egg, lightly beaten
- Sesame or poppy seed or additional dried rosemary, crushed

Measure all dough ingredients into bread machine pan in the order suggested by manufacturer, adding potato flakes with flour. Select dough / manual cycle. When cycle is complete, remove dough to floured surface. If necessary, knead in additional flour to make dough easy to handle.

Divide dough into 12 equal pieces. Roll each piece to 10-inch rope; coil each rope and tuck end under coil. Place rolls 2 inches apart on large greased baking sheet. Cover; let rise in warm, draft-free place until doubled in size, about 45 to 60 minutes. Brush tops with beaten egg; sprinkle with sesame seed. Bake at 375°F for 15 to 20 minutes or until done. Remove from pan; cool on wire rack. *Makes 12 rolls*

Note: Dough can be prepared in 1½ and 2-pound bread machines.

OATMEAL BREAD

- 1¼ to 1⅓ cups milk or water
- 2¼ teaspoons quick-rising yeast (one 1¼ ounce package)
- 2 tablespoons butter or margarine, melted or 1 tablespoon vegetable oil
- 3 cups bread flour
- 1 cup QUAKER® Oats (quick or old fashioned, uncooked)
- 2 tablespoons sugar
- 1 teaspoon salt

Bring all ingredients to room temperature by letting them stand on the counter for about 30 minutes*. Place yeast in bread machine according to directions in manual. Combine flour, oats, sugar and salt in a bowl; mix well. In a separate bowl combine milk and margarine; mix well. Place into bread machine according to manual. When baking, use white bread and light crust setting. *Makes one 1½-pound loaf*

*This can be done quickly by microwaving the ingredients for 15 to 20 seconds.

Maple Fruit Variation: Combine ⅓ cup pancake syrup with margarine and only 1 cup milk. Proceed as directed above. Add ½ cup dried fruit to bread dough partially through kneading cycle according to bread machine manual.

POTATO ROSEMARY ROLLS

CRANBERRY–PECAN WREATH

½ cup milk
1 large egg
¼ cup butter or margarine, cut up
½ teaspoon salt
2½ cups bread flour
¼ cup sugar
2 teaspoons FLEISCHMANN'S® Bread Machine Yeast
Cranberry-Pecan Filling (recipe follows)
Orange Glaze (recipe follows)

Add all ingredients except filling and glaze to bread machine pan in the order suggested by manufacturer. Select dough/manual cycle. When cycle is complete, remove dough to floured surface. If necessary, knead in enough flour to make dough easy to handle. Roll dough to 26×6-inch rectangle; spread Cranberry-Pecan Filling over dough to within ½ inch of edges. Beginning at long end, roll up tightly as for jelly roll. Pinch seam to seal. Form into ring; join ends, pinching to seal. Transfer to greased large baking sheet. Cover and let rise in warm, draft-free place until doubled in size, about 45 to 60 minutes.

Bake at 350°F for 30 to 35 minutes or until done. Remove from pan; cool on wire rack. Drizzle with Orange Glaze; decorate with additional cranberries, orange slices and pecan halves, if desired.

Makes 1 (8-inch) coffee cake

Cranberry-Pecan Filling: In medium saucepan, combine 1 cup fresh or frozen cranberries, finely chopped, ⅔ cup firmly packed brown sugar and ¼ cup butter or margarine. Bring to a boil over medium-high heat. Reduce heat and simmer 4 to 6 minutes or until very thick, stirring frequently. Remove mixture from heat; stir in ½ cup chopped pecans, toasted.

Orange Glaze: In small bowl, cream 1½ tablespoons butter or margarine with 1 cup powdered sugar, sifted. Add 1 to 2 tablespoons milk and 1½ teaspoons freshly grated orange peel. Stir until smooth.

FRENCH ONION BREAD STIX

1⅓ cups *French's®* Taste Toppers™ French Fried Onions, crushed
¼ cup grated Parmesan cheese
1 container (11 ounces) refrigerated soft bread sticks
1 egg white, beaten

1. Preheat oven to 350°F. Combine *Taste Toppers* and cheese in pie plate. Separate dough into 12 pieces on sheet of waxed paper.

2. Brush one side of dough with egg white. Dip pieces wet side down into crumbs, pressing firmly. Baste top surface with egg white and dip into crumbs.

3. Twist pieces to form a spiral. Arrange on ungreased baking sheet. Bake 15 to 20 minutes or until golden brown.

Makes 12 bread sticks

Prep Time: 5 minutes
Cook Time: 15 minutes

GRANDMA'S CINNAMON ROLLS

Rolls
½ cup water
½ cup milk
2 tablespoons butter, at room temperature
1 large egg, at room temperature
¾ teaspoon salt
¼ cup sugar
3 cups bread flour
2¼ teaspoons RED STAR® Active Dry Yeast

Filling
¼ cup butter, melted
6 tablespoons sugar
¼ cup chopped nuts
¾ teaspoon ground cinnamon

Glaze
1 cup powdered sugar
2 tablespoons hot coffee
1½ tablespoons butter, melted
¼ teaspoon maple flavoring

Bread Machine Method
Place room temperature ingredients for rolls in pan in order listed. Select dough cycle. *Do not use the delay timer.* Check dough consistency after 5 minutes of kneading, making adjustments, if necessary.

Hand-Held Mixer Method
Combine yeast, 1 cup flour, ¼ cup sugar and salt. Heat water and milk to 120° to 130°F. Combine dry mixture, water, milk and butter in mixing bowl on low speed. Beat 2 to 3 minutes on medium speed. Add egg; beat 1 minute. By hand, stir in enough remaining flour to make firm dough. Knead on floured surface 5 to 7 minutes or until smooth and elastic. Add additional flour, if necessary.

Stand Mixer Method
Combine yeast, 1 cup flour, ¼ cup sugar and salt. Heat water and milk to 120° to 130°F. Combine dry mixture, water, milk and butter in mixing bowl with paddle or beaters 4 minutes on medium speed. Add egg; beat 1 minute. Gradually add remaining flour and knead with dough hook 5 to 7 minutes or until smooth and elastic.

Food Processor Method
Combine yeast, 1 cup flour, ¼ cup sugar and salt. Use room temperature water and milk. Put dry mixture in processing bowl with steel blade. While motor is running, add water, milk, butter and egg. Process until mixed. Continue processing, adding remaining flour until dough forms a ball.

Rising, Shaping and Baking
Place dough in lightly oiled bowl and turn to grease top. Cover; let rise until dough tests ripe.* Turn dough onto lightly floured surface; punch down to remove air bubbles. Roll or pat into 12×9-inch rectangle. Brush with ¼ cup melted butter. Combine 6 tablespoons sugar, nuts and cinnamon; sprinkle over dough. Starting with shorter side, roll up tightly. Pinch edge to seal. Cut into 12 slices. Place in greased 13×9-inch pan. Cover; let rise until indentation remains when touched. Bake in preheated 375°F oven 20 to 35 minutes.

Meanwhile, combine glaze ingredients; blend until smooth. Remove rolls from pan; drizzle with glaze.

Makes 1 dozen rolls

Place two fingers into the dough and then remove them. If the holes remain the dough is ripe and ready to punch down.

FREEZER ROLLS

1¼ cups warm water (100° to 110°F)
2 envelopes FLEISCHMANN'S® Active Dry Yeast
½ cup warm milk (100° to 110°F)
⅓ cup butter or margarine, softened
½ cup sugar
1½ teaspoons salt
5½ to 6 cups all-purpose flour
2 large eggs

Place ½ cup warm water in large warm bowl. Sprinkle in yeast; stir until dissolved. Add remaining warm water, warm milk, butter, sugar, salt and 2 cups flour. Beat 2 minutes at medium speed of electric mixer. Add eggs and ½ cup flour. Beat at high speed for 2 minutes. Stir in enough remaining flour to make soft dough. Turn out onto lightly floured surface. Knead until smooth and elastic, about 8 to 10 minutes. Cover with plastic wrap; let rest for 20 minutes.

Punch dough down. Shape into desired shapes for dinner rolls. Place on greased baking sheets. Cover with plastic wrap and foil, sealing well. Freeze up to 1 week.*

Once frozen, rolls may be placed in plastic freezer bags.

Remove from freezer; place on greased baking sheets. Cover; let rise in warm, draft-free place until doubled in size, about 1½ hours.

Bake at 350°F for 15 minutes or until done. Remove from baking sheets; cool on wire racks.

Makes about 2 dozen rolls

To bake without freezing: After shaping, let rise in warm, draft-free place, until doubled in size, about 1 hour. Bake according to above directions.

Shaping the Dough for Crescents: Divide dough in half. Roll each half to 14-inch circle. Cut each into 12 pie-shaped wedges. Roll up tightly from wide end. Curve ends slightly to form crescents.

ONION–HERB BAKED BREAD

1 envelope LIPTON® RECIPE SECRETS® Golden Onion Soup Mix
1 medium clove garlic, finely chopped
1 teaspoon dried basil leaves
1 teaspoon dried oregano leaves
⅛ teaspoon pepper
½ cup butter or margarine, softened
1 loaf Italian or French bread (about 16 inches long), halved lengthwise

Preheat oven to 375°F.

In small bowl, thoroughly blend all ingredients except bread; generously spread on bread halves. Arrange bread, cut-side up, on baking sheet. Bake 15 minutes or until golden. Serve warm. *Makes 1 loaf*

Note: Store any remaining spread, covered, in refrigerator for future use.

BANANA–CHOCOLATE CHIP BREAD

1-POUND LOAF

⅓ cup milk
⅓ cup mashed very ripe banana
1 large egg
1 tablespoon butter or margarine
¾ teaspoon salt
2 cups bread flour
¼ cup semisweet chocolate pieces
1½ teaspoons FLEISCHMANN'S® Bread Machine Yeast

1½-POUND LOAF

½ cup milk
½ cup mashed very ripe banana
1 large egg
1 tablespoon butter or margarine
1 teaspoon salt
3 cups bread flour
⅓ cup semisweet chocolate pieces
2 teaspoons FLEISCHMANN'S® Bread Machine Yeast

Use the 1-pound recipe if your machine pan holds 10 cups or less of water. Add ingredients to bread machine pan in the order suggested by manufacturer, adding mashed banana with milk and semisweet chocolate pieces with flour. Recommended cycle: Basic/white bread cycle; medium/normal or light crust color setting. *Makes 1 loaf (8 or 12 slices)*

Note: How this bread turns out depends on your machine. Some machines will make a smooth chocolate-colored bread. Others will leave bits of chocolate chips, and still others will give a marbled loaf.

• Classic Tip •

Are your bananas too ripe? Save them for baking. Mashed bananas may be frozen for up to six months. Simply stir in 1 teaspoon lemon juice for each banana to prevent browning and freeze in an airtight container.

CINNAMON TWISTS

ROLLS

- **1 package DUNCAN HINES® Bakery-Style Cinnamon Swirl Muffin Mix, divided**
- **2 cups all-purpose flour**
- **1 package (¼ ounce) quick-rise yeast**
- **1 egg, slightly beaten**
- **1 cup hot water (120° to 130°F)**
- **2 tablespoons butter or margarine, melted**
- **1 egg white, slightly beaten**
- **1 teaspoon water**

TOPPING

- **1½ cups confectioners' sugar**
- **2½ tablespoons milk**

1. Grease 2 large baking sheets.

2. For rolls, combine muffin mix, flour and yeast in large bowl; set aside.

3. Combine contents of swirl packet from Mix, egg, hot water and melted butter in medium bowl. Stir until thoroughly blended. Pour into flour mixture; stir until thoroughly blended. Invert onto well-floured surface; let rest for 10 minutes. Knead for 10 minutes or until smooth, adding flour as necessary. Divide dough in half. Cut and shape 24 small ropes from each half. Braid 3 ropes to form small twist and place on greased baking sheet. Combine egg white and 1 teaspoon water in small bowl. Brush each twist with egg white mixture and sprinkle with contents of topping packet from Mix. Allow twists to rise 1 hour or until doubled in size.

4. Preheat oven to 375°F.

5. Bake at 375°F for 17 to 20 minutes or until deep golden brown. Remove to cooling racks.

6. For topping, combine confectioners' sugar and milk in small bowl. Stir until smooth. Drizzle over warm rolls. Serve warm or cool completely.

Makes 16 rolls

Tip: For best results, let rolls rise in a warm, draft-free area. A slightly warm oven (130° to 140°F) is ideal.

STATE FAIR CRACKED WHEAT BREAD

- **1⅓ cups water**
- **2 tablespoons butter or margarine**
- **1 teaspoon salt**
- **¼ cup cracked wheat**
- **3 cups bread flour**
- **½ cup whole wheat flour**
- **3 tablespoons nonfat dry milk powder**
- **2 tablespoons firmly packed brown sugar**
- **2 teaspoons FLEISCHMANN'S® Bread Machine Yeast**

Add ingredients to bread machine pan in the order suggested by manufacturer. (If dough is too dry or stiff or too soft or slack, adjust dough consistency.) Recommended cycle: Basic/white bread cycle; medium/normal crust color setting.

Makes 1 (2-pound) loaf

STATE FAIR CRACKED WHEAT BREAD

BLACK PEPPER–ONION BREAD

1-POUND LOAF

- ⅔ cup water
- 1 tablespoon butter or margarine
- ¾ teaspoon salt
- 2 cups bread flour
- 2 tablespoons nonfat dry milk powder
- 2 teaspoons sugar
- 1 teaspoon SPICE ISLANDS® Minced Onions
- ½ teaspoon SPICE ISLANDS® Medium Grind Java Black Pepper*
- ⅛ teaspoon SPICE ISLANDS® Garlic Powder
- 1½ teaspoons FLEISCHMANN'S® Bread Machine Yeast

1½-POUND LOAF

- 1 cup water
- 1 tablespoon butter or margarine
- 1 teaspoon salt
- 3 cups bread flour
- 3 tablespoons nonfat dry milk powder
- 1 tablespoon sugar
- 1½ teaspoons SPICE ISLANDS® Minced Onions
- ¾ teaspoon SPICE ISLANDS® Medium Grind Java Black Pepper*
- ¼ teaspoon SPICE ISLANDS® Garlic Powder
- 2 teaspoons FLEISCHMANN'S® Bread Machine Yeast

If using a finer grind of pepper, reduce the amount to ¼ teaspoon for either loaf size.

Use the 1-pound recipe if your machine pan holds 10 cups or less of water. Add ingredients to bread machine pan in the order suggested by manufacturer. Recommended cycle: Basic/white bread cycle; medium/normal crust color setting. Timed-bake feature can be used. *Makes 1 loaf (8 or 12 slices)*

• Classic Tip •

This robust bread is great for corned beef sandwiches or served with hearty beef stew.

PEANUT BUTTER SCONES

2 cups self-rising flour
½ cup creamy peanut butter
¼ cup granulated sugar
1 teaspoon vanilla
2½ tablespoons oil
2 eggs (or ½ cup egg substitute)
Cinnamon
Additional sugar

Preheat oven to 425°F. Mix all the ingredients except cinnamon and additional sugar together using a fork. Turn the dough out onto an ungreased pizza pan. The dough will look lumpy. Using your hands, shape the dough into a 10-inch circle. Cut the circle into 12 pie slices and separate each piece so they are about ¼ inch apart. Sprinkle each piece with a mixture of cinnamon and sugar. Bake 10 minutes. Serve plain or with butter and jam. *Makes 12 scones*

Favorite recipe from **Peanut Advisory Board**

PAINTED BREAD KNOTS

1 tablespoon *French's*® Classic Yellow® Mustard
1 tablespoon milk
1 container (11 ounces) refrigerated crusty French loaf dough
Coarse salt

1. Preheat oven to 350°F. Combine mustard and milk in small bowl. Cut bread dough into 12 (1-inch) slices. Roll each slice into 8-inch long piece. Tie each into knot.

2. Arrange knots on lightly greased baking sheet. Paint each with mustard mixture. Sprinkle with salt. Bake 20 minutes or until golden. Transfer baking sheet to wire rack and let knots stand on baking sheet until completely cool.

3. Serve with additional mustard.

Makes 12 servings

Prep Time: 10 minutes
Cook Time: 20 minutes

PAINTED BREAD KNOTS

Bread Basket

PARKER HOUSE ROLLS

4¾ to 5¼ cups all-purpose flour
⅓ cup sugar
2 envelopes FLEISCHMANN'S® RapidRise™ Yeast
1½ teaspoons salt
¾ cup milk
¾ cup water
¼ cup butter or margarine
1 large egg
¼ cup butter or margarine, melted

In large bowl, combine 2 cups flour, sugar, undissolved yeast, and salt. Heat milk, water, and ¼ cup butter until very warm (120° to 130°F). Stir into dry ingredients. Beat 2 minutes at medium speed of electric mixer, scraping bowl occasionally. Add egg and ½ cup flour; beat 2 minutes at high speed. Stir in enough remaining flour to make a soft dough. Knead on lightly floured surface until smooth and elastic, about 8 to 10 minutes. Cover*; let rest 10 minutes.

Divide dough in half; roll each half to 12-inch square, about ¼-inch thick. Cut each into 6 (2×12-inch) strips. Cut each strip into 3 (4×2-inch) rectangles. Brush each rectangle with melted butter. Crease rectangles slightly off center with dull edge of knife and fold at crease. Arrange in rows, slightly overlapping, on greased baking sheets, with shorter side of each roll facing down. Allow ¼-inch of space between each row. Cover; let rise in warm, draft-free place until doubled in size, about 30 minutes.

Bake at 400°F for 13 to 15 minutes or until done. Remove from sheets; cool on wire rack. Brush with remaining melted butter. *Makes 36 rolls*

If desired, allow dough to rise in refrigerator 12 to 24 hours.

SAVORY FRENCH BREAD

1 large loaf French bread
¼ cup butter or margarine, softened
½ teaspoon dried basil leaves
½ teaspoon dried dill weed
½ teaspoon chopped dried chives
¼ teaspoon garlic powder
¼ teaspoon paprika
½ teaspoon TABASCO® brand Pepper Sauce

Preheat oven to 400°F. Slice bread diagonally, but do not cut through bottom crust of loaf. Mix remaining ingredients in small bowl. Spread between bread slices; wrap bread in aluminum foil and heat in oven for 15 to 20 minutes. Serve warm. *Makes 6 to 8 servings*

LEMONY WHEATFUL FRUIT BREAD

½ cup (1 stick) margarine, melted
½ cup fat free milk
2 eggs
  Finely grated peel from 1 lemon
2 tablespoons lemon juice
1 cup sugar
2 cups flour
1½ cups POST® SPOON SIZE® Shredded Wheat
  Cereal, finely crushed
1 teaspoon baking soda
¼ teaspoon ground cinnamon
1 cup dried fruit mix (such as prune, apricot, pear),
  chopped

HEAT oven to 350°F. Spray 9×5-inch loaf pan with no stick cooking spray.

MIX margarine, milk, eggs, lemon peel, juice and sugar in large bowl until well blended. Stir in flour, crushed cereal, baking soda and cinnamon until blended. Stir in fruit. Pour into prepared pan.

BAKE 50 minutes or until bread is golden brown and toothpick inserted in center comes out clean. Cool 10 minutes; remove from pan. Cool completely on wire rack. Store wrapped in plastic wrap.

Makes 1 loaf or 12 (¾-inch) slices

Prep Time: 10 minutes
Bake Time: 50 minutes

DILLY OF A BATTER BREAD

3¼ cups all-purpose flour, divided
2 packages RED STAR® Active Dry Yeast or
  QUICK•RISE™ Yeast
2 tablespoons sugar
1 tablespoon instant minced onion
2 teaspoons dill seed
1 teaspoon salt
1 carton (8 ounces) plain yogurt
½ cup water
2 tablespoons shortening
1 egg

In large mixer bowl, combine 1½ cups flour, yeast, sugar, onion, dill seed and salt; mix well. In small saucepan, heat yogurt, water and shortening until very warm (120°-130°F; shortening does not need to melt). Add to flour mixture. Add egg. Blend at low speed until moistened; beat 3 minutes at medium speed. By hand, gradually stir in remaining flour to make a stiff batter.

Spoon into greased 1½- or 2-quart casserole. Cover; let rise in warm place until light and double, about 1 hour (30 minutes for Quick•Rise™ Yeast). Bake at 375°F for 35 to 40 minutes or until golden brown. Remove from casserole; serve warm or cold.   *Makes 1 round loaf*

LEMONY WHEATFUL FRUIT BREAD

OATMEAL BREAKFAST BREAD

1½-POUND LOAF

    1 cup plus 2 tablespoons water
    1 tablespoon vegetable oil
    ⅓ cup maple syrup
    2 teaspoons ground cinnamon
    1 teaspoon salt
    1 cup oatmeal
    3 cups bread flour
    2¼ teaspoons RED STAR® Active Dry Yeast
    1 cup pecans
    1 cup raisins

2-POUND LOAF

    1⅓ cups water
    5 teaspoons vegetable oil
    ½ cup maple syrup
    2½ teaspoons ground cinnamon
    1¼ teaspoons salt
    1¼ cups oatmeal
    4 cups bread flour
    1 tablespoon RED STAR® Active Dry Yeast
    1¼ cups pecans
    1¼ cups raisins

Bread Machine Method

Have liquid ingredients at 80°F and all others at room temperature. Place ingredients in pan in the order specified in your owner's manual. Select basic cycle and medium/normal crust. Pecans and raisins can be added 5 minutes before the end or the last kneading cycle.

Hand-Held Mixer Method

Using ingredients for medium loaf, combine 1 cup flour, oatmeal, yeast, cinnamon and salt. Combine water, syrup and oil; heat to 120° to 130°F. Combine both mixtures in mixing bowl on low speed. Beat 2 to 3 minutes on medium speed. By hand, stir in pecans, raisins and enough remaining flour to make firm dough. Knead on floured surface 5 to 7 minutes or until smooth and elastic. Use additional flour, if necessary.

Stand Mixer Method

Using ingredients for medium loaf, combine 1 cup flour, oatmeal, yeast, cinnamon and salt. Combine water, syrup and oil; heat to 120° to 130°F. Combine both mixtures in mixing bowl with paddle or beaters 4 minutes on medium speed. Gradually add pecans, raisins and remaining flour; knead with dough hooks 5 to 7 minutes or until smooth and elastic. Use additional flour, if necessary.

Food Processor Method

Using ingredients for medium loaf, combine 1 cup flour, oatmeal, yeast, cinnamon and salt. Combine water, syrup and oil. Put dry mixture in processing bowl with steel blade. While motor is running, add liquid mixture. Process until mixed. Continue processing, adding remaining flour until dough forms a ball. Add pecans and raisins; pulse just until mixed. Use additional flour, if necessary.

Rising, Shaping, and Baking

Place dough in lightly oiled bowl and turn to grease top. Cover; let rise until dough tests ripe.* Turn dough onto lightly floured surface; punch down to remove air bubbles. Roll or pat into 14×7-inch rectangle. Starting with shorter side, roll up tightly, pressing dough into roll. Pinch edges and ends to seal. Place in greased 9×5-inch loaf pan. Cover; let rise until indentation remains after touching. Bake in preheated 375°F oven 30 to 40 minutes. Remove from pan; cool.

Makes 1 loaf

*Place two fingers into the dough and then remove them. If the holes remain the dough is ripe and ready to punch down.

Note: Due to the low volume of this loaf, the medium recipe can be used in a small machine.

CHOCOLATE WALNUT COFFEE RINGS

6½ to 7 cups all-purpose flour, divided
½ cup granulated sugar
1½ teaspoons salt
1½ teaspoons ground cinnamon
2 packages active dry yeast
1 cup butter or margarine
1 cup milk
½ cup water
2 eggs
2 egg yolks
2 cups (12-ounce package) NESTLÉ® TOLL
    HOUSE® Semi-Sweet Chocolate Morsels
1 cup chopped walnuts
⅓ cup packed brown sugar
    Vegetable oil
    Glaze (recipe follows)

In large mixer bowl, combine 2 cups flour, granulated sugar, salt, cinnamon and yeast. In small saucepan over low heat, warm butter, milk and water until very warm (120° to 130°F.). On low speed of electric mixer, gradually beat milk mixture into dry ingredients; beat for 2 minutes. Add eggs, egg yolks and 1 cup flour. Beat on high speed for 2 minutes. Stir in about 2½ cups flour to make a stiff dough. Cover; let stand for 20 minutes.

In medium bowl, combine morsels, walnuts and brown sugar. Sprinkle work surface with ½ cup flour. Turn dough onto work surface; sprinkle with additional ½ cup flour. Knead for 2 to 3 minutes; cut dough in half. On floured surface, roll out one dough half into 16×10-inch rectangle. Sprinkle one half morsel mixture to within ½ inch of edges. Starting at wide end, roll up jelly-roll fashion; pinch seam to seal. Place, seam side down, on large greased baking sheet, joining ends to

from a circle. Cut outside edge at 1-inch intervals, two thirds of way through. Turn each slice on its side to overlap. Brush with oil; cover with plastic wrap.

Repeat with remaining dough and filling. Chill for 2 to 24 hours.

Let coffee rings stand uncovered at room temperature for 10 minutes. Bake in preheated 375°F. oven for 25 to 30 minutes or until golden. Remove from baking sheets; cool on wire racks. Drizzle with Glaze.

Makes 2 coffee rings

Glaze: In small bowl, combine 1 cup powdered sugar, 5 to 6 teaspoons milk, ½ teaspoon vanilla extract and dash ground cinnamon; blend until smooth.

· *Classic Tip* ·

For a beautiful drizzle, place Glaze in a plastic food storage bag. Snip off a tiny piece of one corner, then decorate as desired.

MANY GRAINS BREAD

2¾ to 3¼ cups all-purpose flour, divided
3 cups graham/whole wheat flour, divided
2 packages RED STAR® Active Dry Yeast or
    QUICK•RISE™ Yeast
4 teaspoons salt
3 cups water
½ cup dark molasses
¼ cup vegetable oil
½ cup buckwheat flour
½ cup rye flour
½ cup soy flour
½ cup yellow cornmeal
½ cup quick rolled oats
    Butter

Combine 1½ cups all-purpose flour, 2 cups graham/whole wheat flour, yeast, and salt in large bowl; mix well. Heat water, molasses and oil in large saucepan over medium heat until very warm (120° to 130°F). Add to flour mixture. Blend at low speed until moistened; beat 3 minutes at medium speed. By hand, gradually stir in buckwheat, rye and soy flours, cornmeal, oats, remaining graham/whole wheat flour and enough remaining all-purpose flour to make a firm dough. Knead on floured surface 5 to 8 minutes. Place in large greased bowl, turning to grease top. Cover; let rise in warm place about 1 hour or until double in bulk (about 30 minutes for Quick•Rise™ Yeast).

Punch down dough. Divide into 2 parts. On lightly floured surface, shape each half into round loaf.

Place loaves on large greased baking sheet. Cover; let rise in warm place about 40 to 45 minutes or until double in bulk (30 minutes for Quick•Rise™ Yeast).

Preheat oven to 375°F. With sharp knife, make cross slash across top of each loaf. Bake 35 to 40 minutes until bread sounds hollow when tapped. If bread starts to become too dark, cover loosely with foil during last 5 to 10 minutes of baking. Remove from baking sheet. Brush with butter; cool on wire racks.

Makes 2 round loaves

ORIGINAL RANCH® & CHEDDAR BREAD

1 cup HIDDEN VALLEY® Original Ranch® Dressing
2 cups (8 ounces) shredded sharp Cheddar cheese
1 whole loaf (1 pound) French bread (not sour dough)

Stir together dressing and cheese. Cut bread in half lengthwise. Place on a broiler pan and spread dressing mixture evenly over cut side of each half. Broil until lightly brown. Cut each half into 8 pieces.

Makes 16 pieces

Bread Basket

SUNDAY MORNING UPSIDE–DOWN ROLLS

¼ cup warm water (105°F to 115°F)
1 envelope quick-rising yeast
¼ teaspoon sugar
1 cup scalded milk, slightly cooled
½ cup WESSON® Canola Oil
½ cup sugar
3 eggs, beaten
1½ teaspoons salt
4½ cups all-purpose flour
¾ cup (1½ sticks) butter, softened
2 cups packed brown sugar
1 cup maraschino cherries, chopped
1 (16-ounce) jar KNOTT'S BERRY FARM® Light Apricot Pineapple Preserves

Pour water into a large bowl. Sprinkle yeast, then ¼ teaspoon sugar into water; stir well. Let stand 5 to 8 minutes or until mixture is slightly foamy. Meanwhile, in a small bowl, whisk milk, Wesson® Oil, ½ cup sugar, eggs and salt until well blended. Pour milk mixture into yeast mixture; blend well. Gradually add flour to mixture; mix until smooth. Knead dough in bowl (about 5 minutes) until smooth. Add more flour if dough is sticky. Cover with towel and let rise in warm place for 30 minutes or until dough nearly doubles in size. Punch down dough once; cover.

Meanwhile, in small bowl, cream together butter and brown sugar. Spoon (be careful not to pack) 2 teaspoons of creamed sugar mixture into *each* of 24 muffin cups. Sprinkle maraschino cherries over creamed sugar mixture; then add 2 teaspoons Knott's® preserves to *each* muffin cup. Tear small pillows of dough and place on preserves, filling *each* muffin cup to the rim. Cover; let rise about 15 to 20 minutes. Preheat oven to 375°F. Bake for 12 to 15 minutes or until golden brown. Immediately invert rolls onto cookie sheet. *Do not remove rolls from muffin cups.* Allow a few minutes for preserves to drip down the sides. Lift muffin pans from rolls; cool 5 minutes. Remove muffins to wire rack. Serve warm.   *Makes 2 dozen rolls*

WISCONSIN CHEESE PULL–APART BREAD

3 packages (about 3 dozen) frozen bread dough dinner rolls, thawed to room temperature
⅓ cup butter, melted
1 cup freshly grated Wisconsin Parmesan cheese
1 cup shredded Wisconsin Provolone cheese

Roll each dinner roll in butter, then in Parmesan cheese to coat. Arrange half the rolls in well-greased 12-cup fluted tube pan. Sprinkle with Provolone cheese. Top with remaining rolls. Sprinkle with any remaining Parmesan cheese. Let rise about 1 hour or until doubled in bulk.

Preheat oven to 375°F. Bake 35 to 45 minutes or until golden brown. Use table knife to loosen edges of bread. Remove from pan. Serve warm.   *Makes 12 servings*

Tip: Cover edges of bread with foil during last 10 to 15 minutes of baking if crust becomes too dark.

*Favorite recipe from **Wisconsin Milk Marketing Board***

PUMPKIN–NUT BREAD

1-POUND LOAF

- ½ cup canned pumpkin
- ¼ cup milk
- 1 large egg
- 1 tablespoon butter or margarine
- ¾ teaspoon salt
- 1½ cups bread flour
- ½ cup whole wheat flour
- ⅓ cup coarsely chopped pecans or walnuts, toasted*
- 2 tablespoons packed brown sugar
- ¾ teaspoon SPICE ISLANDS® Pumpkin Pie Spice
- 1½ teaspoons FLEISCHMANN'S® Bread Machine Yeast

1½-POUND LOAF

- ¾ cup canned pumpkin
- ⅓ cup milk
- 1 large egg
- 1 tablespoon butter or margarine
- 1 teaspoon salt
- 2⅓ cups bread flour
- ⅔ cup whole wheat flour
- ½ cup coarsely chopped pecans or walnuts, toasted*
- 3 tablespoons packed brown sugar
- 1 teaspoon SPICE ISLANDS® Pumpkin Pie Spice
- 2 teaspoons FLEISCHMANN'S® Bread Machine Yeast

Toasting nuts brings out their full flavor and helps keep them crisp in breads. To toast nuts, spread the chopped nuts in a shallow baking pan large enough to accommodate a single layer. Bake the nuts at 350°F for 5 to 15 minutes or until lightly toasted, stirring several times and checking often. Be sure to cool the nuts before adding to the bread machine.

Use the 1-pound recipe if your machine pan holds 10 cups or less of water. Add ingredients to bread machine pan in the order suggested by manufacturer, adding pumpkin with milk and nuts with flours. (Pumpkin varies in moisture content. If dough is too dry or stiff or too soft or slack, adjust dough consistency—see Adjusting Dough Consistency tip below.) Recommended cycle: Basic/white bread cycle; light or medium/normal crust color setting.

Makes 1 loaf (8 or 12 slices)

Adjusting Dough Consistency: Bread machine dough is slightly stickier than hand-kneaded dough. After mixing for a few minutes, the ingredients should turn into a dough that forms a soft, smooth ball around the blade. If your machine seems to be straining or if the dough appears too dry or stiff, add more liquid in 1-teaspoon increments to achieve the proper consistency. If the dough seems too soft or slack, add additional bread flour in 1-teaspoon increments until the proper consistency is reached. Do not add more than 3 to 4 tablespoons of liquid or flour. The machine cannot compensate for wide variations from the norm and may not bake the larger amount of dough thoroughly.

PUMPERNICKEL RAISIN BREAD

3 tablespoons plus 1 teaspoon GRANDMA'S®
   Gold Molasses, divided
2 packages (¼ ounce each) active dry yeast
1¼ cups warm water (105° to 115°F), divided
2 cups all-purpose flour
1 cup rye flour
2 tablespoons unsweetened cocoa powder
2 teaspoons salt
2 teaspoons caraway seeds
1½ cups golden raisins

Glaze:
1 tablespoon GRANDMA'S® Gold Molasses
1 tablespoon water
2 tablespoons caraway seeds

1. Dissolve 1 teaspoon Grandma's® Gold Molasses and yeast in ¼ cup warm water in small bowl. Let stand until foamy, about 5 minutes.

2. Combine flours, cocoa, salt and 2 teaspoons caraway seeds in 12-cup food processor fitted with dough or steel blade. Add yeast mixture; mix well. Combine remaining 1 cup warm water and 3 tablespoons Grandma's® Gold Molasses in medium bowl.

3. With machine running, pour molasses mixture slowly through food tube. When dough forms a ball, process 1 minute. If dough sticks to side of bowl, add additional flour, 2 tablespoons at a time. If dough is too dry and does not stick together, add water, 1 tablespoon at a time.

4. Place dough in large greased bowl and turn to coat; cover with plastic wrap. Bring large shallow pot of water to a simmer. Remove from heat; place wire rack in pot. Place bowl with dough on rack; cover with towel. Let rise 1 to 1¼ hours or until doubled in bulk.

5. Punch dough down; flatten to ¼-inch thickness. Sprinkle with raisins; roll up dough and knead several times. Shape into 8-inch round; place on greased baking sheet. Place on rack over hot water as directed above; cover with towel. Let rise 1 to 1¼ hours or until doubled.

6. For glaze, combine 1 tablespoon Grandma's® Gold Molasses and 1 tablespoon water. Brush over loaf; sprinkle with 2 tablespoons caraway seeds.

7. Bake in 350°F oven 25 to 30 minutes until bread sounds hollow when tapped. Cool on rack 30 minutes.

Makes 1 large loaf

• Classic Tip •

Cocoa powder should not be confused with cocoa mixes or instant cocoa powder that contain cocoa powder combined with sweeteners and often dried milk powder. Unsweetened cocoa powder can be stored in a tightly closed container in a cool, dark place for up to two years.

FANFARE DINNER ROLLS

1 cup warm water (105°F to 115°F)
2 envelopes quick-rising dry yeast
¼ teaspoon sugar
⅔ cup whole milk, room temperature
⅓ cup sugar
¼ cup WESSON® Canola Oil
1 large egg
1 tablespoon poppy seeds
2½ teaspoons salt
5⅓ cups all-purpose flour
1 cup (2 sticks) chilled unsalted butter, cut into
    thin slices
    WESSON® No-Stick Cooking Spray
3 tablespoons unsalted butter, melted
    Poppy seeds

Pour water into a large bowl. Sprinkle yeast, then ¼ teaspoon sugar into water; stir well. Let stand 5 to 8 minutes or until mixture is slightly foamy. Meanwhile, in a small bowl, whisk milk, ⅓ cup sugar, Wesson® Oil, egg, poppy seeds and salt until well blended. Pour milk mixture into yeast mixture; mix well. Gradually add 1 cup flour to mixture and stir until batter is smooth. In a food processor, combine 4 cups flour and chilled butter; process until mixture resembles a coarse meal. Add to batter and stir until dry ingredients are moistened. Knead dough in bowl (about 5 minutes) until smooth. Add more flour if dough is sticky. Cover with towels and let rise in a warm place for 30 minutes or until dough nearly doubles in size.

Spray 24 muffin cups with Wesson® Cooking Spray. Turn dough onto floured surface; knead about 4 minutes until dough is smooth and elastic. Evenly divide dough into 4 portions. Place 1 portion on floured surface; cover and refrigerate remaining portions. Roll dough to 13×12×1/8-inch rectangle. Cut rectangle lengthwise into six 2-inch strips. Stack strips on top of each other to form 6 layers. Cut stack into 6 equal individual small stacks. Place each stack, cut side down, into muffin cup. Repeat with remaining dough sections. Cover with a towel; let rise in a warm place for 30 minutes or until nearly doubled in size.

Position one rack in the center of oven and the other rack above the first, allowing plenty of space for rolls to continue rising while baking. Preheat oven to 350°F. Brush rolls gently with melted butter; sprinkle with poppy seeds. Bake for 25 minutes until golden brown. Switch muffin pans halfway through bake time. Cool rolls 7 to 10 minutes. Remove rolls from pan; cool on wire rack. Serve warm. *Makes 2 dozen rolls*

Tip: If you have any leftover dough, roll it into balls. Roll each ball lightly in Wesson® Oil and cinnamon-sugar. Place on a cookie sheet and bake until golden brown.

CHOCOLATE CHIP COFFEECAKE

3 cups all-purpose flour
⅓ cup sugar
2 envelopes FLEISCHMANN'S® RapidRise™ Yeast
1 teaspoon salt
½ cup milk
½ cup water
½ cup butter or margarine
2 large eggs
¾ cup semi-sweet chocolate morsels
   Chocolate Nut Topping (recipe follows)

In large bowl, combine 1 cup flour, sugar, undissolved yeast, and salt. Heat milk, water and butter until very warm (120° to 130°F). Gradually add to dry ingredients. Beat 2 minutes at medium speed of electric mixer, scraping bowl occasionally. Add eggs and 1 cup flour; beat 2 minutes at high speed, scraping bowl occasionally. Stir in chocolate morsels and remaining flour to make a soft batter. Turn into greased 13×9×2-inch baking pan. Cover; let rise in warm, draft-free place until doubled in size, about 1 hour.

Bake at 400°F for 15 minutes; remove from oven and sprinkle with Chocolate Nut Topping. Return to oven and bake additional 10 minutes or until done. Cool in pan for 10 minutes. Remove from pan; cool on wire rack.

Makes 1 cake

Chocolate Nut Topping: In medium bowl, cut ½ cup butter into ⅔ cup all-purpose flour until crumbly. Stir in ⅔ cup sugar, 2 teaspoons ground cinnamon, 1 cup semi-sweet chocolate morsels, and 1 cup chopped pecans.

FRUIT–FILLED PETAL ROLLS

1 package BOB EVANS® Frozen White Dinner
   Roll Dough
¼ cup spreadable fruit or fruit pie filling
1 cup powdered sugar
1 tablespoon orange juice

Thaw dough at room temperature 45 minutes to 1 hour; do not allow dough to begin rising. Knead dough until smooth. Stretch dough and roll into 12-inch square. Cut into 9 (4-inch) squares. Grease muffin pan; press dough squares into cups so that corners are standing up. Place 1 rounded teaspoon fruit filling in each cup. Allow rolls to rise according to package directions. Preheat oven to 350°F. Bake 15 minutes or until lightly browned; let cool slightly. For glaze, combine powdered sugar and orange juice until smooth. Brush tops of rolls with glaze. Serve warm or at room temperature with butter or margarine.

Makes 9 rolls

CHOCOLATE CHIP COFFEECAKE

Cakes & Pies

EASY CAPPUCCINO CAKE

1 package (2-layer size) white cake mix
4 tablespoons MAXWELL HOUSE® Instant Coffee, divided
¼ cup milk plus 1 tablespoon milk
4 squares BAKER'S® Semi-Sweet Baking Chocolate, melted
2 tubs (8 ounces each) COOL WHIP® Whipped Topping, thawed, divided

HEAT oven to 350°F.

PREPARE and bake cake mix as directed on package for 8- or 9-inch round pans, adding 2 tablespoons instant coffee to cake mix.

POUR ¼ cup milk and 1 tablespoon instant coffee into small bowl, stirring until coffee is dissolved. Slowly stir into melted chocolate until smooth. Cool completely. Gently stir in 1 tub of whipped topping. Refrigerate 20 minutes, or until well chilled.

MEANWHILE, mix 1 tablespoon milk and 1 tablespoon coffee until dissolved. Gently stir into remaining tub of whipped topping.

COVER one cake layer with chocolate mixture. Place second cake layer on top. Frost top and side of cake with coffee-flavored whipped topping. Refrigerate until ready to serve. *Makes 14 servings*

Variation: If desired, omit the coffee for a delicious plain chocolate filled layer cake.

Prep Time: 25 minutes

HERSHEY'S BEST LOVED CHOCOLATE CHEESECAKE

Quick Chocolate Crumb Crust (recipe follows)
3 (8-ounce) packages cream cheese, softened
1¼ cups sugar
1 container (8 ounces) dairy sour cream
2 teaspoons vanilla extract
½ cup HERSHEY'S Cocoa
2 tablespoons all-purpose flour
3 eggs
Quick Chocolate Drizzle (recipe follows)

1. Prepare Quick Chocolate Crumb Crust. Heat oven to 450°F.

2. Beat cream cheese and sugar until blended. Add sour cream and vanilla; beat until blended. Beat in cocoa and flour. Add eggs, one at a time; beat just until blended. Pour into crust.

3. Bake 10 minutes. *Reduce oven temperature to 250°F;* continue baking 40 minutes. Remove from oven to wire rack. With knife, loosen cake from side of pan. Cool completely; remove side of pan. Prepare Quick Chocolate Drizzle; drizzle over top. Refrigerate 4 to 6 hours. Store covered in refrigerator.

Makes 12 servings

Quick Chocolate Crumb Crust: Combine 1 cup chocolate wafer crumbs and ¼ cup (½ stick) butter or margarine; press onto bottom of 9-inch springform pan. Makes 1 (9-inch) crust.

Quick Chocolate Drizzle: Place ½ cup HERSHEY'S Semi-Sweet Chocolate Chips and 2 teaspoons shortening (do not use butter, margarine, spread or oil) in small microwave-safe bowl. Microwave at HIGH (100%) 30 seconds. If necessary, microwave at HIGH an additional 15 seconds at a time, stirring after each heating, just until chips are melted.

• Classic Tip •

To easily make wafer crumbs, place wafers in a resealable food storage bag. Gently squeeze all the air out of the bag and seal. Place the bag on a counter and gently roll a rolling pin over the bag until fine crumbs are formed.

Cakes & Pies

CARAMEL PECAN SPICE CAKES

Cake
- 1 package DUNCAN HINES® Moist Deluxe® Spice Cake Mix
- 1 package (4-serving size) vanilla instant pudding and pie filling mix
- 4 eggs
- 1 cup water
- ⅓ cup vegetable oil
- 1½ cups pecan pieces, toasted and finely chopped

Caramel Glaze
- 3 tablespoons butter or margarine
- 3 tablespoons brown sugar
- 3 tablespoons granulated sugar
- 3 tablespoons whipping cream
- ½ cup confectioners' sugar
- ¼ teaspoon vanilla extract
- Pecan halves, for garnish
- Maraschino cherry halves, for garnish

1. Preheat oven to 350°F. Grease and flour two 8½×4½×2½-inch loaf pans.

2. For cake, combine cake mix, pudding mix, eggs, water and oil in large bowl. Beat at medium speed with electric mixer for 2 minutes. Stir in toasted pecans. Pour batter into pans. Bake at 350°F for 55 to 60 minutes or until toothpick inserted in center comes out clean. Cool in pans 15 minutes. Loosen loaves from pans. Invert onto cooling rack. Turn right sides up. Cool completely.

3. For caramel glaze, combine butter, brown sugar, granulated sugar and whipping cream in small heavy saucepan. Bring to a boil on medium heat; boil 1 minute. Remove from heat; cool 20 minutes. Add confectioners' sugar and vanilla extract; blend with wooden spoon until smooth and thick. Spread evenly on cooled loaves. Garnish with pecan halves and maraschino cherry halves before glaze sets.

Makes 2 loaves (24 slices)

STRAWBERRY HEAVEN

- 1 purchased tube angel food cake (9 to 10 inch)
- 1 pint strawberries, crushed
- 1 tablespoon 2% lowfat milk
- 1 tub (8 ounces) COOL WHIP LITE® Whipped Topping, thawed*
- Additional strawberries

*If using a homemade angel food cake, use a 12-ounce tub of COOL WHIP LITE Whipped Topping.

CUT cake horizontally into 3 layers. Place bottom cake layer on serving plate.

STIR crushed strawberries and milk into 1 cup of the whipped topping in large bowl with wire whisk until blended.

SPREAD ½ of the strawberry mixture onto cake layer; top with second cake layer. Repeat layers, ending with cake. Frost top and sides of cake with remaining whipped topping.

REFRIGERATE 1 hour or until ready to serve. Garnish with additional strawberries.   *Makes 12 servings*

Cakes & Pies

DOUBLE CHOCOLATE SNACK CAKE

1 package DUNCAN HINES® Moist Deluxe®
  Devil's Food Cake Mix
1 cup white chocolate chips, divided
½ cup semisweet chocolate chips

Preheat oven to 350°F. Grease and flour 13×9-inch pan.

Prepare cake mix as directed on package. Stir in ½ cup white chocolate chips and semisweet chips. Pour into prepared pan. Bake 35 to 40 minutes or until toothpick inserted in center comes out clean. Remove from oven; sprinkle top with remaining ½ cup white chocolate chips. Serve warm or cool completely in pan.

Makes 12 to 16 servings

Tip: For a special dessert, serve cake warm with a scoop of vanilla ice cream or whipped cream garnished with chocolate chips.

FRUITY JELL-O® CAKE

FRUITY JELL-O® CAKE

2 cups chopped strawberries

1 can (20 ounces) crushed pineapple, drained
1 package (8-serving size) or 2 packages (4-serving size each) JELL-O® Brand Strawberry Flavor Gelatin
3 cups miniature marshmallows
1 package (2-layer size) white cake mix
2 eggs

HEAT oven to 350°F.

ARRANGE fruit on bottom of 13×9-inch pan. Sprinkle with gelatin. Cover with marshmallows.

PREPARE cake mix as directed on package, omitting oil and using 2 eggs and water as specified. Spread batter over mixture in pan.

BAKE 50 to 55 minutes. Remove to rack; cool 15 minutes. Serve warm with thawed COOL WHIP Whipped Topping, if desired. *Makes 24 servings*

Prep Time: 15 minutes
Bake Time: 55 minutes

CARROT CAKE

CAKE

- 1¼ pounds carrots, scraped and cut lengthwise into 2-inch pieces (about 8 to 10 medium carrots)*
- 2 cups granulated sugar
- 1½ CRISCO® Sticks or 1½ cups CRISCO® all-vegetable shortening plus additional for greasing
- 4 eggs
- ½ cup water
- 2 cups all-purpose flour
- 1 tablespoon ground cinnamon
- 2 teaspoons baking soda
- 1 teaspoon salt

FROSTING

- 1 package (8 ounces) cream cheese, softened
- ½ Butter Flavor CRISCO® Stick or ½ cup Butter Flavor CRISCO® all-vegetable shortening
- 1 box (1 pound) confectioners' sugar (3½ to 4 cups)
- 1 teaspoon vanilla
- ¼ teaspoon salt

GARNISH (OPTIONAL)

Chopped nuts
Carrot curls

Grate carrots very finely if food processor is unavailable.

1. Heat oven to 350°F. Grease 13×9×2-inch insulated pan. Flour lightly.

2. For cake, place carrots in food processor. Process until very fine and moist. Measure 3 cups carrots.

3. Combine granulated sugar and 1½ cups shortening in large bowl. Beat at medium speed of electric mixer until creamy. Beat in eggs until blended. Beat in water at low speed until blended.

4. Combine flour, cinnamon, baking soda and 1 teaspoon salt in medium bowl. Add to creamed mixture. Beat at low speed until blended.

CARROT CAKE

Beat 2 minutes at medium speed. Add carrots. Beat until well blended. Pour into pan.

5. Bake at 350°F for 40 to 55 minutes or until toothpick inserted in center comes out clean*. *Do not overbake.* Cool 10 minutes before removing from pan. Invert cake on wire rack. Cool completely. Place cake on serving tray.

6. For frosting, combine cream cheese and ½ cup shortening in large bowl. Beat at medium speed until blended. Reduce speed to low. Add confectioners' sugar, vanilla and ¼ teaspoon salt. Beat until blended. Beat at medium speed until frosting is of desired spreading consistency. Frost top and sides of cake.

7. For optional garnish, place nuts and carrot curls on each serving.   *Makes 12 to 16 servings*

If cake is baked in non-insulated pan, baking time will be shorter. Test for doneness at minimum baking time.

MOLTEN MOCHA CAKES

1 package BAKER'S® Semi-Sweet Baking
   Chocolate
1 cup (2 sticks) butter
2 cups powdered sugar
½ cup GENERAL FOODS INTERNATIONAL
   COFFEES®, any flavor
5 eggs
4 egg yolks
¾ cup flour
   Powdered sugar (optional)
   Raspberries (optional)

HEAT oven to 425°F. Butter eight ¾-cup custard cups or soufflé dishes. Place on cookie sheet.

MICROWAVE chocolate and butter in large microwavable bowl on HIGH 2 minutes or until butter is melted. Stir with wire whisk until chocolate is completely melted. Stir in sugar and flavored instant coffee until well blended. Whisk in eggs and egg yolks. Stir in flour. Divide batter among custard cups.

BAKE 14 to 15 minutes or until sides are firm but centers are soft. Let stand 1 minute, then run small knife around cakes to loosen. Invert cakes onto dessert dishes. Sprinkle with powdered sugar and garnish with raspberries, if desired. *Makes 8 cakes*

Make-Ahead: Bake as directed above. Cool slightly, then cover custard cups with plastic wrap. Refrigerate up to 2 days. Place custard cups on cookie sheet. Reheat in 425°F oven for 12 to 13 minutes.

Prep Time: 15 minutes
Bake Time: 15 minutes

CHOCOLATE PUDDING POKE CAKE

1 package (2-layer size) white cake mix
2 egg whites
1⅓ cups water
4 cups cold fat free milk
2 packages (4-serving size each) JELL-O®
   Chocolate Flavor Fat Free Sugar Free Instant
   Reduced Calorie Pudding & Pie Filling

PREPARE cake as directed on package for 13×9-inch baking pan using 2 egg whites and 1⅓ cups water. Remove from oven. Immediately poke holes down through cake to pan with round handle of a wooden spoon. (Or poke holes with a plastic drinking straw, using turning motion to make large holes.) Holes should be at 1-inch intervals.

POUR milk into large bowl. Add pudding mixes. Beat with wire whisk 2 minutes. Quickly pour about ½ of the thin pudding mixture evenly over warm cake and into holes to make stripes. Let remaining pudding mixture stand to thicken slightly. Spoon over top of cake, swirling to "frost" cake.

REFRIGERATE at least 1 hour or until ready to serve. Store cake in refrigerator. *Makes 15 servings*

Prep Time: 30 minutes plus refrigerating

BLACK FOREST CAKE

MAZOLA NO STICK® Cooking Spray
1 package (18.25 ounces) chocolate cake mix plus
   ingredients as label directs
   Fluffy Frosting (recipe follows)
1 can (21 ounces) cherry pie filling
1 tablespoon cherry flavor liqueur (optional)
2 egg whites

1. Preheat oven to 350°F. Spray 2 (9-inch) round cake pans with cooking spray.

2. Prepare and bake cake mix according to package directions for 2 (9-inch) round layers. Cool on wire rack 10 minutes. Remove from pans; cool completely.

3. Prepare Fluffy Frosting.

4. Place one layer right side up on cake plate. Spoon 1-inch-thick ring of Fluffy Frosting around edge of cake.

5. Combine cherry pie filling and liqueur; spoon half onto cake layer, inside frosting ring.

6. Top with second cake layer, bottom side up. Spread thin layer of frosting over top of cake. Spread 2-inch-wide ring of frosting around top edge of cake; generously frost side of cake with remaining frosting. Spoon remaining cherry filling on top of cake, inside frosting.
Makes 12 servings

Prep Time: 30 minutes
Bake Time: 30 minutes, plus cooling

FLUFFY FROSTING

  2 egg whites
⅛ teaspoon salt
  1 cup KARO® Light Corn Syrup
¼ cup sugar
1½ teaspoons vanilla

1. In large bowl with mixer at high speed, beat egg whites and salt until soft peaks form.

2. In small saucepan combine corn syrup and sugar. Stirring constantly, cook over medium-low heat until sugar dissolves and mixture comes to full boil. Remove from heat.

3. Beating constantly, pour hot syrup into egg whites in a fine steady stream. Beat in vanilla. Continue beating until mixture holds stiff peaks. Use immediately. Makes enough to frost a two-layer 8- or 9-inch cake.

Makes about 2 cups

Coconut Frosting: Prepare Fluffy Frosting. Fold in 1 cup flaked coconut.

Spice Frosting: Follow recipe for Fluffy Frosting. Substitute 1 cup KARO® Dark Corn Syrup for light corn syrup. Add ½ teaspoon ground ginger, ¼ teaspoon cinnamon and dash ground cloves with corn syrup.

Prep Time: 15 minutes

BLACK FOREST CAKE

GINGERBREAD CAKE WITH LEMON SAUCE

Cake

  ¼ cup Butter Flavor CRISCO® all-vegetable
       shortening or ¼ Butter Flavor CRISCO® Stick
  ¼ cup firmly packed light brown sugar
  ¼ cup granulated sugar
  1 large egg, slightly beaten
  ½ cup buttermilk
  ¼ cup light molasses
  1 cup all-purpose flour
  2 teaspoons ground ginger
  1 teaspoon ground cinnamon
  ½ teaspoon baking soda
  ¼ teaspoon ground cloves
  ¼ teaspoon freshly grated nutmeg
  ¼ teaspoon salt

Lemon Sauce

  ½ cup granulated sugar
  ¼ cup unsalted butter
  3 tablespoons fresh lemon juice
  1 teaspoon vanilla

1. Heat oven to 375°F. Lightly spray 8-inch square or round cake pan with CRISCO® No-Stick Cooking Spray; set aside.

2. For cake, combine shortening, brown sugar and ¼ cup granulated sugar in large bowl. Beat at medium speed with electric mixer until well blended. Beat in egg, buttermilk and molasses until well blended.

3. Combine flour, ginger, cinnamon, baking soda, cloves, nutmeg and salt in medium bowl. Add to creamed mixture; mix well. Pour batter into prepared pan.

4. Bake at 375°F for 20 to 25 minutes or until wooden pick inserted into center comes out clean. Cool in pan 15 minutes. Turn out onto cooling rack.

5. For Lemon Sauce, combine all ingredients in small saucepan. Bring to boil over medium-high heat, stirring constantly. Reduce heat to low and simmer 5 minutes or until sauce is slightly thickened. Serve sauce over each slice of cake. *Makes 6 to 8 servings*

• Classic Tip •

The history of gingerbread in England dates back to the Middle Ages when fair ladies presented it to knights before they went into tournament battle.

HOT FUDGE SUNDAE CAKE

1 package DUNCAN HINES® Moist Deluxe® Dark Chocolate Fudge Cake Mix
½ gallon brick vanilla ice cream

Fudge Sauce

1 can (12 ounces) evaporated milk
1¼ cups sugar
4 squares (1 ounce each) unsweetened chocolate
¼ cup butter or margarine
1½ teaspoons vanilla extract
¼ teaspoon salt
Whipped cream and maraschino cherries, for garnish

1. Preheat oven to 350°F. Grease and flour 13×9×2-inch pan. Prepare, bake and cool cake following package directions.

2. Remove cake from pan. Split cake in half horizontally. Place bottom layer back in pan. Cut ice cream into even slices and place evenly over bottom cake layer (use all the ice cream). Place remaining cake layer over ice cream. Cover and freeze.

3. **For fudge sauce,** combine evaporated milk and sugar in medium saucepan. Stir constantly on medium heat until mixture comes to a rolling boil. Boil and stir for 1 minute. Add unsweetened chocolate and stir until melted. Beat over medium heat until smooth. Remove from heat. Stir in butter, vanilla and salt.

4. Cut cake into serving squares. For each serving, place cake square on plate; spoon hot fudge sauce on top. Garnish with whipped cream and maraschino cherry. *Makes 12 to 16 servings*

Tip: Fudge sauce may be prepared ahead and refrigerated in tightly sealed jar. Reheat when ready to serve.

HOT FUDGE SUNDAE CAKE

PEPPERMINT CAKE

CAKE
2¼ cups cake flour
2 teaspoons baking powder
1 teaspoon salt
½ teaspoon baking soda
1½ cups sugar
2 tablespoons margarine, softened
½ cup MOTT'S® Natural Apple Sauce
½ cup skim milk
4 egg whites
1 teaspoon vanilla extract

PEPPERMINT FROSTING
1½ cups sugar
¼ cup water
2 egg whites
¼ teaspoon cream of tartar
½ teaspoon peppermint extract
3 tablespoons crushed starlight candies (about 6)

1. Preheat oven to 350°F. Spray 9-inch round cake pan with nonstick cooking spray.

2. To prepare Cake, in medium bowl, combine flour, baking powder, salt and baking soda. In large bowl, beat 1½ cups sugar and margarine with electric mixer at medium speed until blended. Whisk in apple sauce, milk, 4 egg whites and vanilla.

3. Add flour mixture to apple sauce mixture; stir until well blended. Pour batter into prepared pan.

4. Bake 35 to 40 minutes or until toothpick inserted in center comes out clean. Cool completely on wire rack. Split cake horizontally in half to make 2 layers.

5. To prepare Peppermint Frosting, in top of double boiler, whisk together 1½ cups sugar, water, 2 egg whites and cream of tartar. Cook, whisking occasionally, over simmering water 4 minutes or until mixture is hot and sugar is dissolved. Remove from heat; stir in peppermint extract. Beat with electric mixer at high speed 3 minutes or until mixture forms stiff peaks.

6. Place one cake layer on serving plate. Spread with layer of Peppermint Frosting. Top with second cake layer. Frost top and side with remaining Peppermint Frosting. Sprinkle top and side of cake with crushed candies. Cut into 12 slices. Refrigerate leftovers.

Makes 12 servings

HERSHEY'S "PERFECTLY CHOCOLATE" CHOCOLATE CAKE

2 cups sugar
1¾ cups all-purpose flour
¾ cup HERSHEY'S Cocoa or HERSHEY'S Dutch Processed Cocoa
1½ teaspoons baking powder
1½ teaspoons baking soda
1 teaspoon salt
2 eggs
1 cup milk
½ cup vegetable oil
2 teaspoons vanilla extract
1 cup boiling water
"Perfectly Chocolate" Chocolate Frosting (recipe follows)

1. Heat oven to 350°F. Grease and flour two 9-inch round baking pans.*

2. Stir together sugar, flour, cocoa, baking powder, baking soda and salt in large bowl. Add eggs, milk, oil and vanilla; beat on medium speed of mixer 2 minutes. Stir in water. (Batter will be thin.) Pour batter evenly into prepared pans.

3. Bake 30 to 35 minutes or until wooden pick inserted in center comes out clean. Cool 10 minutes; remove from pans to wire racks. Cool completely.

4. Prepare "Perfectly Chocolate" Chocolate Frosting; spread between layers and over top and sides of cake.

Makes 8 to 10 servings

One 13×9×2-inch baking pan may be substituted for 9-inch round baking pans. Prepare as directed above. Bake 35 to 40 minutes. Cool completely in pan on wire rack. Frost as desired.

"PERFECTLY CHOCOLATE" CHOCOLATE FROSTING

1 stick (½ cup) butter or margarine
⅔ cup HERSHEY'S Cocoa
3 cups powdered sugar
⅓ cup milk
1 teaspoon vanilla extract

1. Melt butter. Stir in cocoa. Alternately add powdered sugar and milk, beating to spreading consistency.

2. Add small amount additional milk, if needed. Stir in vanilla. *Makes about 2 cups frosting*

LEMON CHIFFON PIE

⅔ cup boiling water
1 package (4-serving size) JELL-O® Brand Lemon Flavor Gelatin Dessert
2 teaspoons grated lemon peel
2 tablespoons lemon juice
½ cup cold water
Ice cubes
1 tub (8 ounces) COOL WHIP® Whipped Topping, thawed
1 prepared graham cracker crumb crust (6 ounces)

STIR boiling water into gelatin in large bowl at least 2 minutes or until completely dissolved. Stir in lemon peel and juice. Mix cold water and ice to make 1¼ cups. Add to gelatin, stirring until slightly thickened. Remove any remaining ice.

STIR in whipped topping with wire whisk until smooth. Refrigerate 20 to 30 minutes or until mixture is very thick and will mound. Spoon into crust.

REFRIGERATE 6 hours or overnight until firm. Garnish as desired. *Makes 8 servings*

Preparation Time: 20 minutes
Refrigerating Time: 6½ hours

CLASSIC RHUBARB PIE

CRUST
Classic CRISCO® Double Crust (page 303)
FILLING
4 cups red rhubarb, cut into ½- to ¾-inch pieces
1⅓ to 1½ cups sugar, to taste
⅓ cup all-purpose flour
2 tablespoons butter or margarine
GLAZE
1 tablespoon milk
Sugar

1. **For crust,** prepare crust as directed and press bottom crust into 9-inch pie plate leaving overhang. Do not bake. Heat oven to 400°F.

2. **For filling,** combine rhubarb and sugar in large bowl. Mix well. Stir in flour. Spoon into unbaked pie crust. Dot with butter. Moisten pastry edge with water.

3. Cover pie with woven lattice top (see page 00).

4. **For glaze,** brush with milk. Sprinkle with sugar. Cover edge with foil to prevent overbrowning. Bake at 400°F for 20 minutes. *Reduce oven temperature to 325°F.* Remove foil. Bake 30 minutes or until filling in center is bubbly and crust is golden brown (if using frozen rhubarb bake 60 to 70 minutes). *Do not overbake.* Cool until barely warm or to room temperature before serving. *Makes 1 (9-inch) pie*

LEMON CHIFFON PIE

DECADENT TRIPLE LAYER MUD PIE

¼ cup sweetened condensed milk
2 (1-ounce) squares semi-sweet baking chocolate, melted
1 (6-ounce) READY CRUST® Chocolate Pie Crust
¾ cup chopped pecans, toasted
2 cups cold milk
2 (4-serving-size) packages JELL-O® Chocolate Flavor Instant Pudding & Pie Filling
1 (8-ounce) tub COOL WHIP® Whipped Topping, thawed, divided

1. Combine sweetened condensed milk and chocolate in medium bowl; stir until smooth. Pour into crust. Press nuts evenly onto chocolate mixture in crust. Refrigerate 10 minutes.

2. Pour milk into large bowl. Add pudding mixes. Beat with wire whisk 2 minutes or until smooth. (Mixture will be thick.) Spread 1½ cups pudding over chocolate mixture in crust. Immediately stir half of whipped topping into remaining pudding. Spread over pudding in crust. Top with remaining whipped topping.

3. Refrigerate 3 hours or until set. Garnish as desired. Refrigerate leftovers. *Makes 8 servings*

Prep Time: 10 minutes
Chilling Time: 3 hours

DECADENT TRIPLE LAYER MUD PIE

KEY LIME PIE

1¾ cups boiling water
1 package (8-serving size) or 2 packages (4-serving size) JELL-O® Brand Lime Flavor Gelatin Dessert
2 teaspoons grated lime peel
¼ cup lime juice
1 pint (2 cups) vanilla ice cream, softened
1 prepared graham cracker crumb crust (6 ounces)

STIR boiling water into gelatin in large bowl at least 2 minutes until completely dissolved. Stir in lime peel and juice.

STIR in ice cream until melted and smooth. Refrigerate 15 to 20 minutes or until mixture is very thick and will mound. Spoon into crust.

REFRIGERATE 2 hours or until firm. Garnish as desired. *Makes 8 servings*

SWEET POTATO PECAN PIE

1 pound sweet potatoes or yams, cooked and peeled
¼ cup butter or margarine
1 (14-ounce) can EAGLE® BRAND Sweetened Condensed Milk (NOT evaporated milk)
1 teaspoon each ground cinnamon, grated orange peel and vanilla extract
½ teaspoon ground nutmeg
¼ teaspoon salt
1 egg
1 (6-ounce) graham cracker pie crust
Pecan Topping (recipe follows)

1. Preheat oven to 425°F. With mixer, beat hot sweet potatoes and butter until smooth. Add Eagle Brand and remaining ingredients except crust and Pecan Topping; mix well. Pour into crust.

2. Bake 20 minutes. Meanwhile, prepare Pecan Topping.

3. Remove pie from oven; reduce oven to 350°F. Spoon Pecan Topping on pie.

4. Bake 25 minutes longer or until set. Cool. Serve warm or at room temperature. Garnish with orange zest twist, if desired. Refrigerate leftovers.

Makes 1 pie

Pecan Topping: Beat together 1 egg, 2 tablespoons each dark corn syrup and firmly packed brown sugar, 1 tablespoon melted butter and ½ teaspoon maple flavoring. Stir in 1 cup chopped pecans. (Use Pecan Topping in recipe as noted above.)

Prep Time: 30 minutes
Bake Time: 45 minutes

SWEET POTATO PECAN PIE

BOSTON CREAM PIE

CAKE
2¼ cups cake flour
2 teaspoons baking powder
1 teaspoon salt
½ teaspoon baking soda
1½ cups granulated sugar
2 tablespoons margarine, softened
½ cup MOTT'S® Natural Apple Sauce
½ cup skim milk
4 egg whites
1 teaspoon vanilla extract

FILLING
1 (0.9-ounce) package sugar-free instant vanilla
   pudding
1½ cups skim milk

CHOCOLATE GLAZE
1½ cups powdered sugar
2 tablespoons unsweetened cocoa powder
1 tablespoon skim milk
½ teaspoon vanilla extract
   Lemon peel strips (optional)

1. Preheat oven to 350°F. Spray 9-inch round cake pan with nonstick cooking spray.

2. To prepare Cake, in medium bowl, combine flour, baking powder, salt and baking soda.

3. In large bowl, beat granulated sugar and margarine with electric mixer at medium speed until blended. Whisk in apple sauce, ½ cup milk, egg whites and 1 teaspoon vanilla.

4. Add flour mixture to apple sauce mixture; stir until well blended. Pour batter into prepared pan.

5. Bake 35 to 40 minutes or until toothpick inserted in center comes out clean. Cool completely on wire rack. Split cake horizontally in half to make 2 layers.

6. To prepare Filling, prepare pudding mix according to package directions using 1½ cups skim milk. (Or, substitute 1½ cups prepared fat-free vanilla pudding for Filling.)

7. To prepare Chocolate Glaze, in small bowl, sift together powdered sugar and cocoa. Stir in 1 tablespoon milk and ½ teaspoon vanilla. Add water, 1 teaspoon at a time, until of desired spreading consistency. Place one cake layer on serving plate. Spread filling over cake. Top with second cake layer. Spread top of cake with Chocolate Glaze. Let stand until set. Garnish with lemon peel, if desired. Cut into 10 slices. Refrigerate leftovers.   *Makes 10 servings*

COOKIES & CREME CAFÉ PIE

1 package (12.6 ounces) JELL-O® No Bake Cookies & Creme Dessert
⅓ cup butter *or* margarine, melted
1⅓ cups cold milk
¼ cup GENERAL FOODS INTERNATIONAL COFFEE®, Suisse Mocha Flavor, Vanilla Café Flavor or Irish Cream Café Flavor

STIR crust mix and butter thoroughly with spoon in medium bowl until crumbs are well moistened. Press onto bottom and up side of 9-inch pie plate.

POUR cold milk into large bowl. Add filling mix and coffee. Beat with electric mixer on low speed 30 seconds. Beat on high speed 3 minutes. Do not underbeat.

RESERVE ½ cup of the crushed cookies. Gently stir remaining crushed cookies into filling until well blended. Spoon mixture into prepared pie crust. Top with reserved cookies. Refrigerate 4 hours or until firm or freeze 2 hours to serve frozen. *Makes 8 servings*

Preparation Time: 15 minutes plus refrigerating

TURTLE NUT PIE

3 eggs
1 cup KARO® Light Corn Syrup
⅔ cup sugar
⅓ cup (5⅓ tablespoons) margarine or butter, melted
½ teaspoon salt
1 cup pecans
2 squares (1 ounce each) semisweet chocolate, melted
1 (9-inch) frozen deep dish pie crust*
½ cup caramel flavored topping for ice cream

*To use prepared frozen pie crust: Do not thaw. Preheat oven and a cookie sheet. Pour filling into frozen crust. Bake on cookie sheet.

1. Preheat oven to 350°F.

2. In medium bowl with fork, beat eggs slightly. Add corn syrup, sugar, margarine and salt; stir until well blended. Reserve ½ cup egg mixture; set aside.

3. Stir pecans and chocolate into remaining egg mixture; pour into pie crust.

4. Mix caramel topping and reserved egg mixture; carefully pour over pecan filling.

5. Bake 50 to 55 minutes or until filling is set about 3 inches from edge. Cool completely on wire rack.

Makes 8 servings

Prep Time: 20 minutes
Bake Time: 50 minutes, plus cooling

CHERRY–TOPPED LEMON CHEESECAKE PIE

1 (8-ounce) package cream cheese, softened
1 (14-ounce) can EAGLE® BRAND Sweetened
   Condensed Milk (NOT evaporated milk)
⅓ cup REALEMON® Lemon Juice From
   Concentrate
1 teaspoon vanilla extract
1 (6-ounce) ready-made graham cracker crumb pie
   crust
1 (21-ounce) can cherry pie filling, chilled

1. In large bowl, beat cream cheese until fluffy.
Gradually beat in Eagle Brand until smooth. Stir in
ReaLemon and vanilla. Pour into crust. Chill at least
3 hours.

2. To serve, top with cherry pie filling. Store covered in
refrigerator.   *Makes 6 to 8 servings*

Note: For a firmer crust, brush crust with slightly
beaten egg white; bake in 375°F oven 5 minutes. Cool
before pouring filling into crust.

Prep Time: 10 minutes
Chill Time: 3 hours

GRASSHOPPER MINT PIE

GRASSHOPPER MINT PIE

1 (8-ounce) package cream cheese, softened
⅓ cup sugar
1 (8-ounce) tub frozen whipped topping, thawed
1 cup chopped KEEBLER® Fudge Shoppe®
   Grasshopper Cookies
3 drops green food coloring
1 (6-ounce) READY CRUST® Chocolate Pie Crust
   Additional KEEBLER® Fudge Shoppe®
   Grasshopper Cookies, halved, for garnish

1. Mix cream cheese and sugar with electric mixer until
well blended. Fold in whipped topping, chopped
cookies and green food coloring. Spoon into crust.

2. Refrigerate 3 hours or overnight.

3. Garnish with cookie halves. Refrigerate leftovers.

Makes 8 servings

Preparation Time: 15 minutes
Chilling Time: 3 hours

EASY PEANUT BUTTER CHIP PIE

1 package (3 ounces) cream cheese, softened

1 teaspoon lemon juice

1⅔ cups (10-ounce package) REESE'S® Peanut Butter Chips, divided

⅔ cup sweetened condensed milk (not evaporated milk)

1 cup (½ pint) cold whipping cream, divided

1 packaged chocolate or graham cracker crumb crust (6 ounces)

1 tablespoon powdered sugar

1 teaspoon vanilla extract

1. Beat cream cheese and lemon juice in medium bowl until fluffy, about 2 minutes; set aside.

2. Place 1 cup peanut butter chips and sweetened condensed milk in medium microwave-safe bowl. Microwave at HIGH (100%) 45 seconds; stir. If necessary, microwave an additional 15 seconds at a time, stirring after each heating, until chips are melted and mixture is smooth when stirred.

3. Add warm peanut butter mixture to cream cheese mixture. Beat on medium speed until blended, about 1 minute. Beat ½ cup whipping cream in small bowl until stiff; fold into peanut butter mixture. Pour into crust. Cover; refrigerate several hours or overnight until firm.

4. Just before serving, combine remaining ½ cup whipping cream, powdered sugar and vanilla in small bowl. Beat until stiff; spread over filling. Garnish with remaining peanut butter chips. Cover; refrigerate leftover pie. *Makes 6 to 8 servings*

EASY PEANUT BUTTER CHIP PIE

PEACH YOGURT PIE WITH RASPBERRY SAUCE

CRUST
  1 cup graham cracker crumbs
  ¼ cup sugar
  3 tablespoons CRISCO® Oil*
  1¼ teaspoons water

FILLING
  1 quart peach flavor frozen yogurt, softened

SAUCE
  1 package (12 ounces) frozen unsweetened
     raspberries, thawed
  ⅓ cup sugar
  1 teaspoon cornstarch
  ⅛ teaspoon salt
  ¼ teaspoon almond extract

Use your favorite Crisco Oil product.

1. Heat oven to 350°F. Place cooling rack on countertop.

2. For crust, combine graham cracker crumbs, sugar, oil and water in 9-inch pie plate. Mix with fork. Press firmly against bottom and up side of pie plate.

3. Bake at 350°F for 8 minutes. *Do not overbake.* Remove pie plate to cooling rack. Cool completely.

4. For filling, spread softened yogurt into cooled crust. Freeze 2½ to 3 hours or until firm.

5. For sauce, combine raspberries, sugar, cornstarch and salt in small saucepan. Cook and stir over medium heat until mixture comes to a boil and is thickened. Press through sieve to remove seeds. Stir in almond extract. Cool to room temperature. Refrigerate. Drizzle over pie just before serving. Garnish, if desired.

Makes 1 (9-inch) pie (8 servings)

• Classic Tip •

For a richer version of this pie, try substituting chocolate flavor frozen yogurt for the peach flavor frozen yogurt called for in the recipe.

VERY CHERRY PIE

4 cups frozen unsweetened tart cherries
1 cup dried tart cherries
1 cup sugar
2 tablespoons quick-cooking tapioca
½ teaspoon almond extract
   Pastry for double-crust 9-inch pie
¼ teaspoon ground nutmeg
1 tablespoon butter

Combine frozen cherries, dried cherries, sugar, tapioca and almond extract in large mixing bowl; mix well. (It is not necessary to thaw cherries before using.) Let cherry mixture stand 15 minutes.

Line 9-inch pie plate with pastry; fill with cherry mixture. Sprinkle with nutmeg. Dot with butter. Cover with top crust, cutting slits for steam to escape. Or, cut top crust into strips for lattice top and cherry leaf cutouts.

Bake in preheated 375°F oven about 1 hour or until crust is golden brown and filling is bubbly. If necessary, cover edge of crust with foil to prevent overbrowning.

Makes 8 servings

Note: Two (16-ounce) cans unsweetened tart cherries, well drained, can be substituted for frozen tart cherries. Dried cherries are available at gourmet and specialty food stores and at selected supermarkets.

Favorite recipe from **Cherry Marketing Institute**

FROZEN BLACK–BOTTOM–PEANUT BUTTER PIE

37 RITZ® Crackers
 6 tablespoons butter *or* margarine, melted
⅓ cup hot fudge dessert topping, heated slightly to soften
 1 cup creamy peanut butter
 1 cup cold milk
 1 package (4-serving size) JELL-O® Vanilla *or* Chocolate Flavor Instant Pudding & Pie Filling
 1 tub (8 ounces) COOL WHIP® Whipped Topping, thawed
   Chopped peanuts (optional)

CRUSH crackers in zipper-style plastic bag with rolling pin or in food processor. Mix cracker crumbs and butter. Press onto bottom and up side of 9-inch pie plate; chill. Carefully spread fudge topping over crust.

BEAT peanut butter and milk in large bowl with wire whisk until blended. Add pudding mix. Beat with wire whisk 2 minutes or until well blended. Stir in ½ tub whipped topping. Spoon into crust. Spread remaining whipped topping over top.

FREEZE 4 hours. Sprinkle with chopped peanuts.

Makes 8 servings

Great Substitute: Try using chunky peanut butter instead of creamy for extra peanut flavor.

Prep Time: 10 minutes plus refrigerating

VERY CHERRY PIE

FUDGY PECAN PIE

2 (1-ounce) squares unsweetened chocolate
¼ cup (½ stick) butter or margarine
1 (14-ounce) can EAGLE® BRAND Sweetened
    Condensed Milk (NOT evaporated milk)
½ cup hot water
2 eggs, well beaten
1¼ cups pecan halves or pieces
1 teaspoon vanilla extract
⅛ teaspoon salt
1 (9-inch) unbaked pie crust

1. Preheat oven to 350°F. In medium saucepan over low heat, melt chocolate and butter. Stir in Eagle Brand, hot water and eggs; mix well.

2. Remove from heat; stir in pecans, vanilla and salt. Pour into pie crust. Bake 40 to 45 minutes or until center is set. Cool slightly. Serve warm or chilled. Garnish as desired. Store covered in refrigerator.

Makes 1 (9-inch) pie

Prep Time: 15 minutes
Bake Time: 40 to 45 minutes

APPLE-RAISIN COBBLER PIE

APPLE–RAISIN COBBLER PIE

2 (20-ounce) cans apple pie filling
1 cup raisins
¼ teaspoon ground nutmeg
1 (6-ounce) READY CRUST® Shortbread Pie Crust
⅓ cup all-purpose flour
¼ cup packed brown sugar
3 tablespoons butter or margarine, melted
¾ cup chopped walnuts

1. Preheat oven to 375°F.

2. Combine pie filling, raisins and nutmeg in large bowl. Spoon into crust. Combine flour and sugar in small bowl; stir in butter until crumbly. Stir in walnuts; sprinkle over filling.

3. Bake 35 to 45 minutes or until topping is golden.

Makes 8 servings

Prep Time: 10 minutes
Baking Time: 35 minutes

SPARKLING FRUIT TART

1 cup boiling water
1 package (4-serving size) JELL-O® Brand
  Strawberry Flavor Gelatin
1 package (10 ounces) frozen strawberries in syrup
1 can (11 ounces) mandarin orange segments,
  drained
1 small banana, sliced
1 prepared graham cracker pie crust (9-inch)

STIR boiling water into gelatin in large bowl at least
2 minutes until completely dissolved. Add frozen
strawberries. Stir until strawberries thaw and gelatin
becomes slightly thickened (consistency of unbeaten
egg whites).

ARRANGE orange and banana slices on bottom crust.
Carefully spoon gelatin mixture over fruit.

REFRIGERATE 4 hours or until firm. Garnish with
thawed COOL WHIP® Whipped Topping and fresh
strawberry fans, if desired.   *Makes 8 to 10 servings*

Great Substitute: Use a HONEY MAID® Honey
Graham Pie Crust (9 inch) instead of the refrigerated
pie crust.

Prep Time: 15 minutes plus refrigerating

CLASSIC CRISCO® DOUBLE CRUST

2 cups all-purpose flour
1 teaspoon salt
¾ CRISCO® Stick or ¾ cup CRISCO® all-vegetable
  shortening
5 tablespoons cold water (or more as needed)

1. Spoon flour into measuring cup and level. Combine
flour and salt in medium bowl.

2. Cut in ¾ cup shortening using pastry blender or
2 knives until all flour is blended to form pea-size
chunks.

3. Sprinkle with water, 1 tablespoon at a time. Toss
lightly with fork until dough forms a ball. Divide
dough in half.

4. Press dough between hands to form 5- to 6-inch
"pancake." Flour rolling surface and rolling pin lightly.
Roll both halves of dough into circle. Trim one circle of
dough 1 inch larger than upside-down pie plate.
Carefully remove trimmed dough. Set aside to reroll
and use for pastry cutout garnish, if desired.

5. Fold dough into quarters. Unfold and press into pie
plate. Trim edge even with plate. Add desired filling to
unbaked crust. Moisten pastry edge with water. Lift top
crust onto filled pie. Trim ½ inch beyond edge of pie
plate. Fold top edge under bottom crust. Flute. Cut slits
in top crust to allow steam to escape. Follow baking
directions given for that reicpe.

Makes 1 (9-inch) double crust

SUMMER BERRY PIE

¾ cup sugar
3 tablespoons cornstarch
1½ cups water
1 package (4-serving size) JELL-O® Brand Gelatin Dessert, any red flavor
1 cup blueberries
1 cup raspberries
1 cup sliced strawberries
1 prepared graham cracker crumb crust (6 ounces)
2 cups thawed COOL WHIP® Whipped Topping

MIX sugar and cornstarch in medium saucepan. Gradually stir in water until smooth. Stirring constantly, cook on medium heat until mixture comes to boil; boil 1 minute. Remove from heat. Stir in gelatin until completely dissolved. Cool to room temperature. Stir in berries. Pour into crust.

REFRIGERATE 3 hours or until firm. Top with whipped topping. *Makes 8 servings*

Preparation Time: 20 minutes
Refrigerating Time: 3 hours

GEORGIA PEACH PIE

Crust
1 unbaked 10-inch Classic CRISCO® Double Crust (page 303)

Filling
1 can (29 ounces) yellow cling peaches in heavy syrup
3 tablespoons reserved peach syrup
3 tablespoons cornstarch
1 cup sugar, divided
3 eggs
⅓ cup buttermilk
½ cup butter or margarine, melted
1 teaspoon vanilla

Glaze
2 tablespoons butter or margarine, melted
Additional sugar

1. Heat oven to 400°F.

2. For Filling, drain peaches, reserving 3 tablespoons syrup; set aside. Cut peaches into small pieces; place in large bowl. Combine cornstarch and 3 tablespoons sugar in medium bowl. Add 3 tablespoons reserved peach syrup; mix well. Add remaining sugar, eggs and buttermilk; mix well. Stir in ½ cup melted butter and vanilla. Pour over peaches; stir until peaches are coated. Pour filling into unbaked pie crust. Moisten pastry edge with water.

3. Cover pie with top crust. Fold top edge under bottom crust; flute with fingers or fork. Cut slits or designs in top crust to allow steam to escape.

4. For Glaze, brush top crust with 2 tablespoons melted butter. Sprinkle with additional sugar.

5. Bake at 400°F for 45 minutes or until filling in center is bubbly and crust is golden brown. *Do not overbake.* Cool to room temperature before serving.

Makes 1 (10-inch) pie

SUMMER BERRY PIE

Sweet Endings

UPSIDE—DOWN PEAR TART

½ cup sugar
2 tablespoons butter or margarine
2 teaspoons grated lemon peel
5 medium (2½ to 3 pounds) firm Northwest winter pears, peeled, cored and
    cut into eighths
1 tablespoon lemon juice
    Pastry for 9-inch single crust pie
    Vanilla yogurt

Heat sugar over medium heat in heavy 10-inch skillet with oven-safe handle until syrupy and light brown in color. Remove from heat and add butter and lemon peel; stir until butter melts. Arrange pears in two layers over hot sugar mixture in skillet. Fill open spaces with pear slices; sprinkle with lemon juice. Roll pastry to 10-inch round and place over pears. Bake at 425°F 25 to 30 minutes or until pastry is golden brown. Cool, in pan, 30 minutes. If there seems to be too much sauce in pan, pour excess sauce into 1-pint container and reserve to serve over tart. Invert tart onto shallow serving dish. Serve warm with yogurt. *Makes 6 to 8 servings*

*Favorite recipe from **Pear Bureau Northwest***

TRIPLE CHOCOLATE PARFAITS

⅔ cup granulated sugar

¼ cup unsweetened cocoa powder

2½ tablespoons cornstarch

2 cups milk

1 large egg

1 tablespoon butter

1 teaspoon vanilla extract

8 (½-inch) slices packaged chocolate or marbled pound cake

1¼ cups "M&M's"® Milk Chocolate Mini Baking Bits, divided

2 cups thawed frozen nondairy whipped topping

In medium saucepan combine sugar, cocoa powder and cornstarch; stir in milk. Cook over medium heat, stirring often, until mixture comes to a boil. Boil 1 minute, stirring constantly. Remove from heat. In small bowl beat egg lightly; stir in ½ cup hot milk mixture. Stir egg mixture into hot milk mixture in saucepan. Cook over medium heat 2 minutes, stirring constantly. Remove from heat; stir in butter and vanilla. Let pudding cool 15 minutes; stirring occasionally. Just before serving, cut cake into cubes. Divide half of cake cubes among 8 (8-ounce) parfait glasses. Evenly layer half of pudding, ½ cup "M&M's"® Milk Chocolate Mini Baking Bits and 1 cup whipped topping. Repeat layers. Decorate with remaining ¼ cup "M&M's"® Milk Chocolate Mini Baking Bits. Serve immediately.

Makes 8 servings

Tip: If you're short on time, prepare 2 packages (4-serving size each) instant chocolate pudding instead of making this stove-top version. Then assemble the parfaits as directed.

CRANBERRY COBBLER

2 (16-ounce) cans sliced peaches in light syrup, drained

1 (16-ounce) can whole berry cranberry sauce

1 package DUNCAN HINES® Cinnamon Swirl Muffin Mix

½ cup chopped pecans

⅓ cup butter or margarine, melted
Whipped topping or ice cream

Preheat oven to 350°F.

Cut peach slices in half lengthwise. Combine peach slices and cranberry sauce in *ungreased* 9-inch square pan. Knead swirl packet from Mix for 10 seconds.

Squeeze contents evenly over fruit.

Combine muffin mix, contents of topping packet from mix and pecans in large bowl. Add melted butter. Stir until thoroughly blended (mixture will be crumbly). Sprinkle crumbs over fruit. Bake 40 to 45 minutes or until lightly browned and bubbly. Serve warm with whipped topping.

Makes 9 servings

Tip: Store leftovers in the refrigerator. Reheat in microwave oven to serve warm.

FROZEN PUMPKIN SQUARES

1 cup fine gingersnap crumbs
¼ cup finely chopped walnuts
¼ cup (½ stick) butter *or* margarine, melted
1¼ cups cold milk
2 packages (4-serving size each) JELL-O® Vanilla
    Flavor Instant Pudding & Pie Filling
1 cup canned pumpkin
1 teaspoon pumpkin pie spice
1 tub (8 ounces) COOL WHIP® Whipped Topping,
    thawed, divided

MIX crumbs, walnuts and butter in small bowl. Reserve 2 tablespoons for garnish. Press onto bottom of foil-lined 8-inch square pan. Refrigerate.

POUR milk into large bowl. Add pudding mixes, pumpkin and spice. Beat with wire whisk 2 minutes or until well blended. Gently stir in 2¼ cups of the whipped topping. Spread over crust.

FREEZE 4 hours or until firm. Let stand at room temperature 10 minutes or until dessert can be easily cut. Cut into squares. Garnish with remaining whipped topping and sprinkle with reserved crumbs.

Makes 9 servings

Prep Time: 15 minutes
Freeze Time: 4 hours

FROZEN PUMPKIN SQUARE

• Classic Tip •

For easy snacking, wrap frozen squares individually and freeze. Take out as desired for quick snacks.

POACHED PEARS IN CRANBERRY SYRUP

1 quart (4 cups) cranberry juice
1 cup KARO® Light Corn Syrup
8 slices (¼ inch thick) unpeeled fresh ginger
2 cinnamon sticks (2 to 3 inches)
8 slightly underripe pears

1. In heavy 4-quart saucepot combine cranberry juice, corn syrup, ginger and cinnamon sticks; bring to boil over medium-high heat.

2. Peel pears, leaving stems attached. Add to cranberry liquid; cover. Reduce heat and simmer 15 to 20 minutes or until pears are tender. With slotted spoon transfer pears to shallow serving dish.

3. Remove ginger slices and cinnamon sticks. Discard all but 2 cups syrup in saucepot. Bring to boil; boil 10 to 12 minutes or until syrup thickens slightly. Spoon sauce over pears.   *Makes 8 servings*

Prep Time: 40 minutes

POACHED PEAR IN CRANBERRY SYRUP

CREAMY CHOCOLATE DIPPED STRAWBERRIES

1 cup HERSHEY'S Semi-Sweet Chocolate Chips
½ cup HERSHEY'S Premier White Chips
1 tablespoon shortening (do *not* use butter, margarine, spread or oil)
  Fresh strawberries, rinsed and patted dry (about 2 pints)

1. Line tray with wax paper.

2. Place chocolate chips, white chips and shortening in medium microwave-safe bowl. Microwave at HIGH (100%) 1 minute; stir. If necessary, microwave at HIGH

an additional 15 seconds at a time, stirring after each heating, just until chips are melted when stirred. Holding top, dip bottom two-thirds of each strawberry into melted mixture; shake gently to remove excess. Place on prepared tray.

3. Refrigerate about 1 hour or until coating is firm. Cover; refrigerate leftover dipped berries. For best results, use within 24 hours.

Makes about 3 dozen dipped berries

CHOCOLATE PLUNGE

⅔ cup light corn syrup
½ cup whipping (heavy) cream
1 package (8 squares) BAKER'S® Semi-Sweet
    Baking Chocolate *or* 2 package (4 ounces each)
    BAKER'S® GERMAN'S® Sweet Chocolate
    Assorted fresh fruit (strawberries, sliced kiwi
    fruit, pineapple, apple or banana), cookies,
    pound cake cubes or pretzels

MICROWAVE corn syrup and cream in large microwavable bowl on HIGH 1½ minutes or until mixture comes to boil. Add chocolate; stir until completely melted.

SERVE warm as dip with assorted fresh fruit, cookies, cake cubes or pretzels. *Makes 1½ cups*

Chocolate Peanut Butter Plunge: Stir in ½ cup peanut butter with chocolate.

Chocolate Raspberry Plunge: Stir in ¼ cup seedless raspberry jam with chocolate.

Mocha Plunge: Stir in 1 tablespoon MAXWELL HOUSE® Instant Coffee with chocolate.

Prep Time: 5 minutes

LEMON–BLUEBERRY PIE CUPS

6 vanilla wafer cookies
¾ cup canned blueberry pie filling
1 cup boiling water
1 package (4-serving size) JELL-O® Brand Lemon
    Flavor Gelatin
¾ cup cold water
½ tub (8 ounces) COOL WHIP® Whipped Topping,
    thawed

PLACE one vanilla wafer on bottom of each of 6 dessert cups. Top each wafer with 2 tablespoons pie filling. Set aside.

STIR boiling water into gelatin in large bowl at least 2 minutes until completely dissolved.

STIR in cold water. Refrigerate 10 to 15 minutes or until mixture is slightly thickened (consistency of unbeaten egg whites). Stir in ½ of the whipped topping until well blended. Spoon over pie filling in cups.

REFRIGERATE 2 hours or until firm. Garnish with remaining whipped topping, if desired.

Makes 6 servings

Great Substitutes: Try using cherry or pineapple pie filling instead of the blueberry pie filling.

Best of the Season: Garnish each serving with fresh berries, if desired.

Prep Time: 15 minutes
Refrigerate Time: 2¼ hours

PEACH MELBA DESSERT

1½ cups boiling water, divided
2 packages (4-serving size) JELL-O® Brand Raspberry Flavor Sugar Free Low Calorie Gelatin Dessert or JELL-O® Brand Raspberry Flavor Gelatin Dessert, divided
1 container (8 ounces) BREYERS® Vanilla Lowfat Yogurt
1 cup raspberries, divided
1 can (8 ounces) peach slices in juice, undrained
Cold water

STIR ¾ cup boiling water into 1 package of gelatin in large bowl at least 2 minutes or until completely dissolved. Refrigerate about 1 hour or until slightly thickened (consistency of unbeaten egg whites). Stir in yogurt and ½ cup raspberries. Reserve remaining raspberries for garnish. Pour gelatin mixture into serving bowl. Refrigerate about 2 hours or until set but not firm (gelatin should stick to finger when touched and should mound).

MEANWHILE, drain peaches, reserving juice. Add cold water to reserved juice to make 1 cup; set aside. Stir remaining ¾ cup boiling water into remaining package gelatin in large bowl at least 2 minutes until completely dissolved. Stir in measured juice and water. Refrigerate about 1 hour or until slightly thickened (consistency of unbeaten egg whites).

RESERVE several peach slices for garnish; chop remaining peaches. Stir chopped peaches into slightly thickened gelatin. Spoon over gelatin layer in bowl. Refrigerate 3 hours or until firm. Top with reserved peach slices and raspberries. *Makes 8 servings*

Preparation Time: 20 minutes
Refrigerating Time: 6 hours

CHOCOLATE–DIPPED STRAWBERRY PARFAITS

1 package (8 squares) BAKER'S® Semi-Sweet Chocolate
2 teaspoons butter or shortening
3 pints small strawberries, hulled
1 tub (8 ounces) COOL WHIP® Whipped Topping, thawed
Fresh mint leaves

MICROWAVE chocolate and butter in small microwavable bowl on HIGH 1½ to 2 minutes or until chocolate is almost melted, stirring halfway through heating time. Stir until chocolate is completely melted.

DIP strawberries into chocolate to coat at least ½ of the berry. Place on wax paper; let stand until chocolate is firm.

LAYER about 6 chocolate-dipped strawberries and ⅓ cup whipped topping in each of 8 dessert glasses just before serving. Garnish with mint leaves.

Makes 8 servings

PEACH MELBA DESSERT

314

FROZEN PUDDING TORTONI

FROZEN PUDDING TORTONI

1⅔ cups cold half-and-half
½ teaspoon almond extract
1 package (4-serving size) JELL-O® Vanilla Flavor Instant Pudding & Pie Filling
2 cups thawed COOL WHIP® Whipped Topping
¼ cup drained chopped maraschino cherries (optional)
½ cup chopped amaretti cookies (Italian almond-flavored cookies) *or* chopped toasted PLANTERS® Slivered Almonds

POUR half-and-half and almond extract into large bowl. Add pudding mix. Beat with wire whisk 2 minutes or until well blended. Gently stir in whipped topping. Stir in cherries and chopped cookies. Spoon into individual dessert dishes or paper-lined muffin cups.

FREEZE 3 hours or until firm.   *Makes 8 servings*

Great Substitute: Use JELL-O® Pistachio Flavor Instant Pudding instead of Vanilla Flavor. Garnish each serving with a dollop of thawed COOL WHIP® Whipped Topping and additional chopped amaretti cookies, if desired.

Prep Time: 10 minutes plus freezing

CREAMY CARAMEL FLANS

¾ **cup sugar**

4 eggs

1¾ **cups water**

1 (14-ounce) can EAGLE® BRAND Sweetened Condensed Milk (NOT evaporated milk)

1 teaspoon vanilla extract

⅛ **teaspoon salt**

Sugar Garnish (recipe follows, optional)

1. Preheat oven to 350°F. In heavy skillet over medium heat, cook and stir sugar until melted and caramel-colored. Pour into 8 ungreased 6-ounce custard cups, tilting to coat bottoms.

2. In large bowl, beat eggs; stir in water, Eagle Brand, vanilla and salt. Pour into prepared custard cups. Set cups in large shallow pan. Fill pan with 1 inch hot water.

3. Bake 25 minutes or until knife inserted near centers comes out clean. Cool. Chill. To serve, invert flans onto individual serving plates. Top with Sugar Garnish or garnish as desired. Store covered in refrigerator.

Makes 8 servings

Sugar Garnish: Fill a medium-sized metal bowl half-full of ice. In medium-sized saucepan, combine 1 cup sugar with ¼ cup water. Stir; cover and bring to a boil.

Cook over high heat 5 to 6 minutes or until light brown in color. Immediately put pan in ice for 1 minute. Using spoon, carefully drizzle sugar decoratively over foil. Cool. To serve, peel from foil.

Prep Time: 15 minutes
Bake Time: 25 minutes

CREAMY CARAMEL FLAN

CHOCOLATE SOUFFLÉ

½ cup sugar
¼ cup MINUTE® Tapioca
3 squares BAKER'S® Unsweetened Baking
   Chocolate, coarsely chopped
¼ teaspoon salt
2 cups milk
½ teaspoon vanilla
3 eggs, separated
   Boiling water
   White Chocolate Sauce (recipe follows)

HEAT oven to 325°F.

MIX sugar, tapioca, chocolate, salt and milk in medium saucepan. Let stand 5 minutes. Cook on medium heat, stirring constantly, until mixture comes to full boil. Remove from heat. Stir in vanilla.

BEAT egg whites in large bowl with electric mixer on high speed until stiff peaks form; set aside. Beat egg yolks in large bowl with electric mixer on high speed until thick and lemon colored. Stir in tapioca mixture. Fold in beaten egg whites. Pour into 6-cup soufflé dish or 1½-quart baking dish. Place dish in large baking pan, then place in oven. Carefully pour boiling water into pan to come 1 inch up side of soufflé dish.

BAKE 60 to 65 minutes or until firm. Serve warm with White Chocolate Sauce. *Makes 8 servings*

White Chocolate Sauce: Microwave 1 package (6 squares) BAKER'S® Premium White Baking Chocolate and 1 cup whipping (heavy) cream in large microwavable bowl on HIGH 4 minutes, stirring halfway through heating time. Stir with wire whisk until chocolate is melted and mixture is smooth. Makes 1½ cups.

Variation: Chocolate Soufflé can also be baked in 6 (1-cup) soufflé dishes. Bake 40 to 45 minutes or until firm.

Prep Time: 20 minutes
Bake Time: 65 minutes

GRANDMA'S® GINGERBREAD

½ cup shortening or butter
½ cup sugar
1 cup GRANDMA'S® Molasses
2 eggs
2½ cups all-purpose flour
1 teaspoon salt
2 teaspoons baking powder
½ teaspoon baking soda
1 teaspoon ground ginger
2 teaspoons ground cinnamon
½ teaspoon ground cloves
1 cup hot water

Heat oven to 350°F. In medium bowl, blend shortening with sugar, add molasses and eggs. Beat well. Sift dry ingredients, add alternately with water to molasses mixture. Bake in greased 9-inch square pan, about 50 minutes. *Makes 8 servings*

GRANDMA'S® GINGERBREAD

Sweet Endings

TROPICAL TERRINE

1 package (3 ounces) ladyfingers, split, divided
1½ cups boiling water
1 package (8-serving size) or 2 packages (4-serving size) JELL-O® Brand Orange Flavor Sugar Free Low Calorie Gelatin Dessert
1 can (8 ounces) crushed pineapple in juice, undrained
1 cup cold water
2 cups thawed COOL WHIP LITE® Whipped Topping
1 can (11 ounces) mandarin orange segments, drained
Additional thawed COOL WHIP LITE® Whipped Topping
Kiwi slices
Star fruit slices
Pineapple leaves

LINE bottom and sides of 9×5-inch loaf pan with plastic wrap. Add enough ladyfingers, cut sides in, to fit evenly along all sides of pan.

STIR boiling water into gelatin in large bowl 2 minutes or until completely dissolved. Stir in pineapple with juice and cold water. Refrigerate 1¼ hours or until slightly thickened (consistency of unbeaten egg whites). Gently stir in 2 cups whipped topping and oranges. Spoon into prepared pan. Arrange remaining ladyfingers, cut sides down, evenly on top of gelatin mixture.

REFRIGERATE 3 hours or until firm. Place serving plate on top of pan. Invert, holding pan and plate together; shake gently to loosen. Carefully remove pan and plastic wrap. Garnish with additional whipped topping, fruit and pineapple leaves.

Makes 12 servings

COOL TIPS: If you put a dab of shortening in the corners of the loaf pan, the plastic wrap will adhere to the pan more smoothly and easily. To keep its shape, leftover dessert can be returned to the loaf pan and refrigerated.

BAKED APPLES

2 tablespoons sugar
2 tablespoons GRANDMA'S® Molasses
2 tablespoons raisins, chopped
2 tablespoons walnuts, chopped
6 apples, cored

Heat oven to 350°F. In medium bowl, combine sugar, molasses, raisins and walnuts. Fill apple cavities with molasses mixture. Place in 13×9-inch baking dish. Pour ½ cup hot water over the apples and bake 25 minutes or until soft.

Makes 6 servings

STRAWBERRY SHORTCAKE

STRAWBERRY SHORTCAKES

6 tablespoons sugar, divided
1 pint sliced strawberries (about 2 cups)
2⅓ cups BISQUICK® Original Baking Mix
½ cup milk
3 tablespoons butter *or* margarine, melted
1 tub (8 ounces) COOL WHIP® Whipped Topping, thawed

HEAT oven to 425°F.

MIX 3 tablespoons sugar into strawberries; set aside. Stir baking mix, milk, butter and 3 tablespoons sugar in bowl until soft dough forms. Drop by 6 spoonfuls onto ungreased cookie sheet.

BAKE 10 to 12 minutes or until golden brown. Split warm shortcakes; fill and top with strawberries and whipped topping. *Makes 6 servings*

Special Extra: For a more decadent dessert, try adding 1 cup BAKER'S® Semi-Sweet Chocolate Chunks into the baking mix and proceed as directed above. Drizzle with your favorite chocolate sauce.

Prep Time: 6 minutes
Bake Time: 12 minutes

CHEESECAKE CREME DIP

1 package (8 ounces) PHILADELPHIA® Cream Cheese, softened
1 jar (7 ounces) marshmallow creme

MIX cream cheese and marshmallow creme with electric mixer on medium speed until well blended. Refrigerate.

SERVE with assorted cut-up fresh fruit or pound cake cubes. Garnish, if desired. *Makes 1¾ cups*

Prep Time: 5 minutes plus refrigerating

TIRAMISU

6 egg yolks
½ cup sugar
⅓ cup Cognac or brandy
2 cups (15 ounces) SARGENTO® Whole Milk
　Ricotta Cheese
1 cup whipping cream, whipped
32 ladyfingers, split in half
1 tablespoon instant coffee dissolved in ¾ cup
　boiling water
1 tablespoon unsweetened cocoa
　Chocolate curls (optional)

In top of double boiler, whisk together egg yolks, sugar and Cognac. Place pan over simmering water in bottom of double boiler. Cook, whisking constantly, about 2 to 3 minutes until mixture is thickened. Remove top of double boiler; cool yolk mixture completely. In large bowl of electric mixer, beat yolk mixture and Ricotta cheese on medium speed until blended. Fold in whipped cream.

Place half the ladyfingers in bottom of 13×9-inch pan, cut sides up. Brush with half the coffee; spread with half the Ricotta mixture. Repeat layers. Refrigerate 2 hours. Just before serving, dust with cocoa using fine sieve; cut into squares. Garnish with chocolate curls, if desired.   *Makes 16 servings*

Chocolate Curls: To prepare chocolate curls, combine ½ cup semisweet chocolate chips with 2 teaspoons vegetable shortening in 2-cup microwave-safe bowl. Microwave at HIGH 1 minute. Stir until chocolate is completely melted. Spread evenly into a thin layer on small cookie sheet. Let stand until firm. (Do not chill in refrigerator.) Hold small pancake turner upside down at 45° angle to cookie sheet. Run pancake turner across chocolate, allowing chocolate to curl.

TIRAMISU

PINEAPPLE FRUIT TART

¼ cup ground almonds (about 2 tablespoons whole almonds)
¼ cup butter or margarine, softened
¼ cup sugar
2 tablespoons milk
½ teaspoon almond extract
¾ cup all-purpose flour
2 packages (3 ounces each) cream cheese, softened
2 tablespoons sour cream
¼ cup apricot preserves, divided
1 teaspoon vanilla extract
1 can (15¼ ounces) DEL MONTE® Sliced Pineapple In Its Own Juice, drained and cut in halves
2 kiwifruits, peeled, sliced and cut into halves
1 cup sliced strawberries

1. Combine almonds, butter, sugar, milk and almond extract; mix well. Blend in flour. Chill dough 1 hour.

2. Press dough evenly onto bottom and up sides of tart pan with removable bottom.

3. Bake at 350°F, 15 to 18 minutes or until golden brown. Cool.

4. Combine cream cheese, sour cream, 1 tablespoon apricot preserves and vanilla. Spread onto crust. Arrange pineapple, kiwi and strawberries over cream cheese mixture.

5. Heat remaining 3 tablespoons apricot preserves in small saucepan over low heat. Spoon over fruit.

Makes 8 servings

CHOCOLATE MOUSSE

1½ cups cold 2% lowfat milk
1 package (4-serving size) JELL-O® Chocolate Flavor Fat Free Sugar Free Instant Reduced Calorie Pudding & Pie Filling
2 cups thawed COOL WHIP LITE® Whipped Topping
4 fat free chocolate cookies, chopped
   Additional thawed COOL WHIP LITE® Whipped Topping
   Additional chopped fat free chocolate cookies

POUR milk into medium bowl. Add pudding mix. Beat with wire whisk 2 minutes. Gently stir in 2 cups whipped topping. Spoon ½ of the mixture evenly into 6 individual dessert dishes. Sprinkle cookies evenly over pudding. Top with remaining pudding mixture.

REFRIGERATE until ready to serve. Garnish with additional whipped topping and chopped cookies.

Makes 6 servings

SOUTHERN BANANA PUDDING

1 package (4-serving size) JELL-O® Vanilla or
   Banana Cream Flavor Cook & Serve Pudding
   & Pie Filling *(not Instant)*
2½ cups milk
2 egg yolks, well beaten
30 to 35 vanilla wafers
2 large bananas, sliced
2 egg whites
   Dash salt
¼ cup sugar

HEAT oven to 350°F.

STIR pudding mix into milk in medium saucepan. Add
egg yolks. Stirring constantly, cook on medium heat
until mixture comes to full boil. Remove from heat.

ARRANGE layer of cookies on bottom and up side of
1½-quart baking dish. Add layer of banana slices; top
with ⅓ of the pudding. Repeat layers twice, ending
with pudding.

BEAT egg whites and salt in medium bowl with electric
mixer on high speed until foamy. Gradually add sugar,
beating until stiff peaks form. Spoon meringue mixture
lightly onto pudding, spreading to edge of dish to seal.

BAKE 10 to 15 minutes or until meringue is lightly
browned. Serve warm or refrigerate until ready to
serve.   *Makes 8 servings*

Preparation Time: 30 minutes
Baking Time: 15 minutes

NAPOLEONS

1 frozen ready-to-bake puff pastry sheet
1 container (8 ounces) PHILADELPHIA® Soft
   Cream Cheese
¼ cup powdered sugar
¼ teaspoon almond extract
1 cup whipping cream, whipped
½ cup powdered sugar
1 tablespoon milk
1 (1 oz.) square BAKER'S® Semi-Sweet Baking
   Chocolate, melted

THAW puff pastry sheet according to package
directions.

PREHEAT oven to 400°F.

ROLL pastry to 15×12-inch rectangle On lightly
floured surface. Cut lengthwise into thirds.

PLACE pastry strips on large ungreased cookie sheet;
prick pastry generously with fork. Bake 8 to 10 minutes
or until light golden brown.

STIR together cream cheese, ¼ cup sugar and extract in
medium bowl until well blended. Fold in whipped
cream.

SPREAD two pastry strips with cream cheese mixture;
stack. Top with remaining pastry strip.

STIR together ½ cup sugar and milk in small bowl
until smooth. Spread over top pastry strip. Drizzle with
melted chocolate. Chill.   *Makes 10 servings*

CHOCOLATE TOFFEE BAR DESSERT

1 cup flour
½ cup pecans, toasted and finely chopped
¼ cup sugar
½ cup (1 stick) butter or margarine, melted
1 cup toffee bits, divided
2 cups cold milk
2 packages (4-serving size each) JELL-O®
  Chocolate Flavor Instant Pudding & Pie Filling
1 tub (8 ounces) COOL WHIP® Whipped Topping,
  thawed, divided

HEAT oven to 400°F.

MIX flour, pecans, sugar, butter and ½ cup of the toffee bits in large bowl until well mixed. Press firmly onto bottom of 13×9-inch pan. Bake 10 minutes or until lightly browned. Cool.

POUR milk into large bowl. Add pudding mixes. Beat with wire whisk 1 minute or until well blended. Spread 1½ cups pudding on bottom of crust.

GENTLY stir ½ of the whipped topping into remaining pudding. Spread over pudding in pan. Top with remaining whipped topping. Sprinkle with remaining toffee bits.

REFRIGERATE 3 hours or overnight.

Makes 15 servings

Prep Time: 20 minutes
Bake Time: 10 minutes
Refrigerate Time: 3 hours

CHOCOLATE TOFFEE BAR DESSERT

· Classic Tip ·

For a great flavor variation, substitute JELL-O butterscotch Flavor Instant Pudding can be substituted for Chocolate Flavor with delicious results.

RASPBERRY ALMOND TRIFLES

2 cups whipping cream
¼ cup plus 1 tablespoon raspberry liqueur or orange juice, divided
1 (14-ounce) can EAGLE® BRAND Sweetened Condensed Milk (NOT evaporated milk)
2 (3-ounce) packages ladyfingers, separated
1 cup seedless raspberry jam
½ cup sliced almonds, toasted

1. In large bowl, beat whipping cream and 1 tablespoon liqueur until stiff peaks form. Fold in Eagle Brand; set aside.

2. Layer bottom of 12 (4-ounce) custard cups or ramekins with ladyfingers. Brush with some remaining liqueur. Spread half of jam over ladyfingers. Spread evenly with half of cream mixture; sprinkle with half of almonds. Repeat layers with remaining ladyfingers, liqueur, jam, cream mixture and almonds. Cover and chill 2 hours. Store covered in refrigerator.

Makes 12 servings

Prep Time: 20 minutes
Chill Time: 2 hours

RASPBERRY ALMOND TRIFLES

CHERRIES JUBILEE

1¼ cups cold milk
¼ teaspoon almond extract (optional)
1 package (4-serving size) JELL-O® Vanilla Flavor Instant Pudding and Pie Filling
1 tub (8 ounces) COOL WHIP® Whipped Topping, thawed
¾ cup cherry pie filling

POUR milk and almond extract into large bowl. Add pudding mix. Beat with wire whisk 1 to 2 minutes.

STIR in 2 cups of the whipped topping. Spoon whipped topping mixture and pie filling alternately into 6 parfait glasses.

REFRIGERATE until ready to serve. Garnish with remaining whipped topping. *Makes 6 servings*

SPICED CRANBERRY–APPLE SOUR CREAM COBBLER

4 cups cranberries, washed
6 Granny Smith apples, peeled and sliced thin
2 cups tightly packed light brown sugar
1 teaspoon ground cinnamon
1 teaspoon vanilla
¼ teaspoon ground cloves
2 cups plus 1 tablespoon all-purpose flour, divided
4 tablespoons butter, cut into bits
2 teaspoons double acting baking powder
1 teaspoon salt
½ cup CRISCO® all-vegetable shortening or ½ CRISCO® Stick
1½ cups sour cream
2 teaspoons granulated sugar

1. Heat oven to 400°F. Combine cranberries, apples, brown sugar, cinnamon, vanilla, ground cloves and 1 tablespoon flour in 3-quart baking dish; mix evenly. Dot top with butter bits.

2. Stir together remaining 2 cups flour, baking powder and salt in medium bowl. Cut shortening in using pastry blender or 2 knives until medium-size crumbs form. Add sour cream; blend well. (Dough will be sticky.) Drop dough by spoonfuls on top of fruit mixture. Sprinkle with granulated sugar. Bake at 400°F for 20 to 30 minutes, on middle rack, until top is golden. Serve with cinnamon or vanilla ice cream, if desired. *Makes 6 to 8 servings*

Kitchen Hint: Lucky enough to have some leftover cobbler? Store it in the refrigerator for up to two days. Reheat, covered, in a 350°F oven until warm.

CHOCOLATE DIPPED DELIGHTS

2 packages (4 ounces each) BAKER'S® GERMAN'S® Sweet Chocolate *or* 1 package (8 ounces) BAKER'S® Semi-Sweet Baking Chocolate
Assorted dippers such as whole strawberries, peppermint sticks, dried apricots, cookies, pretzels and JET-PUFFED® Marshmallows
4 squares BAKER'S® Premium White Baking Chocolate, melted (optional)

MICROWAVE chocolate in small microwavable bowl on HIGH 2 minutes or until chocolate is almost melted. Stir until chocolate is completely melted.

DIP dippers into chocolate; let excess chocolate drip off. Let stand at room temperature or refrigerate on wax paper-lined cookie sheet 30 minutes or until chocolate is firm. Drizzle with melted white chocolate, if desired. *Makes about 2 dozen*

Great Substitute: Prepare as directed, substituting 1 package (6 squares) BAKER'S Bittersweet Baking Chocolate *or* 1 package (6 squares) BAKER'S Premium White Baking Chocolate for Sweet or Semi-Sweet Chocolate.

Prep Time: 30 minutes plus cooling

SPICED CRANBERRY-APPLE SOUR CREAM COBBLER

Sweet Endings

MARBLED PUMPKIN CHEESECAKE SQUARES

¼ cup reduced-fat cream cheese, softened
2 tablespoons granulated sugar
3 tablespoons egg substitute
1 cup packed brown sugar
½ cup Dried Plum Purée (recipe follows) or prepared dried plum butter
2 egg whites
1½ teaspoons vanilla
1 cup all-purpose flour
1 teaspoon baking powder
¾ teaspoon ground cinnamon
¼ teaspoon ground ginger
¼ teaspoon salt
⅛ teaspoon ground cloves
¾ cup canned pumpkin

Preheat oven to 350°F. Coat 8-inch square baking dish or pan with vegetable cooking spray. In small bowl, beat cream cheese and granulated sugar until blended. Gradually add egg substitute, beating until blended.

Set aside. In large bowl, beat brown sugar, dried plum purée, egg whites and vanilla until well blended. In medium bowl, combine flour, baking powder, cinnamon, ginger, salt and cloves; stir into brown sugar mixture until well blended. Beat in pumpkin. Spread batter evenly in prepared baking dish. Drop heaping tablespoonfuls of cream cheese mixture over batter. Using knife, gently swirl cream cheese mixture into batter. Bake in center of oven 25 to 30 minutes or until pick inserted into center comes out clean. Cool in baking dish 15 minutes. Cut into squares. Serve warm with fat free vanilla ice cream or frozen yogurt, if desired. *Makes 9 servings*

Dried Plum Purée: Combine 1⅓ cups (8 ounces) pitted dried plums and 6 tablespoons hot water in container of food processor or blender. Pulse on and off until dried plums are finely chopped and smooth. Store leftovers in a covered container in the refrigerator for up to two months. Makes 1 cup.

*Favorite recipe from **California Dried Plum Board***

CHOCOLATE CARAMEL PARFAITS

28 chocolate sandwich cookies, crushed (2 cups)
1 tub (8 ounces) COOL WHIP® Whipped Topping, thawed
1 cup caramel sauce or dessert topping
½ cup hot fudge dessert topping
1 cup chopped pecans

LAYER crushed cookies, 2½ cups of the whipped topping, dessert toppings and pecans in 4 (8-ounce) dessert glasses.

REFRIGERATE at least 1 hour or until ready to serve. Garnish with remaining whipped topping.

Makes 4 servings

MARBLED PUMPKIN CHEESECAKE SQUARE

CHERRY CRISP

1 (21-ounce) can cherry pie filling
½ teaspoon almond extract
½ cup all-purpose flour
½ cup firmly packed brown sugar
1 teaspoon ground cinnamon
3 tablespoons butter or margarine, softened
½ cup chopped walnuts
¼ cup flaked coconut
  Ice cream or whipped cream (optional)

Pour cherry pie filling into ungreased 8×8×2-inch baking pan. Stir in almond extract.

Place flour, brown sugar and cinnamon in medium mixing bowl; mix well. Add butter; stir with fork until mixture is crumbly. Stir in walnuts and coconut. Sprinkle mixture over cherry pie filling.

Bake in preheated 350°F oven 25 minutes or until golden brown on top and filling is bubbly. Serve warm or at room temperature. If desired, top with ice cream or whipped cream. *Makes 6 servings*

Note: This recipe can be doubled. Bake in two 8×8×2-inch baking pans or one 13×9×2-inch pan.

*Favorite recipe from **Cherry Marketing Institute***

**TRIPLE CHOCOLATE
BROWNIE SUNDAE**

TRIPLE CHOCOLATE BROWNIE SUNDAE

1 brownie
1 scoop chocolate ice cream
  HERSHEY'S Chocolate Shell Topping
  REDDI-WIP® Real Whipped Cream

• Place brownie on bottom of sundae dish.

• Place ice cream on top of brownie.

• Shake HERSHEY'S Chocolate Shell Topping according to instructions. Squeeze generous amount over ice cream. Allow to harden for 30 seconds.

• Top with REDDI-WIP Real Whipped Cream.

Makes 1 sundae

RICE PUDDING

1¼ cups water, divided
½ cup uncooked long-grain rice
2 cups evaporated skim milk
½ cup granulated sugar
½ cup raisins
½ cup MOTT'S® Natural Apple Sauce
3 tablespoons cornstarch
1 teaspoon vanilla extract
Brown sugar or nutmeg (optional)
Fresh raspberries (optional)
Orange peel strips (optional)

1. In medium saucepan, bring 1 cup water to a boil. Add rice. Reduce heat to low and simmer, covered, 20 minutes or until rice is tender and water is absorbed.

2. Add milk, granulated sugar, raisins and apple sauce. Bring to a boil. Reduce heat to low and simmer for 3 minutes, stirring occasionally.

3. Combine cornstarch and remaining ¼ cup water in small bowl. Stir into rice mixture. Simmer about 20 minutes or until mixture thickens, stirring occasionally. Remove from heat; stir in vanilla. Cool 15 to 20 minutes before serving. Sprinkle each serving with brown sugar or nutmeg and garnish with raspberries and orange peel, if desired. Refrigerate leftovers.   *Makes 8 servings*

RICE PUDDING

LEMON BERRY CHARLOTTE

1 package (8-serving size) or 2 packages (4-serving size) JELL-O® Brand Lemon Flavor Gelatin
1½ cups boiling water
¾ cup cold water
   Ice cubes
1 tub (12 ounces) COOL WHIP® Whipped Topping, thawed
1 cup chopped strawberries
1 package (3 ounces) ladyfingers, split
   Cloth ribbon (optional)
   Strawberry halves (optional)
   Fresh mint leaves (optional)

DISSOLVE gelatin completely in boiling water in large bowl. Mix cold water and ice to make 1¾ cups. Add to gelatin, stirring until ice is melted. Refrigerate 10 minutes or until slightly thickened, if necessary.

STIR in 3½ cups of the whipped topping and strawberries. Spoon into 2-quart saucepan (about 3½ inches deep) which has been lined with plastic wrap.

REFRIGERATE 4 hours or until firm. Invert saucepan onto serving plate; remove plastic wrap. Spread top and sides of dessert with 1 cup of the whipped topping.

PRESS cut sides of ladyfingers into sides of dessert. Tie ribbon around dessert. Garnish with remaining whipped topping, strawberry halves and mint leaves. Store leftover dessert in refrigerator.

Makes 12 servings

DULCE DE LECHE

1 (14-ounce) can EAGLE® BRAND Sweetened Condensed Milk (NOT evaporated milk)
   Assorted dippers, such as cookies, cake, banana chunks, apple slices and/or strawberries

1. Preheat oven to 425°F. Pour Eagle Brand into 9-inch pie plate. Cover with foil; place in larger shallow baking pan. Pour hot water into larger pan to depth of 1 inch.

2. Bake 1 hour or until thick and caramel-colored. Beat until smooth. Cool 1 hour. Refrigerate until serving time. Serve as dip with assorted dippers. Store leftovers covered in refrigerator for up to 1 week.

Makes about 1¼ cups

CAUTION: Never heat an unopened can.

Prep Time: 5 minutes
Bake Time: 1 hour
Cool Time: 1 hour

LEMON BERRY CHARLOTTE

BRANDIED PEACH COBBLER

Filling
  6 cups fresh sliced peaches (3 pounds) *or*
      2 (16-ounce) packages frozen sliced peaches
  ½ **cup sugar**
  ¼ **cup brandy**
  1 **tablespoon cornstarch**
  1 **tablespoon fresh lemon juice**
  1 **teaspoon brandy extract**
  ½ **teaspoon ground cinnamon**
      WESSON® No-Stick Cooking Spray

Topping
  1 **cup all-purpose flour**
  ⅔ **cup sugar**
  1 **tablespoon baking powder**
  1 **teaspoon ground cinnamon**
  ½ **teaspoon salt**
  ½ **cup WESSON® Vegetable Oil**
  ¼ **cup milk**
  ½ **cup chopped pecans**
      Homemade vanilla ice cream

For filling, in a large bowl, combine *all* filling ingredients *except* Wesson® Cooking Spray. Let stand 30 minutes, stirring often. Meanwhile, preheat oven to 375°F and spray an 11×7×2-inch baking dish with Wesson® Cooking Spray.

For topping, in medium bowl, combine flour, sugar, baking powder, cinnamon and salt; mix well. Add Wesson® Oil and milk; blend well. Fold in pecans. Pour peach mixture into baking dish. Evenly drop topping mixture by rounded tablespoons over peach mixture. Bake 45 to 55 minutes or until brown and bubbly. Serve cold or at room temperature with homemade vanilla ice cream.

Makes 6 servings

THE CARAMEL TURTLE

  Pecan halves
  HERSHEY'S Classic Caramel™ Sundae Syrup
  Chocolate ice cream
  HERSHEY'S Chocolate Shell Topping
  REDDI-WIP® Real Whipped Cream

• Cover bottom of ice cream dish with pecan halves.

• Add HERSHEY'S Classic Caramel Sundae Syrup.

• Place scoop of ice cream on top of syrup.

• Shake HERSHEY'S Chocolate Shell Topping according to instructions. Drizzle over ice cream. Allow to harden for 30 seconds. Top with REDDI-WIP Real Whipped Cream.

Makes 1 sundae

LEMON CURD TARTLETS WITH FRESH RASPBERRIES

3 egg yolks
½ cup sugar
⅓ cup fresh lemon juice
1 teaspoon grated lemon peel
6 tablespoons I CAN'T BELIEVE IT'S NOT BUTTER!® Spread, cut in pieces
24 frozen mini phyllo dough shells, thawed
½ cup whipped cream or non-dairy whipped topping
24 fresh raspberries

In top of double boiler, with wire whisk, beat egg yolks, sugar, lemon juice and lemon peel until blended. Stir in I Can't Believe It's Not Butter! Spread. Cook over medium heat, stirring frequently, 10 minutes or until mixture thickens and reaches 160°F.

Turn into large bowl and cover with plastic wrap, pressing wrap on surface of lemon curd; refrigerate to chill completely, about 2 hours.

To serve, evenly fill shells with lemon curd. Garnish with whipped cream and raspberries.

Makes about 2 dozen tartlets

DOUBLE CHOCOLATE BREAD PUDDING

2 packages (4-serving size each) JELL-O® Chocolate Flavor Sugar Free Cook and Serve Pudding & Pie Filling
5 cups fat free milk
5 cups French bread cubes
1 package (4 ounces) BAKER'S® GERMAN'S® Sweet Chocolate, chopped

HEAT oven to 350°F.

STIR pudding mixes into milk with wire whisk in large bowl 1 minute or until well blended. Stir in bread. Pour pudding mixture into 13×9-inch baking dish. Sprinkle evenly with chopped chocolate.

BAKE 40 minutes or until pudding just comes to a boil in the center. Remove from oven. Let stand 10 minutes before serving. Serve warm. Store leftover pudding in refrigerator.   *Makes 12 servings*

How to make individual servings: Make individual servings of bread pudding by baking in custard cups or ramekins. Reduce baking time to 15 to 20 minutes. Garnish with COOL WHIP LITE® or COOL WHIP FREE® Whipped Topping.

Dalmatian Bread Pudding: Substitute JELL-O® Vanilla Flavor Sugar Free Cook and Serve Pudding & Pie Filling for Chocolate Flavor Pudding to create a delicious black and white bread pudding.

Prep Time: 15 minutes
Bake Time: 40 minutes plus standing

LEMON CURD TARTLETS WITH FRESH RASPBERRIES

Cookies & Candies

COCOA-WALNUT CRESCENTS

> 1 cup margarine
> ⅔ cup powdered sugar
> ⅓ cup unsweetened cocoa
> 1 teaspoon vanilla extract
> ⅛ teaspoon salt
> 1⅔ cups all-purpose flour
> 1 cup PLANTERS® Walnuts, finely chopped
> Powdered Sugar Glaze (recipe follows) and chopped PLANTERS® Walnuts, for garnish

1. Beat margarine and sugar in large bowl with mixer at medium speed until light and fluffy. Blend in cocoa, vanilla and salt. Mix in flour and finely chopped walnuts. Wrap; refrigerate 1 hour.

2. Shape rounded teaspoons of dough into crescent shapes, tapering ends. Place on lightly greased baking sheets.

3. Bake in preheated 325°F oven for 15 to 18 minutes. Remove from sheets; cool completely on wire racks. Drizzle with Powdered Sugar Glaze and sprinkle with chopped walnuts, if desired. *Makes 4 dozen cookies*

Powdered Sugar Glaze: Combine 1 cup powdered sugar and 5 to 6 teaspoons water.

Preparation Time: 15 minutes
Chill Time: 1 hour
Cook Time: 15 minutes
Total Time: 1 hour and 30 minutes

JEREMY'S FAMOUS TURTLES

Cookies

3 egg whites
1 egg yolk
1¼ Butter Flavor CRISCO® Sticks or 1¼ cups Butter Flavor CRISCO® all-vegetable shortening plus additional for greasing
¾ cup firmly packed brown sugar
½ cup granulated sugar
1 teaspoon vanilla
1¾ cups all-purpose flour
1 teaspoon baking soda
¾ teaspoon salt
½ cup butterscotch chips
½ cup semi-sweet chocolate chips
½ cup chopped dates
½ cup chopped pecans
½ cup diced dried fruit bits
⅓ cup cinnamon applesauce
¼ cup toasted wheat germ
¼ cup ground shelled sunflower seeds
2 tablespoons honey
3 cups oats (quick or old fashioned), uncooked
8 ounces pecan halves (2 cups)

Coating

1 to 2 egg whites, lightly beaten
½ cup granulated sugar

1. For cookies, place 3 egg whites in medium bowl. Beat at medium speed of electric mixer until frothy. Beat in egg yolk until well blended.

2. Combine 1¼ cups shortening, brown sugar and granulated sugar in large bowl. Beat at medium speed until well blended. Add egg mixture and vanilla. Beat until well blended.

3. Combine flour, baking soda and salt. Add gradually to shortening mixture at low speed. Stir in, 1 at a time, butterscotch chips, chocolate chips, dates, chopped pecans, fruit bits, applesauce, wheat germ, sunflower seeds, honey and oats. Cover. Refrigerate dough 1 hour.

4. Heat oven to 350°F. Grease baking sheets with shortening. Place sheets of foil on countertop for cooling cookies.

5. Shape dough into 1½-inch balls. Cut pecan halves into 4 lengthwise pieces for legs. Save broken pieces for heads and tails.

6. For coating, dip top of cookie ball in beaten egg white, then dip in sugar. Place cookies, sugar side up, 2½ inches apart on prepared baking sheets. Insert lengthwise nut pieces for legs. Flatten slightly. Place nut sliver for tail and rounded nut piece for head.

7. Bake one baking sheet at a time at 350°F for 9 to 11 minutes or until lightly browned. *Do not overbake.* Reposition nuts, if necessary. Cool 30 seconds on baking sheets. Remove cookies to foil to cool completely.   *Makes about 7½ dozen cookies*

CINNAMON ROLL COOKIES

Cinnamon Mixture
- 4 tablespoons granulated sugar
- 1 tablespoon ground cinnamon

Cookie Dough
- 1 cup Butter Flavor CRISCO® all-vegetable shortening or 1 Butter Flavor CRISCO® Stick
- 1 cup firmly packed light brown sugar
- 2 large eggs
- 1 teaspoon vanilla
- 3 cups all-purpose flour
- 2 teaspoons baking powder
- ½ teaspoon salt
- 1 teaspoon ground cinnamon

CINNAMON ROLL COOKIES

1. For cinnamon mixture, combine granulated sugar and 1 tablespoon cinnamon in small bowl; mix well. Set aside.

2. For cookie dough, combine shortening and brown sugar in large bowl. Beat at medium speed with electric mixer until well blended. Beat in eggs and vanilla until well blended.

3. Combine flour, baking powder, salt and 1 teaspoon cinnamon in small bowl. Add to creamed mixture; mix well.

4. Turn dough onto sheet of waxed paper. Spread dough into 9×6-inch rectangle using rubber spatula. Sprinkle with 4 tablespoons cinnamon mixture to within 1 inch from edge. Roll up jelly-roll style into log. Dust log with remaining cinnamon mixture. Wrap tightly in plastic wrap; refrigerate 4 hours or overnight.

5. Heat oven to 375°F. Spray cookie sheets with CRISCO® No-Stick Cooking Spray.

6. Slice dough ¼ inch thick. Place on prepared cookie sheets. Bake at 350°F for 8 minutes or until lightly browned on top. Cool on cookie sheets 4 minutes; transfer to cooling racks.

Makes about 5 dozen cookies

Kitchen Hint: Be careful when working with this dough. It is a stiff dough and can crack easily when rolling. Roll the dough slowly and smooth any cracks with your finger as you go.

PEANUT BUTTER CHOCOLATE CHUNK COOKIES

1¾ cups flour
¾ teaspoon baking soda
¼ teaspoon salt
¾ cup (1½ sticks) butter *or* margarine, softened
1 cup peanut butter
½ cup granulated sugar
½ cup firmly packed brown sugar
1 egg
1 teaspoon vanilla
1 package (12 ounces) BAKER'S® Semi-Sweet
   Chocolate Chunks
1 cup chopped peanuts (optional)

HEAT oven to 375°F.

MIX flour, baking soda and salt in medium bowl; set aside.

BEAT butter, peanut butter and sugars in large bowl with electric mixer on medium speed until light and fluffy. Add egg and vanilla; beat well. Gradually beat in flour mixture. Stir in chocolate chunks and peanuts. Drop by heaping tablespoonfuls onto ungreased cookie sheets.

BAKE 11 to 13 minutes or just until golden brown. Cool on cookie sheets 1 minute. Remove to wire racks and cool completely.   *Makes about 3 dozen*

Storage Know-How: Store in tightly covered container up to 1 week.

Prep Time: 15 minutes
Bake Time: 11 to 13 minutes

PEANUT BUTTER CHOCOLATE CHUNK COOKIES

Cookies & Candies

CHOCOLATE BANANA WALNUT DROPS

½ cup (1 stick) butter or margarine, softened
½ cup solid vegetable shortening
1¼ cups firmly packed light brown sugar
1 large egg
1 medium banana, mashed (about ½ cup)
2¼ cups all-purpose flour
1 teaspoon baking soda
1 teaspoon ground cinnamon
½ teaspoon ground nutmeg
¼ teaspoon salt
2 cups quick-cooking or old-fashioned oats, uncooked
1 cup coarsely chopped walnuts
1¾ cups "M&M's"® Chocolate Mini Baking Bits

Preheat oven to 350°F. In large bowl cream butter, shortening and sugar until light and fluffy; beat in egg and banana. In medium bowl combine flour, baking soda, cinnamon, nutmeg and salt; blend into creamed mixture. Blend in oats and nuts. Stir in "M&M's"® Chocolate Mini Baking Bits. Drop by tablespoonfuls about 2 inches apart onto ungreased cookie sheets. Bake 8 to 10 minutes just until set. Do not overbake. Cool 1 minute on cookie sheets; cool completely on wire racks. Store in tightly covered container.

Makes about 3 dozen cookies

LEMON PECAN COOKIES

1 cup Butter Flavor CRISCO® all-vegetable shortening or 1 Butter Flavor CRISCO® Stick
1½ cups granulated sugar
2 large eggs
3 tablespoons fresh lemon juice
3 cups all-purpose flour
2 teaspoons baking powder
¼ teaspoon salt
1 cup chopped pecans

1. Heat oven to 350°F.

2. Combine shortening and sugar in large bowl. Beat at medium speed with electric mixer until well blended. Beat in eggs and lemon juice until well blended.

3. Combine flour, baking powder and salt in medium bowl. Add to creamed mixture; mix well. Stir in pecans. Spray cookie sheets lightly with CRISCO® No-Stick Cooking Spray. Drop dough by teaspoonfuls about 2 inches apart onto prepared cookie sheets. Bake at 350°F for 10 to 12 minutes or until lightly browned. Cool on cookie sheets 4 minutes; transfer to cooling rack.

Makes about 6 dozen cookies

CHOCOLATE BANANA WALNUT DROPS

ANNA'S ICING OATMEAL SANDWICH COOKIES

Cookies

- ¾ **Butter Flavor CRISCO® Stick or ¾ cup Butter Flavor CRISCO® all-vegetable shortening plus additional for greasing**
- 1¼ **cups firmly packed light brown sugar**
- 1 **egg**
- ⅓ **cup milk**
- 1½ **teaspoons vanilla**
- 3 **cups quick oats, uncooked**
- 1 **cup all-purpose flour**
- ½ **teaspoon baking soda**
- ½ **teaspoon salt**

Frosting

- 2 **cups confectioners' sugar**
- ¼ **Butter Flavor CRISCO® Stick or ¼ cup Butter Flavor CRISCO® all-vegetable shortening**
- ½ **teaspoon vanilla**
  Milk

1. Heat oven to 350°F. Grease baking sheets with shortening. Place sheets of foil on countertop for cooling cookies.

2. For cookies, combine ¾ cup shortening, brown sugar, egg, milk and vanilla in large bowl. Beat at medium speed of electric mixer until well blended.

3. Combine oats, flour, baking soda and salt. Mix into creamed mixture at low speed just until blended.

4. Drop rounded measuring tablespoonfuls of dough 2 inches apart onto prepared baking sheets.

5. Bake one sheet at a time at 375°F for 10 to 12 minutes, or until lightly browned. *Do not overbake.* Cool 2 minutes on baking sheet. Remove cookies to foil to cool completely.

6. For frosting, combine confectioners' sugar, shortening and vanilla in medium bowl. Beat at low speed, adding enough milk for good spreading consistency. Spread on bottoms of half the cookies. Top with remaining cookies.

Makes about 16 sandwich cookies

• Classic Tip •

When baking more then one sheet of cookies at a time, it's best to rotate them for even baking. Halfway through the baking time, rotate the cookie sheets from front to back, as well as from the top rack to the bottom rack.

"BUTTERY" DROP COOKIES

½ **Butter Flavor CRISCO® Stick or ½ cup Butter Flavor CRISCO® all-vegetable shortening plus additional for greasing**
¾ **cup sugar**
 1 **tablespoon milk**
 1 **egg**
½ **teaspoon vanilla**
1¼ **cups all-purpose flour**
¼ **teaspoon salt**
¼ **teaspoon baking powder**

1. Heat oven to 375°F. Grease baking sheet. Place foil on countertop for cooling cookies.

2. Combine shortening, sugar and milk in medium bowl. Beat at medium speed of electric mixer until well blended. Beat in egg and vanilla. Beat until blended.

3. Combine flour, salt and baking powder; mix into creamed mixture at low speed until just blended.

4. Drop dough by level measuring tablespoonfuls 2 inches apart onto baking sheet.

5. Bake 7 to 9 minutes or until set. *Do not overbake.* Cool 2 minutes on baking sheet. Remove to foil to cool completely.   *Makes about 3 dozen cookies*

Note: For larger cookies, drop 2 level measuring tablespoonfuls of dough into a mound for each cookie. Place 3 inches apart on greased cookie sheet. Bake at 375°F for 11 to 13 minutes, or until set. Cool 2 minutes on cookie sheet. Remove to cooling rack.

• Classic Tip •

Plan ahead! Freeze baked cookies in an airtight container or freezer bag for up to six months. You'll always have cookies on hand.

PECAN MINI KISSES CUPS

½ cup (1 stick) butter or margarine, softened
1 package (3 ounces) cream cheese, softened
1 cup all-purpose flour
1 egg
⅔ cup packed light brown sugar
1 tablespoon butter, melted
1 teaspoon vanilla extract
    Dash salt
72 HERSHEY'S MINI KISSES™ Milk Chocolate
    Baking Pieces, divided
½ to ¾ cup coarsely chopped pecans

1. Beat ½ cup softened butter and cream cheese in medium bowl until blended. Add flour; beat well. Cover; refrigerate about 1 hour or until firm enough to handle.

2. Heat oven to 325°F. Stir together egg, brown sugar, 1 tablespoon melted butter, vanilla and salt in small bowl until well blended.

3. Shape chilled dough into 24 balls (1 inch each). Place balls in ungreased small muffin cups (1¾ inches in diameter). Press onto bottoms and up sides of cups. Place 2 Mini Kisses™ in each cup. Spoon about 1 teaspoon pecans over chocolate. Fill each cup with egg mixture.

4. Bake 25 minutes or until filling is set. Lightly press 1 Mini Kiss™ into center of each cookie. Cool in pan on wire rack.

Makes 24 cups

Tip: Use Mini Kisses™ Chocolate to decorate cakes, cupcakes, cookies and pies. Stir into slightly softened ice cream or sprinkle over top of a sundae for an added chocolate taste treat.

Prep Time: 25 minutes
Chill Time: 1 hour
Bake Time: 25 minutes
Cool Time: 1 hour

PECAN MINI KISSES CUPS

PEANUT BUTTER KISSES

1¼ cups firmly packed light brown sugar
¾ cup creamy peanut butter
½ CRISCO® Stick or ½ cup CRISCO® all-vegetable shortening
3 tablespoons milk
1 tablespoon vanilla
1 egg
1¾ cups all-purpose flour
¾ teaspoon baking soda
¾ teaspoon salt
48 chocolate kisses, unwrapped

1. Heat oven to 375°F. Place sheets of foil on countertop for cooling cookies.

2. Combine brown sugar, peanut butter, ½ cup shortening, milk and vanilla in large bowl. Beat at medium speed of electric mixer until well blended. Add egg. Beat just until blended.

3. Combine flour, baking soda and salt. Add to shortening mixture; beat at low speed until just blended.

4. Form dough into 1-inch balls. Roll in granulated sugar. Place 2 inches apart on ungreased baking sheets.

5. Bake one baking sheet at a time at 375°F for 6 minutes. Press chocolate kiss into center of each cookie. Return to oven. Bake 3 minutes. *Do not overbake.* Cool 2 minutes on baking sheets. Remove cookies to foil to cool completely.   *Makes about 3 dozen cookies*

MOM'S BEST OATMEAL COOKIES

¾ Butter Flavor CRISCO® Stick or ¾ cup Butter Flavor CRISCO® all-vegetable shortening plus additional for greasing
1¼ cups firmly packed light brown sugar
1 egg
⅓ cup milk
1½ teaspoons vanilla
3 cups quick oats, uncooked
1 cup all-purpose flour
½ teaspoon baking soda
½ teaspoon salt
¼ teaspoon ground cinnamon
1 cup chopped pecans
⅔ cup flake coconut
⅔ cup sesame seeds

1. Heat oven to 350°F. Grease baking sheets with shortening. Place sheets of foil on countertop for cooling.

2. Combine ¾ cup shortening, brown sugar, egg, milk and vanilla in large mixer bowl. Beat at medium speed of electric mixer until well blended.

3. Combine oats, flour, baking soda, salt and cinnamon. Mix into shortening mixture at low speed just until blended. Stir in pecans, coconut and sesame seeds.

4. Drop by rounded measuring tablespoonfuls of dough 2 inches apart onto prepared baking sheets.

5. Bake one baking sheet at a time at 375°F for 10 to 12 minutes or until lightly browned. *Do not overbake.* Remove cookies to foil to cool completely.

Makes about 2 ½ dozen cookies

PEANUT BUTTER KISSES

Cookies & Candies

VERSATILE CUT-OUT COOKIES

3⅓ cups all-purpose flour
1 tablespoon baking powder
½ teaspoon salt
1 (14-ounce) can EAGLE® BRAND Sweetened Condensed Milk (NOT evaporated milk)
¾ cup (1½ sticks) butter or margarine, softened
2 eggs
2 teaspoons vanilla or 1½ teaspoons almond or lemon extract
Ready-to-spread frosting

1. Preheat oven to 350°F. Grease baking sheets; set aside. In medium bowl, combine flour, baking powder and salt; set aside. In large bowl, beat Eagle Brand, butter, eggs and vanilla until well blended. Add dry ingredients; mix well.

2. On floured surface, lightly knead dough to form smooth ball. Divide into thirds. On well-floured surface, roll out each portion to ⅛-inch thickness. Cut with floured cookie cutter. Place 1 inch apart on prepared sheets.

3. Bake 7 to 9 minutes or until lightly browned around edges. Cool completely. Frost and decorate as desired. Store loosely covered at room temperature.

Makes about 6½ dozen cookies

Sandwich Cookies: Use 2½-inch cookie cutter. Bake as directed above. Sandwich two cookies together with ready-to-spread frosting. Sprinkle with powdered sugar or colored sugar if desired. Makes about 3 dozen.

Prep Time: 15 minutes
Bake Time: 7 to 9 minutes

CHEWY OATMEAL RAISIN COOKIES

1 cup packed light brown sugar
1 cup FLEISCHMANN'S® Original Margarine, softened
¼ cup EGG BEATERS® Healthy Real Egg Product
1 teaspoon vanilla extract
2 cups quick-cooking oats
1½ cups all-purpose flour
1 teaspoon baking soda
1 teaspoon ground cinnamon
1 cup seedless raisins

1. Beat sugar and margarine in large bowl with mixer at medium speed until blended. Beat in Egg Beaters® and vanilla until mixture is smooth.

2. Blend in oats, flour, baking soda and cinnamon. Stir in raisins.

3. Drop batter by tablespoonfuls, 2 inches apart, onto greased baking sheets. Bake in preheated 400°F oven for 5 to 7 minutes or until lightly browned. Remove from sheets; cool on wire racks.

Makes about 3 dozen cookies

Preparation Time: 25 minutes
Cook Time: 5 minutes
Total Time: 45 minutes

EASY LEMON COOKIES

1 package DUNCAN HINES® Moist Deluxe®
   Lemon Cake Mix
2 eggs
½ cup vegetable oil
1 teaspoon grated lemon peel
   Pecan halves, for garnish

1. Preheat oven to 350°F.

2. Combine cake mix, eggs, oil and lemon peel in large bowl. Stir until thoroughly blended. Drop by rounded teaspoonfuls 2 inches apart onto ungreased cookie sheets. Press pecan half in center of each cookie. Bake at 350°F for 9 to 11 minutes or until edges are light golden brown. Cool 1 minute on cookie sheets. Remove to wire racks. Cool completely. Store in airtight container.

Makes 4 dozen cookies

Tip: You may substitute whole almonds or walnut halves for the pecan halves.

EASY LEMON COOKIES

WALNUT CRESCENTS

3¾ cups flour
½ teaspoon ground cinnamon
1½ cups (3 sticks) margarine or butter
¾ cup KARO® Light or Dark Corn Syrup
1 tablespoon vanilla
2¼ cups ground walnuts
1½ cups confectioners' sugar

1. In medium bowl combine flour and cinnamon; set aside.

2. In large bowl with mixer at medium speed, beat margarine until creamy. Gradually beat in corn syrup and vanilla until well blended. Stir in flour mixture and walnuts.

3. Cover; refrigerate several hours or until easy to handle.

4. Preheat oven to 350°F. Shape rounded teaspoonfuls of dough into 2-inch-long rolls. Place 2 inches apart on ungreased cookie sheets, curving to form crescents.

5. Bake 15 to 18 minutes or until bottoms are lightly browned. Remove from cookie sheets; cool completely on wire racks. Roll in confectioners' sugar.

Makes about 8 dozen cookies

Prep Time: 30 minutes, plus chilling
Bake Time: 15 to 18 minutes, plus cooling

CHOCOLATE WHITE CHOCOLATE CHUNK COOKIES

2 cups flour
2 teaspoons CALUMET® Baking Powder
¼ teaspoon salt
¾ cup (1½ sticks) butter *or* margarine, softened
1½ cups firmly packed brown sugar
2 eggs
1 teaspoon vanilla
4 squares BAKER'S® Unsweetened Baking Chocolate, melted, cooled slightly
1 package (12 ounces) BAKER'S® White Chocolate Chunks
1 cup chopped nuts (optional)

HEAT oven to 350°F.

MIX flour, baking powder and salt in medium bowl; set aside.

BEAT butter and sugar in large bowl with electric mixer on medium speed until light and fluffy. Add eggs and vanilla; beat well. Stir in melted chocolate. Gradually beat in flour mixture. Stir in chocolate chunks and nuts. Drop by heaping tablespoonfuls onto ungreased cookie sheets.

BAKE 11 to 12 minutes or until cookies feel set to the touch. Cool on cookie sheets 1 minute. Remove to wire racks and cool completely.   *Makes about 3½ dozen*

Storage Know-How: Store in tightly covered container up to 1 week.

Make-Ahead: After cookies are completely cooled, wrap in plastic wrap and place in an airtight plastic container or zipper-style plastic freezer bag. Cookies can be frozen for up to 1 month. Bring cookies to room temperature before serving.

Prep Time: 15 minutes
Bake Time: 11 to 12 minutes

CHOCOLATE WHITE CHOCOLATE
CHUNK COOKIES

GINGER SNAP OATS

¾ Butter Flavor CRISCO® Stick or ¾ cup Butter Flavor CRISCO® all-vegetable shortening plus additional for greasing
1 cup packed brown sugar
½ cup granulated sugar
½ cup molasses
2 teaspoons vinegar
2 eggs
1¼ cups all-purpose flour
1 tablespoon ground ginger
1½ teaspoons baking soda
½ teaspoon ground cinnamon
¼ teaspoon ground cloves
2¾ cups quick oats (not instant or old-fashioned), uncooked
1½ cups raisins

1. Heat oven to 350°F. Grease baking sheets with shortening. Place sheets of foil on countertop for cooling cookies.

2. Combine ¾ cup shortening, brown sugar, granulated sugar, molasses, vinegar and eggs in large mixer bowl. Beat at medium speed of electric mixer until well blended.

3. Combine flour, ginger, baking soda, cinnamon and cloves. Mix into shortening mixture at low speed until blended. Stir in oats and raisins.

4. Drop dough by rounded teaspoonfuls 2 inches apart onto prepared baking sheets.

5. Bake one baking sheet at a time 350°F for 11 to 14 minutes. *Do not overbake.* Cool 2 minutes on cookie sheets. Remove cookies to foil to cool completely.

Makes about 5 dozen cookies

FUDGY OATMEAL BUTTERSCOTCH COOKIES

1 package (18.25 ounces) devil's food cake mix
1½ cups quick-cooking or old-fashioned oats, uncooked
¾ cup (1½ sticks) butter, melted
2 large eggs
1 tablespoon vegetable oil
1 teaspoon vanilla extract
1¼ cups "M&M's"® Chocolate Mini Baking Bits
1 cup butterscotch chips

Preheat oven to 350°F. In large bowl combine cake mix, oats, butter, eggs, oil and vanilla until well blended. Stir in "M&M's"® Chocolate Mini Baking Bits and butterscotch chips. Drop by heaping tablespoonfuls about 2 inches apart onto ungreased cookie sheets. Bake 10 to 12 minutes. Cool 1 minute on cookie sheets; cool completely on wire racks. Store in tightly covered container. *Makes about 3 dozen cookies*

GINGER SNAP OATS AND MOM'S BEST OATMEAL COOKIES (PAGE 354)

Cookies & Candies

PEANUT BUTTER CHIP TASSIES

1 package (3 ounces) cream cheese, softened
½ cup (1 stick) butter, softened
1 cup all-purpose flour
1 egg, slightly beaten
½ cup sugar
2 tablespoons butter, melted
¼ teaspoon lemon juice
¼ teaspoon vanilla extract
1 cup REESE'S® Peanut Butter Chips, chopped*
6 red candied cherries, quartered (optional)

Do not chop peanut butter chips in food processor or blender.

1. Beat cream cheese and ½ cup butter in medium bowl; stir in flour. Cover; refrigerate about one hour or until dough is firm. Shape into 24 one-inch balls; place each ball into ungreased, small muffin cups (1¾ inches in diameter). Press dough evenly against bottom and sides of each cup.

2. Heat oven to 350°F.

3. Combine egg, sugar, melted butter, lemon juice and vanilla in medium bowl; stir until smooth. Add chopped peanut butter chips. Fill muffin cups ¾ full with mixture.

4. Bake 20 to 25 minutes or until filling is set and lightly browned. Cool completely; remove from pan to wire rack. Garnish with candied cherries, if desired.

Makes about 2 dozen

OATMEAL SCOTCH CHIPPERS

1¼ Butter Flavor CRISCO® Sticks or 1¼ cups Butter Flavor CRISCO® all-vegetable shortening
1½ cups firmly packed brown sugar
1 cup granulated sugar
3 eggs
1¼ cups crunchy peanut butter
4½ cups rolled oats, uncooked
2 teaspoons baking soda
1 cup semisweet chocolate chips
1 cup butterscotch-flavored chips
1 cup chopped walnuts

1. Heat oven to 350°F. Place sheets of foil on countertop for cooling cookies.

2. Combine 1¼ cups shortening, brown sugar and granulated sugar in large bowl. Beat at medium speed of electric mixer until well blended. Beat in eggs. Add peanut butter. Beat until blended.

3. Combine oats and baking soda. Stir into shortening mixture with spoon. Stir in chocolate chips, butterscotch chips and nuts until blended.

4. Drop by rounded teaspoonfuls 2 inches apart onto ungreased baking sheets.

5. Bake one baking sheet at a time at 350°F for 10 to 11 minutes or until lightly browned. *Do not overbake.* Cool 2 minutes on baking sheet. Remove cookies to foil to cool completely. *Makes about 6 dozen cookies*

Cookies & Candies

CREAMY DOUBLE DECKER FUDGE

1 cup REESE'S® Peanut Butter Chips
1 can (14 ounces) sweetened condensed milk
   (not evaporated milk), divided
1 teaspoon vanilla extract, divided
1 cup HERSHEY'S Semi-Sweet Chocolate Chips

1. Line 8-inch square pan with foil.

2. Place peanut butter chips and ⅔ cup sweetened condensed milk in small microwave-safe bowl. Microwave at HIGH (100%) 1 to 1½ minutes, stirring after 1 minute, until chips are melted and mixture is smooth when stirred. Stir in ½ teaspoon vanilla; spread evenly into prepared pan.

3. Place remaining sweetened condensed milk and chocolate chips in another small microwave-safe bowl; repeat above microwave procedure. Stir in remaining ½ teaspoon vanilla; spread evenly over peanut butter layer.

4. Cover; refrigerate until firm. Remove from pan; place on cutting board. Peel off foil. Cut into squares. Store tightly covered in refrigerator.

Makes about 4 dozen pieces or 1½ pounds

Note: For best results, do not double this recipe.

Prep Time: 15 minutes
Cook Time: 3 minutes
Chill Time: 2 hours

CRUNCHY CLUSTERS

1 (12-ounce) package semi-sweet chocolate chips
   or 3 (6-ounce) packages butterscotch-flavored
   chips
1 (14-ounce) can EAGLE® BRAND Sweetened
   Condensed Milk (NOT evaporated milk)
1 (3-ounce) can chow mein noodles or 2 cups
   pretzel sticks, broken into ½-inch pieces
1 cup dry-roasted peanuts or whole roasted
   almonds

1. Line baking sheet with waxed paper. In heavy saucepan over low heat, melt chips with Eagle Brand. Remove from heat.

2. In large bowl, combine noodles and peanuts; stir in chocolate mixture.

3. Drop by tablespoonfuls onto prepared baking sheet; chill 2 hours or until firm. Store loosely covered at room temperature.　　*Makes about 3 dozen*

Microwave Directions: In 2-quart glass measure, combine chips and **Eagle Brand.** Cook on 100% power (HIGH) 3 minutes, stirring after 1½ minutes. Stir until smooth. Proceed as directed above.

Prep Time: 10 minutes
Chill Time: 2 hours

HOLIDAY MARBLE BARK

6 squares BAKER'S® Semi-Sweet Baking
    Chocolate *or* 1 package (6 squares) BAKER'S®
    Bittersweet Baking Chocolate
1 package (6 squares) BAKER'S® Premium White
    Baking Chocolate
1 cup crushed peppermint candies (about
    50 peppermint starlight candies)

MICROWAVE semi-sweet and white chocolates in separate medium microwavable bowls on HIGH 2 minutes or until chocolates are almost melted, stirring halfway through heating time. Stir until chocolates are completely melted.

STIR ½ cup of the peppermint candies into each bowl. Alternately spoon melted chocolates onto wax paper-lined cookie sheet. Swirl chocolates together with knife to marbleize.

REFRIGERATE 1 hour or until firm. Break into pieces.

Makes about 1 pound

How to crush peppermint candies: Place candies in zipper-style plastic bag. Crush with rolling pin or mallet. Or, process in food processor using pulsing action.

Make-Ahead: Can be prepared up to 3 weeks ahead for gift-giving. Store in an airtight container between layers of wax paper in the refrigerator.

Chocolate Peanut Butter Marble Bark: Prepare as directed, omitting peppermint candies. Stir ¼ cup creamy peanut butter into melted white chocolate.

Chocolate Nut Marble Bark: Prepare as directed, substituting 1 cup toasted chopped nuts *or* toasted BAKER'S® ANGEL FLAKE® Coconut for peppermint candies.

Festive Fruit Bark: Prepare as directed, omitting Semi-Sweet Chocolate and peppermint. Use 2 packages (6 squares each) BAKER'S Premium White Chocolate. Stir in ½ cup dried cranberries and ½ cup toasted chopped almonds *or* pistachios.

Prep Time: 20 minutes
Refrigerate Time: 1 hour

MOCHA RUM BALLS

60 NILLA® Wafers, finely rolled (about 2½ cups
    crumbs)
 1 cup powdered sugar
 1 cup PLANTERS® Pecans, finely chopped
½ cup margarine or butter, melted
 2 tablespoons light corn syrup
 2 tablespoons unsweetened cocoa
¼ cup rum
 1 teaspoon instant coffee granules
    Powdered sugar, for coating

1. Mix crumbs, 1 cup powdered sugar, pecans, melted margarine or butter, corn syrup and cocoa in large bowl. Blend rum and instant coffee until coffee granules are dissolved; stir into crumb mixture. Let stand 15 minutes.

2. Shape mixture into 1-inch balls; roll in additional powdered sugar. Store in airtight container, separating layers with waxed paper. Flavor improves with standing.   *Makes about 3 dozen*

Preparation Time: 50 minutes
Total Time: 50 minutes

DIVINITY

2½ cups sugar
½ cup KARO® Light Corn Syrup
½ cup water
¼ teaspoon salt
2 egg whites, at room temperature
1 teaspoon vanilla
1 cup chopped nuts (optional)

1. In 2-quart saucepan combine sugar, corn syrup, water and salt. Stirring constantly, bring to boil over medium heat. Without stirring, cook over low heat (small to medium bubbles breaking across surface of liquid) until temperature on candy thermometer reaches 266°F or small amount of mixture dropped into very cold water forms a hard ball which doesn't flatten until pressed, about 40 minutes.

2. When temperature reaches 260°F, in large bowl with mixer at high speed, beat egg whites until stiff peaks form. Beating at high speed, gradually add hot syrup in a thin steady stream. DO NOT SCRAPE MIXTURE FROM SIDE OF SAUCEPAN INTO BOWL. Continue beating at high speed until mixture begins to lose its gloss, about 3 minutes.

3. Reduce speed to low. Beat in vanilla. Continue beating at low speed until mixture holds a peak and does not spread when dropped from a spoon, about 8 minutes. (If mixture becomes too stiff for mixer, beat with wooden spoon.) Immediately stir in nuts.

4. Working quickly, drop by teaspoonfuls onto waxed paper.* If desired, garnish with walnut pieces or candied cherries. Let stand until set. Store in tightly covered container.   *Makes about 1¼ pounds*

Or, spread in 8- or 9-inch square baking pan lined with plastic wrap. If desired, garnish with walnut pieces or candied cherries. Cool on wire rack. Cut into squares. Store in tightly covered container.

Note: To color Divinity, add few drops food color with vanilla.

Peppermint Divinity: Line 8- or 9-inch square baking pan with plastic wrap. Follow recipe for Divinity. Omit nuts. Immediately after beating, fold in ¼ cup crushed peppermint candy. Pour into prepared pan. Cool on wire rack. Cut into squares.

Peanut Butter Divinity: Follow recipe for Divinity. Omit nuts. Immediately after beating, add ⅓ cup SKIPPY® SUPER CHUNK® or Creamy Peanut Butter; fold just until marbleized.

Dried Cherry or Cranberry Divinity: Follow recipe for Divinity. Omit nuts. Immediately after beating, fold in 1 cup chopped dried cherries or cranberries.

Prep Time: 60 minutes, plus cooling

VERY BEARY PEANUT BRITTLE

2 cups sugar
1 cup water
½ cup light corn syrup
1 tablespoon margarine or butter
½ cup PLANTERS® COCKTAIL Peanuts
1 teaspoon vanilla extract
½ teaspoon baking soda
1 cup TEDDY GRAHAMS® Graham Snacks, any flavor

1. Heat sugar, water, corn syrup and margarine or butter in medium saucepan over medium-low heat, stirring occasionally, until mixture reaches 290°F on candy thermometer.

2. Stir in peanuts; continue to heat to 300°F. Remove from heat; stir in vanilla and baking soda.

3. Thinly spread mixture onto greased baking sheet. Press bear-shaped graham snacks into mixture while still hot.

4. Cool completely; break into bite-size pieces. Store in airtight container for up to 2 weeks.

Makes about 1½ pounds

Preparation Time: 15 minutes
Cook Time: 20 minutes
Cooling Time: 2 hours
Total Time: 2 hours and 35 minutes

CHEERY CHERRY ALMOND—TOPPED FUDGE

1 can (8 ounces) almond paste
1 can (14 ounces) sweetened condensed milk (*not* evaporated milk), divided
Few drops red food color
1¾ cups HERSHEY'S Semi-Sweet Chocolate Chips
Red candied cherry halves
Sliced almonds

1. Line 8-inch square pan with foil, extending foil over edges of pan.

2. Beat almond paste and ¼ cup sweetened condensed milk in small bowl until blended. Add food color; beat until well blended. Refrigerate about 1 hour or until stiff. Spread mixture into prepared pan.

3. Place chocolate chips and remaining sweetened condensed milk in medium microwave-safe bowl. Microwave at HIGH (100%) 1 minute; stir. If necessary, microwave at HIGH an additional 15 seconds at a time, stirring after each heating, just until chips are melted when stirred. Spread over almond paste layer. Cover; refrigerate until firm.

4. Use foil to lift fudge out of pan; peel off foil. Cut fudge into squares; garnish with cherry halves and almonds. Store in tightly covered container in refrigerator. *Makes about 4 dozen pieces*

Raspberry Almond-Topped Fudge: Substitute 1⅔ cups HERSHEY'S Raspberry Chips for chocolate chips.

Note: For best results, do not double this recipe.

VERY BEARY PEANUT BRITTLE

CANDIED ORANGE PEEL

8 to 10 medium thick-skinned oranges, washed
Water
1 teaspoon salt
2 cups sugar
1 cup water
½ cup KARO® Light Corn Syrup
Sugar
Melted semisweet chocolate (optional)

1. Cut oranges just through peel into quarters; remove peel and place in large saucepan. (Reserve oranges for eating or for use in salads and fruit cups.)

2. Cover orange peel with cold water; add salt. Bring to boil; boil 10 minutes. Drain. Boil and drain 2 more times, omitting salt.

3. Gently scrape off moist white membrane with spoon. (Peel should be about ¼ inch thick.) Cut peel into ¼-inch-wide strips.

4. In 3-quart saucepan combine 2 cups sugar, 1 cup water and corn syrup. Stirring constantly, cook over medium heat until sugar is dissolved. Add orange peel. Bring to boil; reduce heat and boil gently 45 minutes. Drain well.

5. A few pieces at a time, roll orange peel in sugar. Arrange in single layer on wire racks. Let dry, lightly covered, in warm place 10 to 12 hours. Store in covered container.

6. If desired, dip 1 end in melted chocolate. Place on waxed paper-lined cookie sheet. Chill 15 minutes or until set.   *Makes about 8 cups*

Prep Time: 2 hours, plus drying

HOLIDAY TRUFFLES

3 tablespoons heavy cream
1 tablespoon instant coffee granules
2 cups semisweet or milk chocolate chips
½ cup FLEISCHMANN'S® Original Margarine
1 teaspoon vanilla extract
Crushed cookie crumbs, chopped nuts, toasted coconut, melted white chocolate, colored sprinkles

1. Blend heavy cream and coffee in small bowl; let stand 5 minutes to dissolve.

2. Melt chocolate chips in medium saucepan over low heat until smooth. Remove from heat. With wire whisk, beat in margarine, heavy cream mixture and vanilla until smooth. Place in bowl; refrigerate until firm, about 3 hours.

3. Shape teaspoonfuls of mixture into balls and coat with cookie crumbs, chopped nuts, coconut, melted white chocolate or colored sprinkles until well coated. Store in airtight container in refrigerator.

Makes 2½ dozen

Prep Time: 30 minutes
Cook Time: 5 minutes
Chill Time: 3 hours
Total Time: 3 hours and 35 minutes

CHOCOLATE PEANUT BUTTER TRUFFLES

1 package (8 squares) BAKER'S® Semi-Sweet Chocolate
½ cup peanut butter
1 tub (8 ounces) COOL WHIP® Whipped Topping, thawed
   Powdered sugar, finely chopped nuts, BAKER'S ANGEL FLAKE® Coconut, unsweetened cocoa or multi-colored sprinkles

MICROWAVE chocolate in large microwavable bowl on HIGH 2 minutes or until chocolate is almost melted, stirring halfway through heating time. Stir until chocolate is completely melted.

STIR in peanut butter until smooth. Cool to room temperature. Stir in whipped topping.

REFRIGERATE 1 hour. Shape into 1-inch balls. Roll in powdered sugar, nuts, coconut, cocoa or sprinkles. Store in refrigerator.   *Makes about 3 dozen*

Cool Christmas Fudge: Prepare as directed above, substituting 4 ounces PHILADELPHIA® Cream Cheese for peanut butter. Stir in ½ cup chopped nuts with whipped topping. Spread in foil-lined 8-inch square pan. Refrigerate 4 hours or until firm. Remove from pan. Cut into squares. Store in refrigerator. Makes about 4 dozen.

KAHLÚA® BONBONS

¼ cup KAHLÚA® Liqueur
4 teaspoons instant coffee powder
¾ cup unsalted butter, softened
1 ounce cream cheese, softened
2 egg yolks
1½ cups powdered sugar
12 ounces semisweet chocolate, chopped
¼ cup vegetable shortening
10 ounces amaretti cookies*, crushed

Amaretti are Italian meringue cookies and can be purchased at Italian or specialty food shops. If desired, substitute an equal amount of finely chopped toasted hazelnuts or almonds.

In small bowl combine Kahlúa® and coffee powder. Let stand 10 minutes. In medium bowl, cream butter with cream cheese until fluffy. Add egg yolks and sugar and beat until smooth. Stir Kahlúa® and coffee powder until powder is completely dissolved. Gradually beat into butter mixture. Drop mixture by rounded teaspoonfuls onto baking sheets or trays lined with waxed paper or plastic wrap. Set in freezer 1 hour or overnight.

When ready to dip, remove from freezer 1 sheet at a time; roll between palms to shape into balls. Return to freezer.

Melt chocolate and shortening in top of double boiler over simmering water, stirring frequently. Cool to lukewarm, stirring occasionally. Place crushed amaretti in bowl.

Using wooden skewer or toothpick, dip bonbon balls, 1 at a time, into warm chocolate. Allow excess chocolate to drip off, then transfer to bowl of amaretti crumbs. Using small spoon, sprinkle crumbs over bonbon to cover completely. Transfer to baking sheets or trays lined with clean plastic wrap. Using second skewer, gently push bonbon off dipping skewer. If hole remains, cover with additional amaretti crumbs. If chocolate becomes too thick, reheat gently as needed. Store bonbons in refrigerator.   *Makes about 4 dozen*

FAST 'N' FABULOUS DARK CHOCOLATE FUDGE

MAZOLA NO STICK® Cooking Spray
½ cup KARO® Light or Dark Corn Syrup
⅓ cup evaporated milk
3 cups (18 ounces) semisweet chocolate chips
¾ cup confectioners' sugar, sifted
2 teaspoons vanilla
1 cup coarsely chopped nuts (optional)

1. Spray 8-inch square baking pan with cooking spray.

2. In 3-quart microwavable bowl, combine corn syrup and evaporated milk; stir until well blended. Microwave on HIGH (100%), 3 minutes.

3. Stir in chocolate chips until melted. Stir in confectioners' sugar, vanilla and nuts. With wooden spoon beat until thick and glossy.

4. Spread in prepared pan. Refrigerate 2 hours or until firm. *Makes 25 squares*

Marvelous Marble Fudge: Omit nuts. Prepare as directed above; spread into prepared pan. Drop ⅓ cup SKIPPY® Creamy Peanut Butter over fudge in small dollops. With small spatula, swirl fudge to marbleize. Chill as above.

Double Peanut Butter Chocolate Fudge: Prepare as directed above. Stir in ⅓ cup SKIPPY® SUPER CHUNK® Peanut Butter. Spread in prepared pan. Drop additional ⅓ cup peanut butter over fudge in small dollops. With small spatula, swirl fudge to marbleize. Chill as above.

Prep Time: 10 minutes, plus chilling

HOLIDAY PEPPERMINT CANDIES

½ package (4 ounces) PHILADELPHIA® Cream Cheese, softened
1 tablespoon butter *or* margarine
1 tablespoon light corn syrup
¼ teaspoon peppermint extract *or* few drops peppermint oil
4 cups powdered sugar
Green and red food coloring
Sifted powdered sugar
Green, red and white decorating icing (optional)

MIX cream cheese, butter, corn syrup and extract in large mixing bowl with electric mixer on medium speed until well blended. Gradually add 4 cups powdered sugar; mix well.

DIVIDE mixture into thirds. Knead a few drops green food coloring into first third; repeat with red food coloring and second third. Wrap each third in plastic wrap.

SHAPE into 1-inch balls, working with 1 color mixture at a time. Place on wax paper-lined cookie sheet. Flatten each ball with bottom of glass that has been lightly dipped in sifted powdered sugar.

REPEAT with remaining mixtures. Decorate with icing. Store candies in refrigerator. *Makes 5 dozen*

Prep Time: 30 minutes plus refrigerating

Acknowledgments

The publisher would like to thank the companies and organizations listed below for the use of their recipes and photographs in this publication.

A.1.® Steak Sauce

Barilla America, Inc.

BelGioioso® Cheese, Inc.

Birds Eye®

Bob Evans®

Butterball® Turkey Company

California Dried Plum Board

Chef Paul Prudhomme's Magic Seasoning Blends®

Cherry Marketing Institute

Clamato® is a registered trademark of Mott's, Inc.

Colorado Potato Administrative Committee

ConAgra Grocery Products Company

Del Monte Corporation

Dole Food Company, Inc.

Duncan Hines® and Moist Deluxe® are registered trademarks of Aurora Foods Inc.

Eagle® Brand

Equal® sweetener

Filippo Berio® Olive Oil

Fleischmann's® Original Spread

Fleischmann's® Yeast

General Mills, Inc.

The Golden Grain Company®

Grandma's® is a registered trademark of Mott's, Inc.

GREY POUPON® Dijon Mustard

Guiltless Gourmet®

Hebrew National®

Heinz U.S.A.

Hershey Foods Corporation

Hillshire Farm®

Holland House® is a registered trademark of Mott's, Inc.

The HV Company

The J.M. Smucker Company

Kahlúa® Liqueur

Keebler® Company

Kellogg Company

Kikkoman International Inc.

The Kingsford Products Company

Kraft Foods Holdings

Lawry's® Foods, Inc.

Lee Kum Kee (USA) Inc.

© Mars, Incorporated 2002

McIlhenny Company (TABASCO® brand Pepper Sauce)

Michigan Bean Commission

Mott's® is a registered trademark of Mott's, Inc.

Mushroom Council

Nabisco Biscuit and Snack Divison

National Honey Board

National Pork Board

National Turkey Federation

Nestlé USA

New Jersey Department of Agriculture

NILLA® Wafers

Norseland, Inc. / Lucini Italia Co.

Peanut Advisory Board

Pear Bureau Northwest

PLANTERS® Nuts

The Procter & Gamble Company

The Quaker® Oatmeal Kitchens

Reckitt Benckiser

Reddi-wip®

RED STAR® Yeast, a product of Lasaffre Yeast Corporation

Riviana Foods Inc.

Sargento® Foods Inc.

StarKist® Seafood Company

The Sugar Association, Inc.

Sunkist Growers

Tyson Foods, Inc.

Uncle Ben's Inc.

Unilever Bestfoods North America

USA Dry Pea & Lentil Council

USA Rice Federation

Veg-All®

Wisconsin Milk Marketing Board

Index

Index

Index

Index

Index

METRIC CONVERSION CHART

VOLUME MEASUREMENTS (dry)

$\frac{1}{8}$ teaspoon = 0.5 mL
$\frac{1}{4}$ teaspoon = 1 mL
$\frac{1}{2}$ teaspoon = 2 mL
$\frac{3}{4}$ teaspoon = 4 mL
1 teaspoon = 5 mL
1 tablespoon = 15 mL
2 tablespoons = 30 mL
$\frac{1}{4}$ cup = 60 mL
$\frac{1}{3}$ cup = 75 mL
$\frac{1}{2}$ cup = 125 mL
$\frac{2}{3}$ cup = 150 mL
$\frac{3}{4}$ cup = 175 mL
1 cup = 250 mL
2 cups = 1 pint = 500 mL
3 cups = 750 mL
4 cups = 1 quart = 1 L

VOLUME MEASUREMENTS (fluid)

1 fluid ounce (2 tablespoons) = 30 mL
4 fluid ounces ($\frac{1}{2}$ cup) = 125 mL
8 fluid ounces (1 cup) = 250 mL
12 fluid ounces (1$\frac{1}{2}$ cups) = 375 mL
16 fluid ounces (2 cups) = 500 mL

WEIGHTS (mass)

$\frac{1}{2}$ ounce = 15 g
1 ounce = 30 g
3 ounces = 90 g
4 ounces = 120 g
8 ounces = 225 g
10 ounces = 285 g
12 ounces = 360 g
16 ounces = 1 pound = 450 g

DIMENSIONS

$\frac{1}{16}$ inch = 2 mm
$\frac{1}{8}$ inch = 3 mm
$\frac{1}{4}$ inch = 6 mm
$\frac{1}{2}$ inch = 1.5 cm
$\frac{3}{4}$ inch = 2 cm
1 inch = 2.5 cm

OVEN TEMPERATURES

250°F = 120°C
275°F = 140°C
300°F = 150°C
325°F = 160°C
350°F = 180°C
375°F = 190°C
400°F = 200°C
425°F = 220°C
450°F = 230°C

BAKING PAN SIZES

Utensil	Size in Inches/Quarts	Metric Volume	Size in Centimeters
Baking or Cake Pan (square or rectangular)	8 × 8 × 2	2 L	20 × 20 × 5
	9 × 9 × 2	2.5 L	23 × 23 × 5
	12 × 8 × 2	3 L	30 × 20 × 5
	13 × 9 × 2	3.5 L	33 × 23 × 5
Loaf Pan	8 × 4 × 3	1.5 L	20 × 10 × 7
	9 × 5 × 3	2 L	23 × 13 × 7
Round Layer Cake Pan	8 × 1½	1.2 L	20 × 4
	9 × 1½	1.5 L	23 × 4
Pie Plate	8 × 1¼	750 mL	20 × 3
	9 × 1¼	1 L	23 × 3
Baking Dish or Casserole	1 quart	1 L	—
	1½ quart	1.5 L	—
	2 quart	2 L	—